Marilynne Robinson's Worldly Gospel

New Directions in Religion and Literature

This series aims to showcase new work at the forefront of religion and literature through short studies written by leading and rising scholars in the field. Books will pursue a variety of theoretical approaches as they engage with writing from different religious and literary traditions. Collectively, the series will offer a timely critical intervention to the interdisciplinary crossover between religion and literature, speaking to wider contemporary interests and mapping out new directions for the field in the early twenty-first century.

Series editors: Emma Mason and Mark Knight

Also available in the series:

The New Atheist Novel, Arthur Bradley and Andrew Tate
Blake. Wordsworth. Religion, Jonathan Roberts
Do the Gods Wear Capes?, Ben Saunders
England's Secular Scripture, Jo Carruthers
Victorian Parables, Susan E. Colón
The Late Walter Benjamin, John Schad
Dante and the Sense of Transgression, William Franke
The Glyph and the Gramophone, Luke Ferretter
John Cage and Buddhist Ecopoetics, Peter Jaeger
Rewriting the Old Testament in Anglo-Saxon Verse, Samantha Zacher
Forgiveness in Victorian Literature, Richard Hughes Gibson
The Gospel According to the Novelist, Magdalena Mączyńska
Jewish Feeling, Richa Dwor
Beyond the Willing Suspension of Disbelief, Michael Tomko
The Gospel According to David Foster Wallace, Adam S. Miller
Pentecostal Modernism, Stephen Shapiro and Philip Barnard
The Bible in the American Short Story, Lesleigh Cushing Stahlberg and Peter S. Hawkins
Faith in Poetry, Michael D. Hurley
Jeanette Winterson and Religion, Emily McAvan
Religion and American Literature since the 1950s, Mark Eaton
Esoteric Islam in Modern French Thought, Ziad Elmarsafy
The Rhetoric of Conversion in English Puritan Writing, David Parry
Djuna Barnes and Theology, Zhao Ng
Food and Fasting in Victorian Religion and Literature, Lesa Scholl
The Economy of Religion in American Literature, Andrew Ball
Christian Heresy, James Joyce, and the Modernist Literary Imagination, Gregory Erikson

Forthcoming:

Weird Faith in 19th Century Literature, Mark Knight and Emma Mason

Marilynne Robinson's Worldly Gospel

A Philosophical Account of Her Christian Vision

Ryan S. Kemp
Jordan Rodgers

BLOOMSBURY ACADEMIC
LONDON • NEW YORK • OXFORD • NEW DELHI • SYDNEY

BLOOMSBURY ACADEMIC
Bloomsbury Publishing Plc
50 Bedford Square, London, WC1B 3DP, UK
1385 Broadway, New York, NY 10018, USA
29 Earlsfort Terrace, Dublin 2, Ireland

BLOOMSBURY, BLOOMSBURY ACADEMIC and the Diana logo are
trademarks of Bloomsbury Publishing Plc

First published in Great Britain 2023
Paperback edition published 2024

Copyright © Ryan S. Kemp and Jordan Rodgers, 2023, 2024

Ryan S. Kemp and Jordan Rodgers have asserted their right under the Copyright,
Designs and Patents Act, 1988, to be identified as Author of this work.

For legal purposes the Acknowledgments on p. xi constitute an extension
of this copyright page.

Series design by Eleanor Rose

Cover image: *Le jardin du docteur Gachet à Auvers sur Oise (Auvers-sur-Oise)*,
Vincent van Gogh, 1890, 0,73x0,52 m, musee d'Orsay, Paris.

All rights reserved. No part of this publication may be reproduced or transmitted
in any form or by any means, electronic or mechanical, including photocopying,
recording, or any information storage or retrieval system, without prior
permission in writing from the publishers.

Bloomsbury Publishing Plc does not have any control over, or responsibility for,
any third-party websites referred to or in this book. All internet addresses given
in this book were correct at the time of going to press. The author and publisher
regret any inconvenience caused if addresses have changed or sites have ceased
to exist, but can accept no responsibility for any such changes.

A catalogue record for this book is available from the British Library.

Library of Congress Cataloging-in-Publication Data

Names: Kemp, Ryan S., author. | Rodgers, Jordan M., author.
Title: Marilynne Robinson's worldly gospel : a philosophical account of her Christian vision / Ryan S. Kemp,
and Jordan Rodgers. Description: London ; New York : Bloomsbury Academic, 2023. |
Includes bibliographical references and index. | Summary: "In her five novels and
many essays, Marilynne Robinson develops a distinctive Christian vision animated by a powerfully affirmative
and sacramental attitude toward the physical world and everyday human life. An in-depth philosophical
exploration of her work - from Gilead to her extensive non-fiction writing - Marilynne Robinson's Worldly Gospel
reads the author's theology as articulating a compelling response to the claim that Christianity is
an otherworldly religion whose adherents seek through it to escape the misfortunes of this life.
Ryan Kemp and Jordan Rodgers argue that Robinson's work challenges the modern atheistic tradition
dating back to Friedrich Nietzsche to present a unique form of contemporary faith that seeks to affirm the
world rather than deny its claims"– Provided by publisher.
Identifiers: LCCN 2022031275 | ISBN 9781350106956 (hardback) | ISBN 9781350318397 (paperback) |
ISBN 9781350106963 (ebook) | ISBN 9781350106970 (epub) | ISBN 9781350106987
Subjects: LCSH: Robinson, Marilynne–Criticism and interpretation. |
Robinson, Marilynne–Religion. | Christianity in literature. | American fiction–21st century–History
and criticism. Classification: LCC PS3568.O3125 Z755 2023 | DDC 813/.54–dc23/eng/20220921
LC record available at https://lccn.loc.gov/2022031275

ISBN: HB: 978-1-3501-0695-6
PB: 978-1-3503-1839-7
ePDF: 978-1-3501-0696-3
eBook: 978-1-3501-0697-0

Series: New Directions in Religion and Literature

Typeset by Deanta Global Publishing Services, Chennai, India

To find out more about our authors and books visit www.bloomsbury.com and
sign up for our newsletters

Ryan: *For my children—Ella, Olivia, Violet, and Wyatt.*
"O taste and see that the Lord is good."

Jordan: *For Samantha, Simone, Sylvie, and Vita, whose beauty takes no effort to see.*

"'And when they wanted wine, the mother of Jesus saith unto him, They have no wine'. . ., *Alyosha overheard.*

Ah, yes, I've been missing it and I didn't want to miss it, I love that passage: it's Cana of Galilee, the first miracle. . . . Ah, that miracle, ah, that lovely miracle! Not grief, but men's joy Christ visited when he worked his first miracle, he helped men's joy. . . . 'He who loves men, loves their joy . . .'"

—Fyodor Dostoevsky, *The Brothers Karamazov*

Contents

Acknowledgments	viii
Introduction	1
1 The Life-Denial Critique of Christianity: Feuerbach and Nietzsche	13
2 *Housekeeping*: Lessons in Life-Denial	51
3 *Gilead*: More Beauty than Our Eyes Can Bear	81
4 O Sinner, Come *Home*	113
5 *Jack*: A Glorious Presence	147
6 *Lila*: More Life than We Can Bear	173
Conclusion: Our Fantastic Condition	205
Works Cited	213
Index	221

Acknowledgments

Ryan: In the few years since graduate school, I have been fortunate to befriend a handful of people who have pushed me to write with more humanity. This book is an attempt to do just that and with the best of writing partners—my dear friend Jordan Rodgers. Jordan was one of the few people in graduate school who never really succumbed to the temptation to write "academically," and he was also the one who introduced me to the work of Marilynne Robinson. His steady companionship, warm intelligence, and artistic conscience have been a gift during the last few years. If this book manages anything resembling grace, it is due to his pen.

I would like also to take the opportunity to acknowledge a few others who have encouraged me during the writing process.

Thanks, first, to my wife, Jessica. She is the real writer in the family, and her encouragement and example always push me to speak more truly. If not for her, and in a way that I can't entirely explain, the joy I experience in writing would be deeply diminished.

Thanks to my grandparents, Leroy and Jean Kemp, who were diligent and insightful discussion partners during the writing process. When they learned I was writing a book about Marilynne Robinson, they proceeded to read all of the novels in short order. They had studied opinions about *Jack* long before I finished reading it.

Thanks to my friends James Gordon, Greg Lynch, and Adam Wood for allowing me to interrupt our last fishing trip with writing breaks and nagging questions about "existence" and "souls" and other Robinson-related exotica. (Greg, I promise to get back to business on our next outing.)

Thanks to all the students with whom I have discussed Robinson's novels over the past six years, but especially: Colton Bernasol, David Bjorklund, Drew Bjorklund, Connor Brown, Tessa Coker, Michael Contreras, Jerusha Crone, Daniel Giles, Cameron Harro, Lonzie Helms,

Laura Howard, Caleb Kirby, Hannah Lambert, Collin Maldonado, Miles Trujillo, George Turkington, and Carrie Weldy. Megan Kim deserves her own line of thanks as she put in many hours reading and commenting on the manuscript. She is a true poet and has a sensitive ear that I soon learned to trust implicitly.

Finally, both Jordan and I would like to express special thanks to three friends with whom we spent a weekend discussing a late draft of this book: Mark Jonas, Alex Loney, and Michael Morgan. Thanks to each of you for your time and especially your loving attention. The companionship and conversation of that weekend more than justified the work of writing this book.

Jordan: The writing of this book coincided with a volatile time in my life. Aside from the pandemic, which upended us all in various ways and certainly didn't make an exception of me, the time during which this book was written saw me become a father thrice over, and begin and (probably) end my career in academia. Both of those experiences are, I think, present in what we've written, and it could not be as it is if not for the existence of my daughters, nor do I think I would have written it if I had felt at home in the academic world.

Of course, my main debt is to my writing partner, Ryan Kemp. As we write in the Introduction, this book began as an offhand comment I made to Ryan after my first lovestruck reading of Marilynne Robinson's *Gilead*. I was smitten with John Ames, and I said that I thought even Nietzsche would have had to respect him. I forgot the comment more or less as soon as it was made. But I am grateful to Ryan that he didn't. This book exists because he reached out to me a couple of years later, out of the blue and after we had parted ways to take up our first academic positions, he in Illinois and I in Pennsylvania. He told me that what I had said had stuck with him, and that he wanted to write together with me and explore the idea. His reaching out to me meant more than he could have known then. It was gratifying to know that he valued my writing enough to want to attach my name to his. And the book project has felt to me like a lifeline over these years, an always available reminder that the work I was doing was worthwhile. Ryan gave me that, and as if that wasn't enough, he was also a delightful writing partner: hardworking, confident, and unfailingly encouraging. I can only hope that I've helped him make this book live up to his expectations for it.

I have always remembered a bit of writing advice that I imagine is actually quite common, but which came to me through Kurt Vonnegut: write with an audience of one in mind. It is probably a sign of my failures as a writer of academic prose that I couldn't ever really decide who I was writing for. This one, though, is written for my wife, Samantha. Our conversations about Robinson's books, and about religious questions more generally, are the true wellspring of my ideas for this book, and I imagine most of what is really valuable in it comes from them. I have written with the thought in mind that when the book was done it might mean something to her. Anyone else who finds something in it to like is icing on the cake, as far as I'm concerned.

I'd like also to thank my parents, Mike and Donna Rodgers. My overall way of looking at the world was probably shaped more by the long conversations I had with them about religion when I was home over school breaks during college years, often going deep into the night, than by anything that has happened since or is likely still to happen. I hope they'll have Robinson's novels read before this book is in their hands. (If you haven't, Mom and Dad, put this down now.)

Thanks are due as well to my former colleague at King's College (PA), Bernard Prusak, for being both a valuable and necessary mentor and a tireless advocate for me during tough years, but also and most importantly for being enthusiastic about this project from its early stages. Conversations with Bernard about the book proposal were important for getting my ideas clear early, and Bernard set up two opportunities for me to present early versions of some of this material publicly at King's, in 2017 and 2019. I want to thank as well the audience members of the 2019 talk at King's, and single out for special thanks Melanie Shepherd, Katherine Filbert, and Regan Reitsma.

Acknowledgments

The authors are grateful to Marilynne Robinson and Farrar, Strauss and Giroux for permission to quote from the following works:

Excerpts from GILEAD by Marilynne Robinson. Copyright © 2004 by Marilynne Robinson. Reprinted by permission of Farrar, Straus and Giroux. All Rights Reserved.

Excerpts from HOME by Marilynne Robinson. Copyright © 2008by Marilynne Robinson. Reprinted by permission of Farrar, Straus and Giroux. All Rights Reserved.

Excerpts from HOUSEKEEPING by Marilynne Robinson. Copyright © 1981 by Marilynne Robinson. Reprinted by permission of Farrar, Straus and Giroux. All Rights Reserved.

Excerpts from LILA by Marilynne Robinson. Copyright © 2014 by Marilynne Robinson. Reprinted by permission of Farrar, Straus and Giroux. All Rights Reserved.

Excerpts from JACK by Marilynne Robinson. Copyright © 2020 by Marilynne Robinson. Reprinted by permission of Farrar, Straus and Giroux. All Rights Reserved.

Introduction

The idea for this book might as well have come out of nowhere. It began as a stray comment, made years ago, in a casual department lounge conversation: in *Gilead*, Marilynne Robinson had written a character—the Congregationalist pastor John Ames—whose Christian vision even Nietzsche, the great philosophical critic of Christianity, might respect. For Nietzsche, as we will discuss at some length in Chapter 1, the most important philosophical issue is that of the value of life; his condemnation of Christianity stems from his conviction that it encourages its adherents to *deny* this life—that is, to be especially attentive to what is unsatisfying and incomplete in it, and to live in a way that will minimize attachment to it, and emphasize expectation of an afterlife that will be perfectly satisfying and complete. But one of the most striking features of *Gilead* is Ames's joyous relation to his own, small, transient life. Ames clearly believes in the afterlife and allows himself musings about what it might be like—he is, after all, not long for this world, and the novel exists as a long letter to his young son who will not read it until after he is gone. He has, it seems, as much reason as anyone could have to want to forget about this life and spend his remaining days dreaming of the next. But instead, what is most striking and enthralling about Ames is his remarkable affection for the world he is about to leave, and a virtuosic attentiveness to the moments in which it can reveal its value. Somehow, Ames's Christian beliefs seem to intensify rather than diminish his love for this life. The passage in the novel that was most striking for us occurs when Ames finds himself "thinking about existence," and remembering a particular moonlit walk in his small hometown along a road lined with oak trees, from which a flood of acorns fell with a kind of bizarre, extravagant violence. The memory inspires in him a philosophical reflection about the relation of this life to the next:

> I feel sometimes as if I were a child who opens its eyes on the world once and sees amazing things it will never know any names for and then has to close its eyes again. I know this is all mere apparition compared to what awaits us, but it is only lovelier for that. There is a human beauty in it. And I can't believe that, when we have all been changed and put on incorruptibility, we will forget our fantastic condition of mortality and impermanence, the great bright dream of procreating and perishing that meant the whole world to us. In eternity this world will be Troy, I believe, and all that has passed here will be the epic of the universe, the ballad they sing in the streets. Because I don't imagine any reality putting this one in the shade entirely, and I think piety forbids me to try. (*Gilead* 57)

Here was a kind of life-affirmation which contained the pathos at which Nietzsche's own philosophy seemed to aim. Ames's vision (and through it, the novel's) didn't just present a particular strain of Christianity to which Nietzsche's critique simply happened not to apply very persuasively; rather, what we thought we had found in Robinson's novel was a stirring response to Nietzsche's own problem—how to affirm life in what Nietzsche calls our "nihilistic" modern world. That would mean suggesting something a bit bolder, namely, that the very religion Nietzsche thought had saddled us with our current predicament might itself, in a different form, show us the way back out of it.

Hence that stray comment: not just that Nietzsche wouldn't object very strenuously to Ames but might actually respect him. The idea was, in its way, quite straightforward, though we worried that it might prove a bit too idiosyncratic to serve as an interpretive lens for Robinson's novel. We were well aware that Robinson herself almost never referred to Nietzsche in her writing. But what had started as an offhand remark began, when we dwelled on it, to develop a life of its own, suggesting justifications for itself.

Nietzsche's critique of a "nihilistic" modernity seemed to us important, and his view that this nihilism grew initially out of certain tendencies inherent in Christianity, at least as a socio-historical institution, resonated with our own personal experience. Both of us were intimately familiar with the way in which many use Christianity for purely consolatory purposes, more or less as a kind of refined painkiller, a promise of a serene afterlife that makes the pervasive suffering and disappointment of the present more endurable. We were all too familiar as well with the moralism that often accompanies this outlook, a moralism that likes to dress itself up in lofty language about narrow paths and divine ideals, but in practice often limits its moral vision to a set of simple rules (or worse, political allegiances), the following of which guarantees a spot in heaven, while allowing the believer to ignore, or at least pretend to ignore, the more harrowing and anxiety-inducing aspects of the human condition, and with them the *people* whose life circumstances force them to deal with that condition more directly. Not only that, but it seemed to us that this mindset—world-weary and depressed, on the hunt for "hacks" to reduce the complexity of life down to a livable formula—is hardly unique to modern Christians, and in fact infects a great deal of the secular age in which we live. A Christian worldview of this kind really is a capitulation to the modern forces that Christians have typically claimed to oppose.

And indeed, it is this connection between Christianity and secular modernity that makes Nietzsche's critique in particular so important. It would perhaps have been more natural and timelier to cast Robinson's fiction as a response to the critiques of Christianity, and of religious belief in general, of the so-called "New Atheists," Daniel Dennett, Sam Harris, Richard Dawkins, and Christopher Hitchens.[1] But in fact, in terms of philosophical argument there is really not much "new" in these atheists. Arguably, their popularity is the result not of any new arguments or trenchant critiques, but of their writing in an age when the *political* dangers of fundamentalist religion to modern secular liberalism have seemed more imminent. (Indeed, part of what is "new" in the new atheists is their willingness to critique Islamic religion just as, if not more harshly than Christian fundamentalism.) All four new atheists are good, modern, secular liberals, and all four totally neglect the cultural relationship between secular liberalism and historical Christianity that so exercised the creative energies of Nietzsche, and that ultimately explain the roots of what he saw as the real and lasting problems of the modern age.[2] Nietzsche is in this way a far "newer" atheist than they, and thus by far the more satisfying counterpoint to Robinson's deeply Christian fiction which, as we will seek to show, *is* responsive to these Nietzschean worries.

Some other recent authors are closer to speaking to these concerns and might themselves have formed an interesting counterpoint to Robinson's fiction. One is the duo Hubert Dreyfus and Sean Kelly, whose *All Things Shining: Reading the Western Classics to Find Meaning in a Secular Age* (2011) explicitly invokes Nietzsche's prophecy of the death of God as one of its jumping off points. Dreyfus and Kelly, like Nietzsche, criticize Christianity for its moralism and otherworldliness, and seek in their book to revive a kind of Greek polytheism for the modern, disenchanted age, one that would see and celebrate the "shining" things of this life once again. Their celebratory mood perhaps shares some affinity with John Ames, and their diagnosis of the ills of modernity appeal to all the right reference points. Perhaps more directly relevant, though it only glancingly mentions Nietzsche, is Martin Hägglund's *This Life: Secular Faith and Spiritual Freedom* (2019). Hägglund's critique of religion is broad in scope—for him, not just Christianity but religion itself (including, e.g., Judaism, Islam, Buddhism) ought to be defined in terms of its devaluation of "this life":

> [T]he common denominator for what I call *religious* forms of faith is a devaluation of our finite lives as a lower form of being. All world religions hold that the highest form of existence or the most desirable form of life is eternal rather than finite. To be religious . . . is to regard our finitude as a lack, an illusion, or a fallen state of being. (Hägglund 2019, 6)

Hägglund's book is an attempt to get us to reject "religion" in this sense, but not "faith"—for him there is a secular faith which consists in embracing our finitude rather than running from it, in freely committing ourselves to bringing about what we value in this life, and doing so despite the sobering realization that our achievements are contingent and reversible. Much of his book is an attempt to lay out what this would look like politically; his own deeply Marxist form of democratic socialism is built around the idea of freeing up our time from wage labor, so that we have the time to determine for ourselves what we value and then seek to realize it. Our achievements, he insists, are meaningful only on the condition of their fragility and our finitude—what we are seeking to achieve or preserve (Hägglund explicitly refers to the impending climate disaster throughout) is and must be finite, and thus we can only really be committed if we are prepared to treat finite things as valuable in themselves, and not as mere means to something eternal. But this is just what "religion" in his sense denies.

Why Nietzsche, then, rather than Dreyfus and Kelly or Hägglund? There are a few reasons for this that can be indicated in advance. We join many others in finding Dreyfus and Kelly's ultimate position to be unsatisfying, culminating as it does in a celebration of things like the "whooshing" feeling of being in a cheering crowd and the joys of drinking coffee from a perfectly constructed cup. And their critique of monotheistic religion, borrowed mostly from thinkers like Nietzsche, is less sympathetic than it might be, and thus less likely to find a worthwhile conversation partner in Robinson.[3] Hägglund does address monotheism more directly (if still perhaps too dismissively[4]), and his response to the problems of modernity is more serious, but that response is also much more political. This is not necessarily a mark against Hägglund's claims generally, but it does render his theoretical framework more foreign to Robinson's concerns, which, as we shall see, revolve far more around the problems of private individuals than those of the public sphere. In this, Robinson is like Nietzsche, who was also exercised more by the concerns of the individual and has even been referred to by some commentators as anti-political.[5]

What seems revelatory in *Gilead* is the fact that it portrays humble, homely, indeed outwardly quite boring and politically nonrepresentative individuals, but in a way that renders them interesting precisely because their lives are infused with a meaning that is deeply, unmistakably Christian. Their faith, if they have it, draws them "back into life," to use Ames's phrase, rather than facilitating flight from it. It is perhaps this that explains one of the more curious aspects of the reception of Robinson's novels, which is that they have been received enthusiastically by secular, even aggressively atheist, readers. And it seems that that interest has been *because* of their obvious, earnest religiosity, rather than in spite of it. For example, Mark O'Connell, himself a "more or less fully paid-up atheist," writes, "I have read and loved a lot of literature about religion and religious experience—Tolstoy, Dostoevsky, Flannery O'Connor, the Bible—but it's only with Robinson that I have actually felt what it must be like to live with a sense of the divine" (O'Connell 2012).[6] Why is this? We will suggest that the answer is to be found in the Nietzschean conflict between life-denial and life-affirmation. Our instincts as denizens of the modern, thoroughly secular world are life-denying, in a sense that transcends whether we personally identify as Christians or atheists.[7] A vision of the world that genuinely seeks to clarify the stakes of affirming life and embody that affirmation, rather than simply to advance our culture wars to their next stage of escalation, is bound to speak to us. But that vision will speak to us all the more effectively if we understand the stakes of the predicament it's trying to address and what it would mean to face it honestly. That is what the Nietzschean context can give us, as readers of Robinson's novels and as modern people trying to figure out how we will live.

Our project began as a short piece focused only on *Gilead*, and on the person of John Ames. At the time, Ames was to be the unproblematic hero of the story. But a good reader of Robinson's corpus, and arguably even a close reader of *Gilead* itself, ought to have known that the story we wanted to tell could not, in the end, be so simple. Since *Gilead*, Robinson has written three more novels that take place in the same universe, revolve around the same characters, and cover many of the same plot points. The four Gilead novels—*Gilead, Home, Lila,* and *Jack*—obviously speak to and with each other, but also complicate each other. One of the key ways in which they do so, we will argue, is by complicating the status of John Ames. Ames appears in his own voice in *Gilead*, and that voice is so intoxicating as if to suggest, at times, that he is to serve as some incandescent, self-standing ideal. A careful reader will note, of course, that he has faults, but his readiness to admit to them almost seems itself another mark of his ideal status. However, as a reading of the later novels progressively reveals, Ames also has shortcomings of which he is not fully aware or at least is not concerned to highlight in *Gilead*; not only that but even some of his most important strengths, above all his ability to *see* life and the world around him as luminously valuable, are due not just to his own good nature but to the important influence of other characters in the novel, above all his wife, Lila. By the end of the four Gilead novels, it is arguable that characters like Lila, Glory, and Della are, in some important respects, closer than Ames to the religious ideal Robinson is trying to depict. And all of this still ignores *Housekeeping*, Robinson's first (and for many still her greatest) novel, which is itself in part a rumination on the dangers of life-denial. The development of our initial insight—that Ames was a Christian character deserving of Nietzschean respect—could thus only proceed by dealing with all of Robinson's novels. It turns out that it is not just the character of Ames but Robinson's fiction as a *whole* that is the proper and satisfying response to Nietzschean worries about the nihilism of Christianity, and modern life more generally. Such, at least, will be our contention in this book.

In Chapter 1, "The Life-Denial Critique of Christianity: Feuerbach and Nietzsche," we lay out the philosophical background that will inform our approach to Robinson's novels. The chapter has two parts. The first concerns the German philosopher Ludwig Feuerbach, a crucial linking point for our justification of reading Robinson through a Nietzschean lens. Despite the critical intent of Feuerbach's infamous book *The Essence of Christianity* (first ed., 1841), John Ames has a qualified but strong admiration for it, and Feuerbach's thought plays an important role in the life of Ames's brother, who becomes a professor and philosophical scholar of Feuerbach's work. Feuerbach is also an important early influence on Nietzsche and develops what is in some ways an early version of Nietzsche's "life-denial" critique of Christianity. Thus, we explain in some detail Feuerbach's so-called "projective" theory of religion, in a way that focuses on the elements of it that allow it both to inspire Nietzsche's own critique and to have its surprisingly salutary effect on Ames's theological views. In the second part of the chapter, we turn to Nietzsche himself, detailing the influence Feuerbach had on Nietzsche's conception of the practical problems posed by the Christian religion as he knew it, and then the sophisticated and dramatic critique of it that he developed in texts like *On the Genealogy of Morals* (first ed., 1887). We also deal with some of Nietzsche's own positive views, especially concerning his commitment to "love of fate" (*amor fati*), which will play a key role as well in our understanding of Robinson's novels.

In Chapter 2, "*Housekeeping*: Lessons in Life-Denial," we begin to apply that framework to Robinson's first novel. We argue that *Housekeeping*'s Ruth and Lucille, reeling in the wake of the suicide of their mother, offer two different examples of Nietzschean life-denial, though largely unconnected from any explicit Christian framework. Lucille denies life by allowing herself to be absorbed into her social world, ignoring the dangers of time and change by means of unreflective participation in the settled world of middle-class convention. Ruth, on the other hand, tries to nullify her loss by divesting herself of anything that can be taken from her. Ruth "keeps" her house by abandoning it. One ignores the reality of loss, while the other tries to imagine she has nothing to lose. Ruth's flight is the more honest one, and points in very oblique ways to more satisfying solutions, but both seek to disengage from the world in order to protect themselves from it. They thus raise a question that will guide much of Robinson's subsequent fiction: Is it possible to love life without falsifying it?

In Chapter 3, "*Gilead*: More Beauty than Our Eyes Can Bear," we highlight the Congregationalist pastor John Ames's attempts to give that leading question an affirmative answer. Ames's vision of life, exemplified best in his ecstatic descriptions of the natural world, is at once deeply informed by the Christian tradition in which he was raised and unflinchingly directed toward the people and things around him. Our main task is to explain what it is about Ames's life that allows him to adopt this posture of affirmation. We argue that it is largely due to the unique way in which his Christianity prompts him to revere the world and take joy in it. With this general conclusion in view, we look, first, to explain the particular ways Ames connects religion and joy and then, second, to show how this theoretical understanding is affirmed practically in Ames's own experience. The first task involves a close consideration of Ames's interaction with Feuerbach, while the second is an exploration of how these philosophical questions are addressed practically and in real time as Ames struggles to embrace the novel's prodigal son, his namesake, John ("Jack") Ames Boughton. Ames's ability to confront the failings of his past, culminating in his forgiveness of Jack, is the fulfillment of his "argument" with Feuerbach. A truly religious life is always and inevitably "drawn back into the world" (*Gilead* 238).

In Chapter 4, "O Sinner, Come *Home*," we turn our focus to two characters who have been drawn back into their family home: Jack and Glory Boughton. Though for many *Home* might naturally seem to be something of a step down from the dizzying existential heights of *Housekeeping* and *Gilead*, we argue that it plays an important role in complicating *Gilead*'s romantic portrayal of town life and the versions of Christianity that find their home therein. The Boughton household is in many ways a hostile place for Glory and Jack, a place that is more the cause of their weariness than a prospect for its relief. The reasons for this are themselves complex. Jack's rejection of Christianity (and, what for him amounts to the same thing, the family home) seems less rooted in any particular metaphysical skepticism than a loneliness brought on by the empty invocation of traditional pieties about sin and forgiveness by his father and others around him. He suspects that the sin that Christianity promises salvation from is not really the quite serious sins that *he* has committed. As such, his father's Christianity cannot help but appear hypocritical. It claims to reckon with the sins of humanity but is really only strong enough to deal with the socially respectable sins of quaint Midwesterners. By the end of the novel, Jack's sister Glory comes to see the limitations of these empty pieties and, in doing so, models a form of Christian forgiveness so beautiful in its conception that it imbues her present life with intense meaning and transforms the Boughton home into a place of genuine grace.

In Chapter 5, "*Jack*: A Glorious Presence," we depart from Robinson's publication order to consider in more detail the kind of love so powerfully developed in the character of Glory. Our focus is on Della Miles and some of the concerns her loyalty to Jack raises about the love extolled in the world of Gilead more generally. The worry is that the love displayed by Della (and by implication Ames and Glory) is in some important way disconnected from the actual world and, thus, more life-*denying* than affirming. Instead of being sensitive to the specificity of its object, such love often seems to look through it, being grounded in some nebulous and timeless feature like a person's "existence" or "soul." In response to this worry, we mount a defense of Della, arguing that her love for Jack is intimately connected to his particular characteristics. Since these characteristics have, to many, seemed rather unremarkable on the whole, we also attempt to clarify the background conditions that make Della especially open to loving someone like Jack. In order to do this, we draw attention to Della's poetic background, especially her affection for the poetry of Paul Laurence Dunbar. In the end, we conclude that Della models a kind of creative attention that Robinson regards as essential to the cultivation of a genuine love of life.

In Chapter 6, "*Lila*: More Life than We Can Bear," we end our analysis with a character who seems, in many ways, to be the culmination of Robinson's life-affirming vision: Lila. Lila marks the return of the outsider, a character—not so different from *Housekeeping*'s Ruth—who is shown a path back to community and restoration. This chapter looks to shine light on Lila's strength and grace by steadily developing the arc that spans her early experiences of shame and loneliness to the eventual restoration she discovers with Ames. We see this restoration confirmed in Lila's baptism but locate this in an unlikely place: the moment she "washes it off." This reverse-baptism is where Robinson locates the true *imitatio Christi*: a divine magnanimity that courts judgment out of love for others. Finally, we explore the way in which the love that drives Lila to her reverse-baptism expands through her gradual embrace of Christian concepts, especially the idea of "resurrection." We also see how Ames, under pressure from Lila, recommends a biblical hermeneutic that emphasizes worldly praxis. This, it turns out, is just one of several places where Lila seems to have as much to teach Ames as he does her.

Finally, in the "Conclusion: Our Fantastic Condition," we draw together the various threads of our Nietzschean analysis of Robinson's fiction. Both Nietzsche and Robinson encourage an effort to see the people around us, and life as a whole, as something beautiful, and thus something to be loved, and both see that project as running counter to some of the dominant currents of modern life and thought. Nietzsche sees a particular historical form of Christianity as the cause of these currents, but does not see, as Robinson's fiction can show us, that Christianity can also muster powerful resources for fighting them. We close the chapter, and our book, with the suggestion that Robinson and Nietzsche's efforts to articulate a vision of a new, freer way of life are more effective together than they could be separately.

Notes

1 See Dawkins (2006), Dennett (2007), Harris (2005), Hitchens (2009). For discussion of fictional responses to the new atheists, see Bradley and Tate (2010).
2 Because of this, Robinson has (rightly) been quite dismissive of them. See for instance her remarks about atheism in Robinson et al. (2018–19).
3 This dissatisfaction with their ultimate position is given nice expression by Kyla Ebels-Duggan: "[Dreyfus and Kelly's] engaging reading of selections from the Western canon leaves everyone right where they were. It neither addresses the monotheist nor delivers the despairing secularist" (Ebels-Duggan 2011).

4 The historian Peter Gordon responds thus to Hägglund's claim that religious believers denigrate this life in looking to the next one, in his review of *This Life* in *The Nation*: "For many religious believers, the recognition of a higher meaning beyond life is precisely why they care so much about their moral and political conduct in this world" (Gordon 2019).

5 See, for instance, Hunt (1985) and Leiter (2002, 295–7).

6 See also the comment of Peg Boyers in Marilynne Robinson et al. (2018–2019): "If only, if only: to have that kind of robust faith that is actually smart enough to have doubt. If I could find my way to a religious belief I'd want it represented by Marilynne."

7 See Garret Keizer, reviewing Robinson's *Home*: "Had I an atheist friend who asked, 'Can you tell me please what this religion business is all about, not as some metaphysical hypothesis or historical phenomenon, but what it really means to *be religious*?' I might hand him or her a copy of Marilynne Robinson's novel *Gilead*. 'Read this,' I'd say, 'and it will give you a pretty good idea.'

And had I a religious friend, a co-religionist friend, who asked, 'Can you tell me please what's wrong with us, not the obvious corruptions of the gospel that any sophomore skeptic can point out, but the fundamental sicknesses that live so close to the core of our faith that one has to wonder if they're not essential to the faith itself?' I might recommend Robinson's latest novel *Home*. 'Read this,' I'd say, 'and it might give you a clue'" (Keizer 2009).

# 1

The Life-Denial Critique of Christianity
Feuerbach and Nietzsche

Marilynne Robinson never explicitly refers to Friedrich Nietzsche in her novels, despite the fact that those novels can be quite allusive. And she only very rarely mentions him in her essayistic work. There is no reason to believe that he played any explicit formative role in the development of her thought or her novelistic practice. Nevertheless, we want to argue that he *should* play such a role in our reading of her. The reasons for this are twofold: first, Nietzsche stands as the dramatic peak of a line of critical thinking about Christianity that was prominent especially in Germany throughout the nineteenth century, and this critique deeply informs Robinson's own sense of that against which her Christian vision ought to be defined.[1] This is apparent in the many and surprisingly positive references in *Gilead* to Ludwig Feuerbach, the German philosopher who did more than perhaps anyone in the nineteenth century to initiate that critique. Second, Nietzsche's own positive program, sketchy though it remains, shares important structural affinities with the position at which Robinson arrives, especially in its goal of an affirmative attitude toward what John Ames, in Robinson's *Gilead*, ecstatically refers to as "this life, this world" (*Gilead* 9).

This chapter has three main goals. The first is to explain in some detail Feuerbach's so-called "projective" theory of religion, as he developed it in his infamous *The Essence of Christianity* (*Das Wesen des Christentums*; first edition, 1841). The second is to detail the influence Feuerbach had on Nietzsche, and how Nietzsche himself developed the life-denial critique of Christianity in his own highly sophisticated and dramatic form, in works like *On the Genealogy of Morals* (first edition, 1887). The third is to point to Nietzsche's programmatic claims about how the problems posed by this life-denial for our lives in the modern world should and should not be addressed, and to suggest some ways in which those claims might point to the need for something like Robinson's fiction.

1 Ludwig Feuerbach: "God, Who Is My Being"

We are clearly meant to be somewhat surprised that John Ames has a certain affection for Feuerbach. Feuerbach is, after all, known mostly for his atheism; *The Essence of Christianity* made a huge impression when it was published precisely because of the frankness of its rejection of orthodox belief in God.[2] Though the perception of its "danger" for religious believers had perhaps somewhat diminished by the time in which the narrative of *Gilead* takes place, it is not at all strange that Ames's brother Edward considers himself to be doing something a bit risqué in giving his little brother such a book. And yet, here is Ames speaking to his young son:

> Feuerbach is a famous atheist, but he is about as good on the joyful aspects of religion as anybody, and he loves the world. Of course he thinks religion could just stand out of the way and let joy exist pure and undisguised. That is his one error, and it is significant. But he is marvelous on the subject of joy, and also on its religious expressions. (*Gilead* 23–4)

This attitude sets the stage for our analysis. Feuerbach is, it seems, not merely an unsuccessful critic of religion/Christianity but a positive source, "as good as any" on the "joyful" aspects of religion, which are certainly the central aspects of Ames's own religion. Late in *Gilead*, after Ames has undergone his reconciliation with the troubled Jack Boughton, he leaves him a copy of Feuerbach's *Essence*, with a passage underlined: "Only that which is apart from my own being is capable of being doubted by me. How then can I doubt of God, who is my being? To doubt of God is to doubt myself" (*Gilead* 239; cf. Feuerbach (1957, 239)).[3]

However, one cannot glean all the important details of Feuerbach's position from Ames's stray observations concerning him in *Gilead*, many of which center on the way Feuerbach interprets the Christian sacrament of baptism (to which we will return below). What then are these details? What was Feuerbach's position, and why *was* it taken to be so dangerous, both in his own time and in that of Ames's adolescence?

Feuerbach is sometimes called a proponent of a "projectionist" theory of religion, though the term "projection" appears somewhat seldom in his book. The claim that this term attempts to capture, however, is relatively simple and faithful to his intent. In Feuerbach's view, belief in God has its origin in an imaginative projection, on the part of human beings, of certain valued aspects of their human nature, onto a being conceived of as external to humanity. Predicates that are traditionally applied to God—for example, his omniscience, omnipotence, all-loving benevolence—are applicable to human beings in a limited form. We are knowers, but do not know all; we have power, but it is limited; we are capable of loving our fellow human beings, but often fall into hatred instead. We recognize these limitations *as* limitations, however, because we have a conception not just of ourselves as individuals but of human nature, that is, humanity as a species.[4] Human nature is, in Feuerbach's view, limitless: "Every limitation of the reason, or in general of the nature of man, rests on a delusion, an error" (EC 7). But this fact does not necessarily lend consolation to us, since we are all individuals with very real limitations, who do not perfectly exemplify the capabilities of our species. Religion in Feuerbach's view is born of dissatisfaction with that limited state, a dissatisfaction that he believes can only be addressed by the imagination. The imagination projects the perfected version of these fundamentally human predicates onto a divine being, posited as transcendent of human consciousness. But this projection happens immediately and instinctively, not as a result of deliberation or a conscious mental process: "The essence of religion is the immediate, involuntary, unconscious contemplation of the human nature as another, a distinct nature" (EC 213).

Feuerbach does not object to this imaginative act of projection simply as such. What he says of belief in divine revelation in particular—it "is a childlike belief, and is only respectable so long as it is childlike"—holds for his view of religious belief in general (EC 208). It is "childlike," insofar as it is not yet anything like a rational articulation of a metaphysical belief grounded in real evidence; it is, rather, belief in an object based purely on feeling. But that feeling—a yearning to transcend individual limitation—is universal and contains, even if only implicitly, a deep affirmation of the value of humanity. That this must be so is evident in Feuerbach's description of the phenomenological content of the feeling: "[t]he divine nature which is discerned by feeling is in truth nothing else than feeling enraptured, in ecstasy with itself—feeling intoxicated with joy, blissful in its own plenitude" (EC 9).[5] The belief in God that the feeling naturally engenders is, in Feuerbach's view, obviously not rationally justifiable, but he does not object to it on those grounds, at least not initially. Rather, he says that it is "man's earliest and also indirect form of self-knowledge" (EC 13). Because the object of the projection is *in fact* human nature, though it (falsely) presents itself as a nature transcendent of humanity, its development and articulation ought to lead to a higher human self-knowledge, guided and nourished still by that primordial feeling of rapture, ecstasy, plenitude. The reason, in fact, that Feuerbach finds it essential to formulate a theory of religion in the first place is precisely to assist in the project of rendering this anthropological impetus explicit. His goal is not to undermine the natural impulses that give birth to religious practice and religious thinking but to make explicit the positive value judgments concerning humanity implicit in them. Though his project is obviously at odds with religious orthodoxy, and to that extent is "negative" and "destructive," it is so "only in relation to the *un*human, not to the human elements of religion" (EC xxxvi).

The second possible future of the religious impulse, that guided by its "unhuman" elements, finds its modern and most virulent expression in theology (and especially *Christian* theology). Theology is, for Feuerbach, the fruitless and necessarily contradictory attempt to make the object of religion's imaginative projection the subject of purportedly "scientific" reflection.[6] This project has purely theoretical problems, and Feuerbach spends a good part of the second half of *The Essence of Christianity* detailing them. But what is most important for our purposes is the *practical* problem it raises. The initial impetus of the religious projection was, recall, a feeling of dissatisfaction on the part of individual human beings concerning their limitations. The projected god is a consolation for this, but *only* if the god is itself recognizably human. The religious imagination, as Feuerbach depicts it, is *essentially* anthropomorphic: it does not shrink from attributing human mental activities, emotional responses, and physical capacities to the god, if these are things it values in human beings and wishes were perfected in them.[7] But when the god is turned into an object of intellectual reflection, all these qualities are rendered suspect. Because the ideal and perfected form of human nature does not present itself to us as an object of sensuous perception, and indeed since everything that presents itself to sensuous perception is in fact limited and imperfect, the divine must exist in some way utterly unfamiliar to us.[8] The initially posited separation of God and man was something "involuntary and harmless," but now becomes "an intentional, excogitated separation" (EC 197). The anthropomorphism of applying human predicates to the god is seen as intellectually suspect—either the god cannot have anything truly predicated of him (negative theology) or at best the predicates apply to him only analogically (the more influential view of Aquinas). Either way, the now theologized religion becomes the bringer not of consolation but of alienation from my true nature. I am limited, and God is not, but that is no consolation to me, since there is an impassible gulf between him and me. The continued articulation of theological categories only serves to render this central problem ever clearer and more intolerable. In the context of Christianity, it is here that we can find the origin of beliefs like that of original sin and the consequent need for salvation, and views about the last judgment and the afterlife.[9] Belief in God becomes an expression not of affirmation of human life, as it was in the initial, "childlike" phase, but of explicit *denial* of human life, insofar as it finds itself inadequate compared to the external standard set by the divine being.

Christianity serves as the most dramatic example of both the best and worst tendencies of the religious impulse. It is crucial to the religious impulse that gives birth to imaginative projection that the God thereby imagined is not indifferent to the concerns of humans. Christianity posits not just that God cares in some sense about us and responds to our prayers but that he *loves* us, indeed just *is* love. And the "us" that he loves is not one particular tribe or nation but humanity as such. Thus Christianity more than any other religion expressed a deification of indiscriminate love of human beings as such, especially in accounts of the life of Jesus Christ. Just as importantly, the emphasis Christianity places on God becoming human in the *physical person* of Jesus Christ, though it caused a number of intractable problems for the theologians, inevitably suggested a high valuation of humanity, and ultimately that "[m]an was already in God, was already God himself, before God became man, i.e., showed himself as man" (EC 50).[10] Insofar as Feuerbach sought to bring to fruition the desire for human self-knowledge and self-affirmation inherent in the religious impulse, he thus saw the Christian religion as of epochal importance. The goal of the anthropological program was to bring to realization the Christian ideal of love of one's fellow man, not as the action of God, or of ourselves in the transformed state of some future life, but in *this* life, *this* world.[11]

But Christianity was also, especially in its modern form, deeply corrupted by the theological program. Especially when taken in its official and state-sanctioned forms, modern Christianity for Feuerbach was far more a creature of theology than the childlike impulses which initially had given birth to it. The attempt to develop a rationalistic or scientific system out of the claims of religion, to make of religion an activity of the intellect rather than of human feeling, led inevitably to "an inexhaustible mine of falsehoods, illusions, contradictions, and sophisms" (EC 214), whose result is a complete undermining of the original religious impulse. That impulse, recall, is an affirmative one, an attempt to deal productively with the problem of human limitation by positing and attempting to develop a relationship with a being who transcends those limitations but whose goodness is nonetheless grounded in peculiarly human modes of value (knowledge, power, love). But theology, by insisting on treating the posited being as an object of scientific analysis, betrays this impulse and in fact leads to a denial of the value of human life and despair in the face of our limitations. Proofs of the existence of God seek to establish as the conclusion of an argument something that ought to be an immediate, phenomenal reality to the religious believer, and thus have the effect of separating man further from God and in the end encouraging atheism (EC 198–201). Belief in the necessity of special divine revelation gives further expression to that separation: God, since he is without human limitation and wholly other than us, is claimed to be inaccessible to us by the pitiful means of normal human inquiry, which is ultimately vain and fruitless; if he is to be known, it must be because he reveals himself to us (EC 206–9). God, far from confirming for us our deep value as knowing, making, and loving beings, in fact makes us all the more conscious of our failings and their inevitability. God transcends the depravity and sinfulness inherent in the limited beings humans are, and must hate in us that which we have insufficient power to overcome. The Christian comes to see herself as unsalvageable by her own efforts, so that active love of self and fellow human beings is replaced by a passive faith in the saving power of God. That faith, as it becomes more influenced by the overintellectualization of the theological impulse, inevitably becomes highly partisan and sectarian, such that Christians "must therefore love only Christians—others only as possible Christians" (EC 254). Christians become "blind to what there is of goodness and truth lying at the foundation of heathen worship" (EC 256). Thus, the object of their love is emphatically *not*, as Jesus has advised, human beings but only humans insofar as they have submitted themselves to something that is not them, that is beyond them and transcends them (i.e., God). Though Jesus and the disciples sought to define their religion in a way that transcended tribalism, the result of the theologization of the religion is a kind of intellectualized tribalism, whose ultimate meaning is and must be a denial of the value of humanity.

Against this intellectualized and life-denying view of religion, Feuerbach posits an "anthropology," or a renewed study of the features and capabilities of the human being. This project would be guided not by the negative value judgment of human limitation but the positive value judgment, immediately present already in the initial imaginative projection of religion, of a humanity freed from those limitations:

> The necessary turning point of history is therefore the open confession, that the consciousness of God is nothing else than the consciousness of the species; that man can and should raise himself only above the limits of his individuality, and not above the laws, the positive essential conditions of his species; that there is no other essence which man can think, dream of, imagine, feel, believe in, wish for, love and adore as the *absolute*, than the essence of human nature itself. (EC 270)

What is needed then to make this open confession possible is a kind of reversal of the original movement religion had enacted—what had been projected onto God as entirely other than us must be reapplied to its real source in humanity. What traditional modern religion regards as mystical, spiritual values are in fact, when understood in this way, thoroughly human and indeed quite quotidian.

Feuerbach displays this at the close of his book by means of a discussion of the Christian sacraments of baptism and the Lord's supper, the "characteristic symbols of the Christian religion" (EC 275). Baptism ought to be seen as a means of celebrating the value of water, the "universal element of life" (EC 276). Indeed, Feuerbach suggests that the Christian practice itself is a relic of pagan nature-worshipping practices, which came closer to the profound truth it is supposed to represent, the "wonderful but natural effect of water on man" (EC 275). This effect is not just physical (though of course it is also that); water also has "moral and intellectual" effects, revealed to us in its power to cleanse, and symbolically to wash away malign forces and refresh us for new efforts. It also is "the readiest means of making friends with nature," of feeling immediately to ourselves the truth that we are born from and dependent on nature and the rest of life. Simple bathing is, or can be, a profound experience: "the profoundest secrets lie in common everyday things, such as supranaturalistic religion and speculation ignore" (EC 276). But while baptism reminds us of our dependence on nature, the Lord's supper reminds us of the ways in which human beings are set apart from the rest of nature. It symbolizes this by means of bread and wine, two substances that exist only because of human ingenuity and labor. Through them we are to "adore the supernatural power of mind, of consciousness, of man" (EC 277). That power, though it is set over against nature, is not independent of it—the flour for the bread and the grape for the wine are products of nature, and so humanity only gives form to an existing matter. But that form is essential for them to serve as sustenance for us; thus, the bread and wine "typify to us the truth that Man is the true God and Savior of man" (EC 277). Just as the simple act of bathing is exalted in baptism, the act of eating and drinking is exalted in the Lord's supper, elevated by this conception to the status of "a religious act" (EC 277).

Feuerbach knew that these ideas were bound to be mocked by his early readers. He anticipates that some will be "inclined to smile" at the thought that such simple things could bear such weighty significance. And indeed, in a preface added to the second edition of his book in 1843, Feuerbach is already responding to such critics, who charge that his work ends in the seemingly banal proposition that "bathing, eating, and drinking are the *summa summarum*" of religion (EC xli). It is telling that Feuerbach's response is to double down—that is indeed his position, and his critics' mistake to see the proposition as banal. First, as has already been said, what is common and everyday is not necessarily for that reason uninteresting or insignificant. And, more pointedly, it is easier to see the deep significance of water and food when they are taken away, when daily acts of bathing, eating, and drinking are "unnaturally, violently interrupted" (EC 277). Hunger, thirst, and uncleanliness can destroy the life and motivation of the human being;

experiencing want of any of them is sufficient to motivate one to see the sense in celebrating their presence, to "vindicate to common things an uncommon significance, *to life, as such, a religious import*" (EC 278).[12]

2 Friedrich Nietzsche: "I Seek God!"

Nietzsche's analysis of religious belief, like Feuerbach's, is informed by a deep sympathy with some of what he takes to be the underlying aims of religion (though precisely *what* he takes these to be is quite different, as we shall see).[13] At the same time, Nietzsche was able to express his capacious vision in an image- and symbol-rich language that gave it a dramatic and even prophetic force of which Feuerbach was incapable. Thus, though Feuerbach's *Essence of Christianity* achieved a significant level of popularity and influence more or less immediately upon publication, and Nietzsche's works took a long time to find readers, the latter have proved to be the more widely and enduringly popular, and the ones that seem to call more forcefully for some kind of response from their readers.

Nietzsche's penchant for drama is on full display in the 125th aphorism in *The Gay Science* (1882), entitled "The madman":

> Have you not heard of that madman who lit a lantern in the bright morning hours, ran to the market place, and cried incessantly: "I seek God! I seek God!"—As many of those who did not believe in God were standing around just then, he provoked much laughter. Has he got lost? asked one. Did he lose his way like a child? asked another. Or is he hiding? Is he afraid of us? Has he gone on a voyage? emigrated?— Thus they yelled and laughed.
>
> The madman jumped into their midst and pierced them with his eyes. "Whither is God?" he cried; "I will tell you. *We have killed him*— you and I. All of us are his murderers. But how did we do this? How could we drink up the sea? Who gave us the sponge to wipe away the entire horizon? What were we doing when we unchained this earth from its sun? Whither is it moving now? Whither are we moving? Away

from all suns? Are we not plunging continually? Backward, sideward, forward, in all directions? Is there still any up or down? Are we not straying, as through an infinite nothing? Do we not feel the breath of empty space? Has it not become colder? Is not night continually closing in on us? Do we not need to light lanterns in the morning? Do we hear nothing as yet of the noise of the gravediggers who are burying God? Do we smell nothing as yet of the divine decomposition? Gods, too, decompose. God is dead. God remains dead. And we have killed him.

"How shall we comfort ourselves, the murderers of all murderers? What was holiest and mightiest of all that the world has yet owned has bled to death under our knives: who will wipe this blood off us? What water is there for us to clean ourselves? What festivals of atonement, what sacred games shall we have to invent? Is not the greatness of this deed too great for us? Must we ourselves not become gods simply to appear worthy of it? There has never been a greater deed; and whoever is born after us—for the sake of this deed he will belong to a higher history than all history hitherto."

Here the madman fell silent and looked again at his listeners; and they, too, were silent and stared at him in astonishment. At last he threw his lantern on the ground, and it broke into pieces and went out. "I have come too early," he said then; "my time is not yet. This tremendous event is still on its way, still wandering; it has not yet reached the ears of men. Lightning and thunder require time; the light of the stars requires time; deeds, though done, still require time to be seen and heard. This deed is still more distant from them than most distant stars—*and yet they have done it themselves.*"

It has been related further that on the same day the madman forced his way into several churches and there struck up his *requiem aeternam deo*. Led out and called to account, he is said always to have replied nothing but: "What after all are these churches now if they are not the tombs and sepulchers of God?" (GS 125)[14]

The passage is justly famous and obviously contains a great deal worth commenting upon. For now, it is worth focusing on two elements of the story. First, though one might expect the "God is dead" line to be an insult directed at religious believers, the madman's proclamation is in fact directed at atheists. The madman is worried primarily not about people who believe in God but about people who think that religious belief is a matter for blasé mockery. This is typical of Nietzsche's treatment of religion. He thinks that the Christian religion has been a disaster of epic proportions for humanity and does not consider himself above mocking it from time to time, but he never takes it with anything but absolute seriousness, and he never doubts that the Christian religion speaks to something deep in us, something that will have to be addressed even after that belief has died. The Christian religion is, as the madman says, what was "holiest and mightiest of all that the world has yet owned," and we should not make fun of its drama of "festivals of atonement" and "sacred games," but rather think about how we might create them anew in the future. It is significant for understanding Nietzsche's thought that he is just as concerned with attacking certain secular responses to the death of Christian belief as he is with attacking the belief itself, perhaps even more so.

The other aspect of the passage worth emphasizing for now is its vagueness about the so-called "killing" of God. The collective "we," which Nietzsche elsewhere makes clear refers primarily to modern Europeans,[15] have done something, the effect of which is the death of Christian religious belief, but what is it, exactly? To what historical phenomenon is the madman (and through him, Nietzsche) alluding? Is he thinking of scientific or philosophical arguments? Changes in social organization? Political upheavals? Are we to take it that the madman (and through him, Nietzsche) thinks that Christian belief has been *disproven*, somehow? One of the frustrating things for a Christian reader of Nietzsche is his consistent silence on this point. Revealingly, he says elsewhere in *The Gay Science* that "What decides against Christianity now is our taste, not our reasons" (GS 132). But what was this taste? And, since it did in fact give birth to reasons of a kind, what were those reasons? Why did Nietzsche reject Christianity?

Nietzsche was born in 1844, in the small town of Röcken in Saxony.[16] Feuerbach had published his *Essence of Christianity* just three years earlier, and by 1844 it was every religious radical's favorite book. But

Nietzsche himself would know nothing of this until much later, well after the initial cultural shockwaves let loose by Feuerbach's book had subsided. The household into which he was born was deeply pious—his father, Carl Ludwig, was a Lutheran Pietist minister, and a follower of the more sentimentalist, less rationalist *Erweckungsbewegung* or "Awakened Movement" within that tradition.[17] However, Carl Ludwig Nietzsche died in 1849, when Nietzsche was not yet five years old. Not long after, in 1850, Nietzsche's only brother, still just a baby, followed his father to the grave. The Nietzsches (now Friedrich himself, his mother Fransziska, his elder sister Elisabeth, and his paternal grandmother Erdmuthe), who had lived in a parsonage in Röcken tied to the elder Nietzsche's ministerial position, moved after his death to the larger town of Naumburg. Though the early death of a much beloved father who was a minister to boot obviously played some role in Nietzsche's later thinking about religion, the fact that he was now being raised in a house full of women was at least as important, if not more. Nietzsche's later misogyny will not be our primary concern, but it is worthy of note that his critique of the "weakness" of Christian morality often went in concert with criticism of what Nietzsche regarded as "feminine."[18] His relations with his mother, grandmother, and sister seem to have been mostly happy, but he also seems to have associated them and their sex with unreflective piety and a dependence on the comforts of family life, both of which he sought to outgrow.

Though the young Nietzsche himself may have been planning in a loose sense to follow his father into the ministry,[19] his career as a strikingly independent thinker began early. During his time at Schulpforta, the prestigious school close to Naumburg, Nietzsche made close friends with two other pupils, Wilhelm Pinder and Gustav Krug, and set up a literary society called "*Germania*," whose primary purpose was to serve as a forum for the boys to share and critique each other's literary and artistic compositions. Among Nietzsche's contributions were some striking philosophical and religious essays, which already evinced a freethinker's separation from the more instinctive and comfortable Christianity in which he had been raised. Nietzsche asked for two of

Feuerbach's works, including *The Essence of Christianity*, as birthday presents in 1861, and likely read them not long after. In a draft of a letter to Pinder and Krug from the following April, Nietzsche declares himself in sympathy with some of Feuerbach's basic ideas—that Christianity is "essentially a matter of the heart" rather than the intellect, that its dogmas are merely "symbols" expressing deeper anthropological truths, and most importantly for our purposes, that belief in the supernatural is in fact an alien addition to this anthropological essence, such that "the illusion of the supernatural has placed the human spirit in a false relationship to the earthly world." Nietzsche closes the letter with the claim that "Humanity will become manly through arduous doubts and battles; it recognizes in itself 'the beginning, the middle, the end of religion.'"[20]

Though these words still expressed a kind of cautious attachment to the values of Christianity (suitably masculinized), they would already have been quite enough to scandalize his family. This process was accelerated during Nietzsche's early years at university at Bonn. There, in 1865, Nietzsche read for the first time David Friedrich Strauss's infamous *Das Leben Jesu, kritisch bearbeitet* ("The Life of Jesus, Critically Examined"), in which Strauss applied the critical-historical methods developed in classical philology (which was to be Nietzsche's primary area of study) to the analysis of biblical texts, and specifically the four gospels. In doing so, Strauss highlighted numerous contradictions in the biblical texts, denied the divinity of Jesus, and claimed that the accounts of his miracles were attempts at mythmaking rather than reports of actual events. Nietzsche apparently came home to his family over the Easter holidays of 1865 brandishing the book; in May of that year, his sister writes him, saying, "I really regret your bringing the unhappy Strauss with you on holiday, and that I've heard so much about him from you" (quoted in Young 2010, 59). Elisabeth goes on to express her dismay at Strauss's (and now Nietzsche's) doubt and criticism of "the loftiest things," and that for her this development is as if a "firm protective wall has fallen, and one now stands before a broad, map-less, confusing, mist-enshrouded desert where there is nothing firm." Clearly the pathos of the madman fable owes something to this evocative description of Elisabeth's, and it clearly spoke to Nietzsche then as well. In his response to her, he makes clear that the path he is taking is dangerous, but that it must be if it is really aimed at truth: "Here the ways of men divide: if you wish to strive for peace of soul and happiness, then believe; if you wish to be a disciple of truth, then inquire" (quoted in Young 2010, 60).

Taking up the stance of the fearless, intrepid inquirer made Nietzsche ripe for one last influence, that of the pessimist Arthur Schopenhauer, and especially his work *The World as Will and Representation*. Nietzsche later said of Schopenhauer that one of the things he respected most about him was that he was the first "admitted and uncompromising atheist" among the Germans: "the ungodliness of existence counted for him as something given, palpable, indisputable" (GS 357). Schopenhauer's conception of the "ungodliness of existence" is straightforward enough to state briefly. Schopenhauer's view was that the whole of the objective world was a manifestation of an underlying will, or will-to-live, which was characterized by an infinite striving, impossible to finally satisfy. Thus, our life and life itself is, at root, a kind of continuous suffering, whether in the form of the pain of not having what one strives for or of the boredom of lacking something for which to strive.[21] And worst of all, nothing awaits the end of this process as its final consummation or redemption; the striving goes on forever, never satisfied, even when the particular manifestation of it that I am ceases in death. Existence is finite, fundamentally unpleasant to us, and has no purpose. Even Feuerbach and Strauss, who had boldly questioned prior religious dogmas, had not gone this far. They had maintained a form of teleological optimism from the Christian worldview, insisting only that certain orthodox religious beliefs (in the afterlife, in miracles, etc.) in fact got in the way of humans achieving their ends. Schopenhauer argued that there was no final end to achieve after all; ceasing to believe in God will bring us no nearer to happiness than believing in him did. The only way out was, by way of various ascetic practices, to seek to deny the insatiable will altogether.

One might have expected the committed atheist Schopenhauer to be hostile to Christianity, and indeed he was hostile to its supernatural claims. But he also found in Christianity one of the strongest statements, in mythological form, of what he took to be basic pessimistic truths. In particular, he saw the great Christian drama of humanity "falling" into original sin with Adam, only to be "saved" by the intervention of a God, to be a mythological statement of his own view:

> The doctrine of original sin (affirmation of the will) and of salvation (denial of the will) is really the great truth which constitutes the kernel of Christianity, while the rest is in the main only clothing and covering, or something accessory. (Schopenhauer 1969, vol. I, 405)

Schopenhauer's basic idea is that the Christian teaching that human beings are subject to original sin (perhaps most strongly expressed in the Calvinist doctrine of the "total depravity" of human beings) is a way of capturing in mythological form the pessimistic thought that human life is essentially unsatisfiable striving (and hence endless suffering), and that affirming that life can only lead to more suffering. The doctrine of the salvation of human beings by the grace of God is, similarly, a way of capturing the thought that there is nothing that humans themselves can do to fix the problem; they can only come to know their powerlessness, and through that perhaps quiet their wills (a knowledge Schopenhauer thinks is expressed in the Lutheran doctrine of *sola fide*, i.e., that "only faith" can save us, and not good deeds).

For Schopenhauer, these doctrines are the "kernel" of Christian teaching, while all else that attaches to it is a mere "shell." (In fact, Schopenhauer says that "There is nothing in which we have to distinguish the kernel from the shell so much as in Christianity" (1969, vol. II, 625).) In the New Testament, "the world is generally spoken of as something to which we do not belong, which we do not love, the ruler of which, in fact, is the devil" (1969, vol. II, 624). Schopenhauer sees this negative attitude toward the world especially in Christian teachings about sex, which he sees as the central manifestation of attachment to the will to live, and to which Christians, in his view, were fundamentally opposed. This is clearest in the praise of celibacy as the highest virtue, and the consequent requirement that priests remain celibate, thus marking their ascetic detachment from the will to live. This strict teaching, Schopenhauer suggests, was most firmly adhered to during the time of the early church fathers (of which he seems to have preferred Augustine), but the spread of Christianity to the masses and its rise to greater political power inevitably meant a loosening of this ethical teaching. Thus Christendom, as many authors after him were to agree, was the enemy of true Christianity. Schopenhauer goes so far as to consign all of Protestantism to the status of "shell" rather than "kernel": the Protestants drop the celibacy requirement for their leaders, and have increasingly developed a more naively optimistic worldview overall, in which God will give us a "much pleasanter world" if only we "conform to his will in certain respects," so that Christianity becomes "a religion for comfortable, married, and civilized Protestant parsons" (1969).

Nietzsche was of course himself the product of just such a "comfortable, married, and civilized" Protestantism, and it is likely that such passages in Schopenhauer put him in mind of his discussion with his sister in May 1865, in which he had drawn the contrast between the comforts of orthodox Christian belief and the dangerous but inspiring path of the inquirer. Schopenhauer had now given him a model in that vein, an intrepid inquirer consumed so completely by the desire for the truth about life that he was willing to follow it to the un-Christian, "ungodly," even utterly demoralizing end. And we often find Schopenhauer's view of Christianity repeated in Nietzsche's works, not always with attributions to Schopenhauer: that the Old and New Testaments have fundamentally different messages (BGE 52), that Christianity preaches hostility to the world and especially to the sexual impulse (TI, "Ancients," 4), and that the core of Christianity is ascetic (GM, third essay). Only the value judgments are reversed: while Schopenhauer saw these points as marks in favor of Christianity, Nietzsche most certainly did not.

Feuerbach, as we have seen, saw the essence of Christianity not in asceticism and life-denial but in a childlike affirmation of the real values of life (albeit wrongly projected onto a transcendent deity). The doctrines that Schopenhauer (and later Nietzsche) saw as essential to Christianity—original sin and the consequent need for salvation—Feuerbach saw as later theological accretions inimical to the initial, life-affirming impetus of the religion. Though Nietzsche only rarely mentioned Feuerbach in his published writings, while repeatedly engaging with Schopenhauer, Nietzsche did not just drop Feuerbach for Schopenhauer, nor was he ever a blind follower of either of them. The originality of Nietzsche's critical treatment of Christianity, and ultimately that treatment's fertility in his larger project of a critique of the asceticism of modern life as a whole, stems in large part from the way in which these two volatile influences interacted in his psyche. Nietzsche internalized from an early age Feuerbach's life-affirming vitalism, but that view was complicated and sharpened by a desire to have the courage to see life as it is and not to fall prey to naive illusions. That desire was certainly fueled by Schopenhauer's example, but it was not created by it. Already in his personal life Nietzsche was inclined to regard Christianity, at least as he had experienced it in his family (and perhaps especially in his sister), as just such a naive illusion, believed in primarily not for its truth but for the peculiar kind of comfort and consolation it promised to bestow on our lives, full of suffering as they are. And it is important for Nietzsche's later development that Schopenhauer did *not* renounce this yearning for consolation. He too thought there was a "need" in humanity to make sense of suffering and death that only religion (for the masses) or the true pessimistic philosophy (for the truly learned) could satisfy, by preaching that that suffering had a cosmic meaning and was shared by all. Nietzsche rejected this too, and thus ultimately came to see even Schopenhauer's philosophy as corrupted by the life-denying spirit that had animated Christianity, and that the latter was the true enemy of a healthy and vigorous modern Europe.

And so, Nietzsche opposed that enemy, with all of the rhetorical ammunition at his considerable disposal. He keeps none of that ammunition in reserve in his late work, *The Antichrist*:

> The Christian idea of God—God as a god of the sick, God as spider, God as spirit—is one of the most corrupt conceptions of God the world has ever seen; this may even represent a new low in the declining development of the types of god. God having degenerated into a *contradiction of life* instead of its transfiguration and eternal *yes*! God as declared aversion to life, to nature, to the will to life! God as the formula for every slander against "the here and now," for every lie about the "beyond"! God as the deification of nothingness, the canonization of the will to nothingness! (A 18)

Nietzsche thus takes his distinctive task to be not only to attack Christianity philosophically but to understand it as an historical phenomenon, both in its origins and in its legacy in secular, post-Christian Europe. In what follows, we will present three intertwining themes of Nietzsche's critique, all of which serve to elaborate on the life-denial charge and to make clear the key claims of his historical analysis. They are (i) Christianity's peculiar focus on *morality*; (ii) the use of the concept of "sin," and the doctrine of original sin in particular; and (iii) belief in a (moralized) afterlife.

Morality: Christianity is for Nietzsche a religion marked by an obsession with morality—it has, he says, a "determination" to "sanction *only* moral values," at the expense of all others (BT, "Attempt at a Self-Criticism," 5).[22] Nietzsche thinks it is key to the diagnosis of what ails an increasingly secular late modern Europe that its culture is highly moralized, too, and that that is precisely because it is a post-Christian society. How then did this close connection come about? In what ways does Christianity betray itself as being a thoroughly "moral" religion?

The best way to approach this point is by way of comparison of Christianity with another religious system for which Nietzsche obviously had more respect: Greek polytheism. Nietzsche's first published work,

The Birth of Tragedy, goes out of its way to emphasize the nonmoralistic impulses that gave birth to the Olympian gods:

> Anyone who approaches these Olympians with another religion in his heart and proceeds to look for signs of moral loftiness in them, or indeed holiness, or incorporeal spirituality, or a loving gaze filled with compassion, will soon be forced to turn his back on them in dismay and disappointment. Nothing here reminds us of asceticism, of spirituality and duty; everything here speaks only of over-brimming, indeed triumphant existence, where everything that exists has been deified, regardless of whether it is good or evil. (BT 3)

Nietzsche's fairly simple point is that the Greek deities are poorly suited to being univocal moral exemplars;[23] not only are they constantly embroiled in disagreements, and often outright war, they also act in ways that go against what we would take to be traditional moral precepts—especially those concerning sex—and seem to exult in doing so rather than feeling shame or guilt. It is, for Nietzsche, precisely the fact that impulses both "good" and "evil" are "deified" in them that lends them their great significance. In Nietzsche's view, the Greeks had an intimation of Schopenhauer's pessimistic wisdom, which he (like Schopenhauer) saw most clearly expressed in the story of Silenus, the satyr and companion of Dionysus, whose secret wisdom was that it was best never to have been born, second best to die soon. But unlike Schopenhauer, who saw the Olympian gods as a simple recapitulation to naive optimism, Nietzsche thought that the Greeks created their gods not out of a need for moral guidance but because they were consumed by the thought that existence was a torment, and needed a vision, however imaginary, of a life worth living: "Thus gods justify the life of men by living it themselves—the only satisfactory theodicy! Under the bright sunshine of such gods existence is felt to be worth attaining" (BT). It is telling that Nietzsche here invokes the notion of theodicy—a Christian concept with obviously moral implications. Milton may have set out to "justifie the wayes of God to men" in *Paradise Lost*, in the sense of showing how a good God could allow the existence of evil, but Homer in the *Illiad* and *Odyssey* embarked on a very different project: to justify the ways of man, both good and evil, to *themselves*, by transfiguring them into the ways of gods. Homer's success is the result not of compelling moral argument but of aesthetic greatness—it is the inspiring glory of his portrait of the gods that gives them their power.

But polytheism did more than just save the Greeks from pessimistic despair. Polytheism gave the Greeks an opportunity, rare among premodern cultures, to express the drive of the individual to "posit his *own* ideal and to derive from it his own law, joys and rights" (GS 143). That drive is usually regarded with hostility by such cultures, insofar as it encourages the possibilities of acting contrary to societal custom, to the "one and ultimate norm" of human being enshrined in those customs. But polytheism, that "wonderful art and power of creating gods," allows the individual for the first time to see herself *as* an individual. The gods provide a number of different possible ideals by which to live, and in so doing give cover for the individual to seek out a life determined by her own deepest desires rather than those of the social group. This was "the invaluable preliminary exercise for the justification of the egoism and sovereignty of the individual," since "the freedom one conceded to a god in his relation to other gods one finally gave to oneself in relation to laws, customs and neighbors." That freedom is precisely what monotheistic religion tries to stifle for good; it is "the rigid consequence of the teachings of a normal human type," and seeks to "[translate] the morality of custom definitively into flesh and blood." Humans are, Nietzsche suggests, alone among the animals in having "no eternal horizons and perspectives," but we have the disastrous capability, by means of monotheism, of placing eternal limitations on ourselves. We are capable, by means of that dangerous tool, of closing off all possible opportunities for the nourishment of the drive to posit individual ideals. We are capable, that is, of making ourselves over entirely into "herd animals."

No religion has taken this course with more determination than Christianity. Far from taking its God to be one god among many, it sees the gods of all other religions as not really gods at all; either they are an anticipation of the Christian God (e.g., the Jewish Yahweh) or they are false gods, even demons (e.g., the Olympians). It may sound very ecumenical and egalitarian when Paul says that there is neither Jew nor Greek, since "ye all are one in Christ Jesus" (Gal. 3:28), but latent in the statement is the claim that Christian morality just *is* morality.[24] The Christian God is a commander of a set of precepts which claim to be not merely the customs of a particular people but the moral laws of all mankind. And he is the supreme moral judge, who gives rewards to the "good" and punishments to the "evil" in the afterlife. The great success of Christianity throughout the whole of Europe is, in Nietzsche's eyes, largely to be interpreted as the great success of this rigidly moral picture of the world. Europeans, out of a bafflingly complex set of forces and motivations—although fear of suffering plays perhaps an outsize role[25]—have increasingly been guided by the idea that there is just one good way for a human being to be, and in Nietzsche's view that idea has gained rather than lost momentum as Europe has secularized. Thus, its culture has stagnated, since all individual creative impulses which might have pointed to some next stage of cultural development are regarded with hostility.

Sin: That hostility is impossible to distinguish from the Christian concept of sin. In Christianity, "sin" is a name both for the act of transgressing God's commands (i.e., for doing "evil" in the sense alluded to above) and for the state of being of a human's soul insofar as she exists at a distance from the presence of God. This dual meaning is no accident, for Christianity teaches not just that human beings sometimes sin (e.g., sometimes "miss the mark," as the original Greek term *hamartia* suggests) but that they exist *in sin*, or are themselves essentially *sinful*. Thus the doctrine of "original sin"—the claim that human beings have inherited from the first human being a nature inevitably inclined to moral error—is one of the most distinctive features of the Christian religion.

Nietzsche's disdain for the Christian doctrine of sin is central to his much celebrated "genealogy" of morality, and in all three of its phases. In the first treatise of the *Genealogy*, Nietzsche suggests that the value opposition "good and evil," as opposed to the opposition "good and bad," is dependent on the feeling of *ressentiment* engendered in physically weaker peoples when they are enslaved and oppressed by a master class. Since their physical weakness denies them the chance of any outward revenge, the slaves engage in an "imaginary revenge" (GM I:10). This imaginary revenge takes the form of a new mode of evaluation of human action—"slave morality"—which begins by declaring *evil* precisely those strong and vitally powerful instincts that allow the masters to oppress the slaves. Central to slave morality is the idea that the masters are persons separate from these instincts, and thus capable of refraining from acting on them; the slaves, by contrast, reinterpret their weakness as the "strength" of self-control, of denying themselves expression of vital instinct.

This evil, however, is not yet the Christian doctrine of sin. For that, Nietzsche argues in the second essay, two historical precedents are necessary. First is the development of what he calls the "bad conscience"—the feeling that an inner impulse is problematic, inimical to one, or to be distrusted. Nietzsche suggests that the phenomenon has its origin in the restrictions of social life and the need for peace among peoples, which deny individuals the ability to express outwardly their highly individualized instincts for lust and power. This denial of outward expression necessitates that these drives and instincts turn inward for nourishment—this they do, and in the process an individual agent with internal complexity and internal depths is born. Now it is possible for that individual to set certain parts or aspects of themselves against one another, to have one seek to gain power over another, to regard another as an enemy, and so on.

Parallel to this development is that of the origin of belief in gods. Nietzsche claims that tribal deities are the earliest kinds of gods, and that belief in them is the result of a deep feeling of indebtedness to the ancestors who founded one's tribe. Early on, one seeks to repay one's debt to these ancestors by following the societal codes and customs that have been handed down. But as time passes and the tribe thrives, the sense of indebtedness grows, and the founding ancestor's reality becomes more spectral and insidiously powerful, until he is "transfigured" into a god (GM II:19). The suspicion grows, too, that such a great debt to such a distant being might never be fully repaid, and so the attempts to repay become more extravagant and even violent (for example, human sacrifice), and ever more motivated by *fear* rather than gratitude.[26]

The Christian doctrine of sin, and of God's willingness to sacrifice himself to save us from it, is put forward by Nietzsche as a real "stroke of genius" precisely because the worldview it generates can serve as the logical conclusion of both historical developments at once (GM II:21). The Christian idea is that the debt to God is in principle incapable of being discharged or "redeemed"—one incurs the debt and feels guilt not just because one is a member of a particular tribe and owes its founders, or because one has transgressed one of its codes (all of which could in principle at least be made good by the individual), but simply because one exists as a member of the human race, as a descendant of Adam. To exist is thus to be guilty before God, to have inherited this existential debt. The *feeling* of that guilt/debt is supplied more than adequately by the feeling of those inner enemies that the bad conscience has conjured—one conceives of those vital, animal instincts that the slaves regarded as evil, that were denied outward expression by social life, as "hostility, rebellion, insurrection against the 'lord,' the 'father,' the primal ancestor and beginning of the world" (GM II:22). One can and should seek to fight them, and the ancient human delight in cruelty and the infliction of suffering guarantees that the fight is in a masochistic sense a satisfying one. But it can have no complete success; the only way out, the only real redemption, comes by means of the most extravagant of sacrifices: God himself, in the form of Jesus Christ, must be sacrificed on the cross for the sins of humankind, "the creditor sacrificing himself for his debtor, out of *love* . . . out of love for his debtor!" (GM II:21).

The third treatise, on the meaning of ascetic ideals, places all of these developments in the context of a history of life-denial. The priest serves as the model of the ascetic ideal in action:

> he relates our life (together with that to which it belongs: "nature," "world," the entire sphere of becoming and of transitoriness) to an entirely different kind of existence, which it opposes and excludes,

unless, perhaps, it were to turn against itself, *to negate itself*: in this case, the case of an ascetic life, life is held to be a bridge for that other existence. The ascetic treats life as a wrong path that one must finally retrace back to the point where it begins; or as an error that one refutes through deeds—*should* refute: for he *demands* that one go along with him; where he can, he forces *his* valuation of existence. (GM III:11)

The priest enacts this self-negation of life in part by the impressiveness of his own example—he may make a prominent and mysterious display of his own ability to neglect and even attack the most basic of his vital impulses (through practices of fasting, chastity, and even self-flagellation). But his most important role is as a leader of the weakly, sick, and oppressed masses, who suffer from their physiologically inferior state and seek a meaning for that suffering. Though they cannot, in most cases, live up to the model of the priest's exceptional behavior, they readily accept his diagnosis of their condition, which is that their suffering is their own fault. The priest is "the true artist of the feeling of guilt" and makes explicit the doctrine of sin, which "has so far been the greatest event in the history of the sick soul: in it we have the most dangerous and doom-laden feat of religious interpretation" (GM III:20). This interpretation sets in motion a whole moral interpretation of the world, according to which all that makes the material, sensuous, transient human life what it is is to be regarded as evil, as something to be distrusted, as needing to be redeemed, and yet as impossible to redeem, except by God. Not just creativity and assertion of individuality but *life itself* in its most central manifestations is to be conceived of as sinful, as rebellion against God. The story of Christianity's ascendance is thus the story of the success of this life-denying ideal; devotion to it means "hatred of the human, still more of the animal, still more of the material . . . abhorrence of the senses, of reason itself . . . fear of happiness and of beauty . . . longing away from all appearance, change, becoming, death, wish, longing itself" (GM III:28). Its aim is the deification of nothingness itself. Thus, the infamous term "nihilism" gains an increasingly prominent place in Nietzsche's analysis, both in his last published works and especially in the notebooks in which he worked out drafts of future publications.

Belief in the Afterlife: The culmination of this whole way of thinking is a thorough devaluation of this life and world, since it contains all of the objectionable features listed earlier (the material, the sensuous, change, death, longing, etc.). Nietzsche calls it a fundamentally Jewish mindset that first "coined an insult out of the word 'world'" (BGE 195), but this insult lives on and is brought to its highest prominence in Christianity itself. Jesus tells his disciples that he is "not of the world," and that they are not either, and that the world has "hated" them (Jn 17:14). One of the Johannine epistles counsels as follows:

> Love not the world, neither the things that are in the world. If any man love the world, the love of the Father is not in him. For all that is in the world, the lust of the flesh, and the lust of the eyes, and the pride of life, is not of the Father, but is of the world. And the world passeth away, and the lust thereof: but he that doeth the will of God abideth for ever. (1 Jn 2:15-17)

And, Paul writes:

> But God hath chosen the foolish things of the world to confound the wise; and God hath chosen the weak things of the world to confound the things which are mighty; And base things of the world, and things which are despised, hath God chosen, yea, and things which are not, to bring to nought things that are: That no flesh should glory in his presence. (1 Cor. 1:27-28)[27]

This negative view of the world is combined in early Christianity with a lively eschatological imagination, one markedly less prominent in the gospels than in the rest of the New Testament.[28] When the writer of I John says that the world "passeth away," he likely means not only to call attention to its transience in a general, philosophical sense but also to its imminent demise. The second coming of Christ, the destruction of this world, the judgment of souls—all of these are coming soon, perhaps before the early Christian's own natural death. Then she will see played out the great moral drama of heaven and hell.

The foolish and weak and despised of this world, those who shun (because they are incapable of it) true lust of the flesh and pride of life, are rewarded with a "life" other than this life, a "world" beyond this world. This world, it turns out, was nothing but an insignificant prelude to the *real* thing, a life of eternal bliss that does not contain all of the frustrated striving, pain, and inner turmoil of this wretched life, which can be safely forgotten once we have transcended it. (In his *Thus Spoke Zarathustra*, Nietzsche has Zarathustra say of the creators of afterworlds that they are motivated mostly by "a poor unknowing weariness that no longer even wants to will" (Z, "Afterworldly").) What it *does* contain is, on Nietzsche's view, in principle impossible to specify, since a life without suffering, bodily limitation, and mortality is in fact no life at all. It would be, as Paul so eloquently put it, the nullification of the things that are by the things that are not.[29] The best sign of the weariness and weakness of those who are drawn to believing in it is, perhaps, precisely this, that the negative characterization—freedom from suffering—suffices for them.

What of those who *did* have the lust of the flesh and the pride of life, and the adulation of this world? Their fate is, naturally, far easier and more enjoyable to describe. In short, they will face the fate that the weak and oppressed faced in this life, but to a far worse degree. They will suffer gruesomely, and eternally. Nietzsche quotes the church father Tertullian, who with great relish and feverishness imagines pagan gods, kings, government officials, philosophers, and poets being brought low before Christ and his followers, and having the instruments of torture once used on the early Christians turned against *them* (GM I:15). Thomas Aquinas, as Nietzsche notes, suggests that the saints in heaven will both look upon and rejoice in the suffering of the damned in heaven, because it is only in contrasting their own happiness with it that they can know that happiness adequately.[30] Dante let his imagination go to its most extravagant and creative lengths in his *Inferno*, and though he had placed over the entrance to that torture chamber the claim that it was created by eternal love, he would have done better, Nietzsche suggests, to say that heaven was created by eternal hate, by the *ressentiment* of oppressed peoples creating an imaginary revenge. Thus, all that the Christian can say positively about heaven is that it will involve a view of hell, in which those who persecuted them in this life get what they deserve.

3 After Christianity—Secular Ascetics versus Religious Aesthetics?

It is relatively common for critics of Christianity to point to hell as proof of the religion's moral bankruptcy.[31] But while Nietzsche certainly intended by his analysis to poke holes in the Christian's moral self-conception, in fact something else bothered him more: the vacuousness of the ascetic ideal. The ideal itself possesses no intrinsic value—it is useful in the very limited sense that it takes the suffering of life and gives it a meaning, at least powerful enough to serve as an alternative to "suicidal nihilism" (GM III:28). But it is a desperate alternative—striving to realize it doesn't actually save people from that suffering or make them any happier, and, even worse, it seems to trap them into never-ending servitude to it. Its success is in fact due simply to the fact that it has faced no competition; there has been no competing, life-affirming ideal for us to strive for instead, and there remains none.

Nietzsche closes his genealogy of morality by considering someone who disagrees with him on this last point. For we moderns might argue that we *do* now have a competing ideal, a faith in the killer of God itself, modern science. The scientific worldview, after all, is thoroughly secular and "this-worldly": it needs no sin and no world beyond this one, and it does not deny but rather affirms the senses, in their capacity as avenues to (scientific) truth. Devotion to this truth at all costs is the moderns' new faith, their new, nonascetic ideal. Nietzsche's compelling response is that this unconditional devotion to scientific truth is in fact itself a further development of the ascetic ideal, which now removes some of its religious trappings so as to reveal its "more incomprehensible, more spiritual, more ensnaring" form (GM III:25). The ascetic ideal in this new secular form needn't be about sacrificing this life for the next one but can exist as pure and unadorned commitment to self-abasement and self-belittlement. Modern science doesn't need to insist on the sinfulness of humanity to further this project. In fact, its very insistence on having no relationship to religion whatsoever opens up new avenues of self-abasement. The world it discloses is not planned by God, and humans have no peculiar significance in it at all. They are but peculiar specks of stardust crawling about on a somewhat larger speck of stardust, itself moving about chaotically in a vast universe that cares not for the well-being of humans or anything else. Humans are not essentially different from the other animals, and even what they took to be the very special ability unique to them called "knowledge" is really only an extension and systematization, hardly noteworthy in the grand scheme of things, of animal sense perception. Their only notable achievement is to have discovered all this about themselves, to have avoided in the end being deceived as to the state of their utter insignificance. And so they devote themselves to the project of proving this insignificance to themselves, of refusing to be the dupes of their previous delusions of grandeur.[32] Often enough, they lose themselves in the largely mechanical labor of accumulating facts so that they can forget the horror of the grand scheme to which their labor is in service. Those who really are honestly and consciously devoted to that grand scheme are devotees to "the truth" in as grand, abstract, unconditional, and unargued-for a sense as the Christians taught one to be devoted to God. They preach as fervently as any Christian priest that there is no justified "pride of life," that humans are inevitably error-prone and self-frustrated creatures. Only the pure, unconditional truth will set them free, but it will be only the freedom finally to see themselves as the lowly, disappointing creatures they are.[33]

Nietzsche finds himself in no small internal conflict over this final result of his genealogy. Nietzsche describes these devotees to truth—these "pale atheists," as he calls them—in terms that are unmistakably both pejorative and descriptive of his former self. He, too, as early on as his discussions about religion with his sister during his college years, had been inspired by the self-image of the inquirer who would follow the truth no matter where it led. And that "will to truth," as he liked to call it, had clearly inspired his original philosophical work. But what his genealogy had effectively revealed is that the ethos that informed that will was, in fact, a modified (indeed *intensified*) version of the very asceticism that he had, following Feuerbach and others, objected to so strongly in Christianity. A "this-worldly asceticism," as the sociologist Max Weber was later to call it, a totally non-religious commitment to life-denial, was not only possible but perhaps unavoidable, indeed was perhaps coming to be *the* central problem of modern life, the "iron cage" [*stahlhartes Gehäuse*] in which we all find ourselves trapped.[34] Getting rid of our religious beliefs, becoming fully secular, "killing God"—none of this serves on its own as a solution to the underlying problem.

For the philosopher committed, as Nietzsche was, to the affirmation of life, a more fundamental reorientation is necessary. What we moderns need is not an ever more pious commitment to (scientific) truth at all costs but a competing, life-affirming ideal. But to do that, we need a new way of *life*, and not just a new set of ideas (or an old set that has finally been interpreted the right way). Philosophy, theology, or science on its own won't help, since the problem lies deeper, in our unthinking commitment to an ideal that has shaped our habitual ways of thinking of ourselves and acting in the world. For this and other reasons, Nietzsche tended to place his hopes for cultural renewal in art. Art, insofar as it develops fictions and illusions, has a more complicated but less ascetic relationship to the search for truth, and it works hard to address us not merely as disembodied intellects but in our entirety as living, breathing, feeling human beings. Nietzsche says at the end of his *Genealogy* that "the complete, genuine antagonism" is between Plato and Homer—the former as the enemy of art, and the proto-Christian life-denier, in his positing of a transcendent world of unchanging Forms, and the latter as the "involuntary deifier" of life, of "*golden* nature" (GM III:25). How, then, can we revive that Homeric spirit? To borrow the words of

Robinson's John Ames, quoted at the beginning of our book, how can we find our way to a place where this life would be like Troy, like the "ballad they sing in the streets" in heaven? (*Gilead* 57).[35]

Nietzsche's own attempts to answer this question, to begin imagining a post-ascetic future, are cast in suggestive but often frustratingly vague language. Though he is an incisive genealogist and cultural critic, his success at founding some new, anti-ascetic movement is, at best, mixed. Nietzsche's most extensive effort occurs in his deeply personal and impressionistic work *Thus Spoke Zarathustra*, an adequate analysis of which would be too complicated for us to attempt here. Among its many striking features is that it is the only fictional work Nietzsche ever wrote, and that it is totally saturated with religious imagery and rhetorical tropes. Zarathustra, like Nietzsche's madman, is horrified by the blasé nature of modern secularism; he worries not so much that they are still too religious but that they are not religious enough (that is, not as aware as they must be of the point of religion, and of how much we lose when it is gone). He gives vent to powerfully charged religious language, in part to communicate the urgency of the situation, but also perhaps because this is the means that we have to convey passionate engagement with life and devotion to ideals. While Nietzsche would have of course found it hard to imagine how a committed Christian could respond adequately to his worries about modern life, the idea of writing fiction with explicit religious language and imagery in order to respond to them was not exactly foreign to him.

One of Nietzsche's suggestive asides will serve as a guidepost for our analysis of Robinson's novels. In one important passage, a kind of new year's resolution, Nietzsche suggests that his love from now on should be a love of fate: "I want to learn more and more how to see what is necessary in things as what is beautiful in them—thus I will be one of those who make things beautiful. *Amor fati*: let that be my love from now on!" The goal, Nietzsche says, is one day to "want only to be a Yes-sayer!" (GS 276). What is perhaps most important for Nietzsche is that this affirmative attitude, this love of fate, cannot just be willed straightforwardly; rather, an *aesthetic* effort is necessary. One cannot simply decide on a whim to say "Yes" to life—one needs first to render it "beautiful," to be able to see it in such a way that it appears as aesthetically valuable. Obviously art in its usual sense will play a role—one of the things artists do for us is to show us things that we wouldn't typically take to be beautiful, but in a way such that they *do* appear beautiful to us. But this particular effect of art bears a general lesson for our everyday perception of the world—much in the world that appears to us irredeemably bad is in fact redeemable, can in fact be rendered beautiful if seen in the right way. It is in fact one of Nietzsche's objections to Christianity that its insistence on the sin of this world and its inadequacy with respect to the next performs something like the opposite of this procedure—it takes an ambivalent world, capable of aesthetic transformation, and makes it look ugly instead of beautiful: "the Christian decision to find the world ugly and bad has made the world ugly and bad" (GS 130). This is at once a claim about Christianity and about the power of human perception—our decisions about how to view the world are not neutral but change the character of what we perceive. It leaves open the possibility that we could make the world beautiful and good in part by being committed to perceiving it in a different way. But that is hardly a decision that can be made on a whim. It involves orienting one's whole life toward it, and there is a great deal of residual asceticism in our inner lives that fights against it. That inner asceticism would teach us that it is naive folly and vain presumption to think that the world is beautiful and good and that we have some role to play in making it so, and that it is wise in the end not to be too hopeful about the world or prideful about humanity. Nietzsche is motivated by a different conception of wisdom; it is perhaps best expressed in a passage from Emerson, which Nietzsche used as the epigraph to *The Gay Science*:

> To the poet and sage, all things are friendly and hallowed, all experiences profitable, all days holy, all men divine.[36]

Notes

1 The history of that critique is long, complicated, and still understudied. The best treatment of it may still be Löwith (1991, 327–88).

2 The book's impact was huge. See Gregory (1977) for a general account of the materialist movement Feuerbach's book initiated.
3 Feuerbach (1957) will be cited in the rest of this chapter by the abbreviation "EC" and page number.
4 In fact, in Feuerbach's view it is precisely this consciousness of our membership in a species that separates us from the other animals, who have no such consciousness (see EC 1–2). This view was obviously influential on Marx's famous view that human beings are *"Gattungswesen"* (species-beings), developed in his *Economic and Philosophical Manuscripts* of 1844.
5 It is presumably in passages such as this that Ames would have found and approved of Feuerbach's treatment of "joy" in religion.
6 "The essence of religion is the immediate, involuntary, unconscious contemplation of the human nature as another, a distinct nature. But when this projected image of human nature is made an object of reflection, of theology, it becomes an inexhaustible mine of falsehoods, illusions, contradictions, and sophisms" (EC 213–14).
7 "He who earnestly believes in the divine existence is not shocked at the attributing of even gross sensuous qualities to God" (EC 15).
8 As Karl Barth, a favorite theologian of Ames (and Robinson), and himself an admirer of Feuerbach, liked to put it, there exists an "infinite qualitative difference" between God and us. See Barth (1933) for use of the phrase.
9 Feuerbach's critical analysis of the alienated state of modern theologically informed religious belief is obviously deeply influenced by the chapter on "unhappy consciousness" in Hegel's *Phenomenology of Spirit*. For a judicious treatment of that influence, see Ameriks (2000, 259–64).
10 Here too Feuerbach is clearly influenced by Hegel, who had stressed the centrality of the incarnation to Christianity in the "Religion" chapter of his *Phenomenology of Spirit*: "this incarnation of the divine being . . . is the simple content of the absolute [or Christian] religion" (Hegel 1977, 459).
11 Thus it should be no surprise that Feuerbach's views were enormously influential on would-be socialists and revolutionaries of the mid- to late-nineteenth century, many of whom were motivated to critique political injustices by a sense of Christian love for those upon whom those injustices had been perpetrated, even if they themselves were no longer believing Christians. See for instance the young Dostoevsky's interactions

with young atheist Russian socialists, as described in Frank (1976, 159–98).

12 Though Feuerbach leaves it unsaid, his message here has obvious social implications. It is only because some of us are so free from the want he describes that it can appear to us that food and water, and our physical well-being more generally, is something banal and uninteresting. But of course others are not so well off, and social and religious institutions in modern Europe played an important role in perpetuating that state of affairs. Feuerbach's social and political philosophy was not particularly well developed at the time of the writing of *The Essence of Christianity*, but this implicit message was heard loud and clear by its enthusiastic readers.

13 In this, of course, Feuerbach and Nietzsche distinguish themselves from the so-called "new atheists" of our own day. For some brief discussion of the latter, see the Introduction.

14 See the Nietzsche entries in the works cited section for the abbreviations we will use for Nietzsche's works. They are cited by section number, unless otherwise noted.

15 Cf. GS, 343.

16 Unless otherwise noted, the biographical details referred to here are drawn from Young (2010).

17 For further discussion, see Blue (2016, 20 ff.).

18 See for instance his late excoriation of George Eliot (whose values he rightly saw as basically Christian), who he called a "moralistic female" (TI, "Skirmishes," 5); and the second section of "How the 'True World' Finally Became a Fable" (TI, "Fable"). Eliot was also the first English translator of both Feuerbach's *Essence of Christianity* and Strauss's *Life of Jesus*, two texts that played important roles in Nietzsche's own development, as we shall see in the following.

19 Elisabeth claims so, but see Blue (2016, 58).

20 See Blue (2016, 140–1) for discussion of the letter and the influence of Feuerbach. Nietzsche is quoting more or less directly from the last lines of part I of *The Essence of Christianity*.

21 See Schopenhauer (1969, vol. I, §57).

22 Nietzsche doesn't claim that Christianity is alone among religions in this focus. Cf. WP, 146: "In itself, religion has nothing to do with morality: but both descendants of the Jewish religion [Nietzsche means Christianity

and Islam] are essentially moralistic religions—such as offer precepts about how one ought to live, and create a hearing for their demands by rewards and punishments."

23 This is not to suggest that they don't serve as exemplars who provide practical guidance of some kind or other, however, as we shall see. But the kind of guidance they give is not "moral," in the sense Nietzsche intends. Plato's *Euthyphro* already bears witness to the problem—Euthyphro wants to use the example of Zeus overthrowing his father (Cronus) as a justification for his bringing suit against his own father, and Socrates is clearly worried about the implications of this procedure for a religion with such unruly and often unscrupulous deities. See Plato (2002, 4–7).

24 All biblical quotations come from the King James Version.

25 Cf. BGE 49, 201–2.

26 It is worth noting here that Nietzsche saw this contrast between fear and gratitude as an important feature that distinguished Christianity from Hellenic religion: "What is amazing about the religiosity of ancient Greeks is the excessive amount of gratitude that flows out from it:—it takes a very noble type of person to face nature and life like *this*!—Later, when the rabble gained prominence in Greece, religion became overgrown with *fear* as well, and Christianity was on the horizon" (BGE 49).

27 Nietzsche explicitly ties this verse to his treatment of life-denial in the *Genealogy* at A 45, in which he skewers a number of passages from the New Testament that, in his view, give the game away.

28 Indeed, Nietzsche's treatment of Jesus in *The Antichrist* is highly ambivalent—he is much closer to the Buddha than to Paul, who is consumed by *ressentiment* and twists Jesus's life to his own, more recognizably priestly and ascetic ends.

29 See A 43: "When the emphasis of life is put on the 'beyond' rather than on life itself—when it is put *on nothingness*—, then the emphasis has been completely removed from life. The enormous lie of personal immortality destroys all reason, everything natural in the instincts,—everything beneficial and life-enhancing in the instincts, everything that guarantees the future, now arouses mistrust. To live *in this way*, so that there is no *point* to life any more, *this* now becomes the 'meaning' of life."

30 Aquinas goes out of his way to argue that the saints do not rejoice directly in the suffering of the damned, since this would be a sign of hatred (see

Summa Theologiae, Supplementum Tertiae Partis, Q. 94 Art. 3). Rather, the saints rejoice directly in "the Divine justice and their own deliverance," and it is only because the punishment of the damned is part of that justice that, indirectly, the sight of it pleases. But even Aquinas quotes Ps. 58:10: "The righteous shall rejoice when he seeth the vengeance."

31 It is even increasingly common for universalist *Christians* to point to it as a proof of nonuniversalist Christianity's moral bankruptcy. For a particularly strident recent statement, see Hart (2019).

32 Cf. BGE, 55, where Nietzsche describes the process as a three-rung "ladder of religious cruelty": (i) human sacrifice (especially of loved ones, firstborns) to the gods; (ii) sacrifice of one's strongest natural instincts to God or gods; and finally (iii) sacrifice of "all comfort and hope, everything holy or healing, any faith in a hidden harmony or a future filled with justice and bliss" in order to "worship rocks, stupidity, gravity, fate, or nothingness out of sheer cruelty to themselves." This last sacrifice is a sacrifice of God "to nothingness." Though in this earlier work Nietzsche only identifies the second stage with asceticism, it is clear by the time he writes the end of GM that he has identified the last stage as a furthering of the goals of asceticism.

33 On this point, it is worth noting that Robinson has herself stressed similar themes, critiquing modern scientism for presenting us with an essentially dispiriting (and also false, of course) picture of the significance of human beings in the cosmos. Her most sustained statement of this is Robinson (2011).

34 See Weber (2011, 177).

35 Robinson herself, a "theological" novelist in some sense or other, as we shall see, would be unlikely to accept this antagonism between theology and art, at least in the final analysis. But she is at one with Nietzsche in thinking that art has a duty to address the whole person, and that living up to that duty often involves suggesting radically new ways of living and thinking. Robinson does not sound so far from Nietzsche, for example, in saying the following about literature: "[M]uch literature is, in a very sort of strict, etymological sense of the word, *subversive*. It wants very much for you to think about something in a way that you would not otherwise. The same is true of poetry. And sometimes people who subscribe to goodness in a programmatic way are resistant to surprise . . . Art sort

of produces that great overturning whenever it's good art" (Larsen & Johnson, eds. (2019), 183). Though she suggests that Christianity itself is subversive in this way, it is worth noting that she does *not* say that theology itself has this tight relation to subversiveness.

36 The quotation is taken loosely from "History," in Emerson's *Essays: First Series*. For Nietzsche's loose version, as translated by Walter Kaufmann, and some discussion, see Nietzsche (1974, 7–8). Emerson's exact wording is: "To the poet, to the philosopher, to the saint, all things are friendly and sacred, all events profitable, all days holy, all men divine" (Emerson 1983, 242).

2

Housekeeping
Lessons in Life-Denial

With its opening line—"My name is Ruth"—readers are invited to put *Housekeeping*'s narrator in conversation with one of American literature's most revered fictional voices. Ishmael, Melville's "desperado philosopher,"[1] is of course not just a character in a great American novel; he is, for many, *the* American character in *the* American novel. His bravado, wit, and "free and easy"[2] independence embody and extend what it means to be an American in the mid-nineteenth century and beyond. This suggests, of course, that to be American in its fullest and most elevated sense is—among other things—to be masculine. It is the personalities and activities of men that shape how we understand American agency. It is here that we begin to appreciate the full scope of Robinson's ambition: not only does she present herself as Melville's literary peer but she announces that a female voice will contribute the next lines of the American story.

Housekeeping's earliest interpreters were quick to notice and appreciate these transgressive elements. Coalescing under the heading of what we might loosely call "feminist" readings, Ruth is christened the "new American Eve."[3] In this role she represents the fulfillment of a form of uniquely American self-reliance that leaves behind the suffocating strictures of the domestic sphere to embrace a kind of freedom traditionally reserved for white men. However, unlike the American Adam, whose emancipation extends to his own ancestry and family, the American Eve escapes with her family, for the sake of family. Thus, on this reading of the novel, Robinson "extends the American range"[4]: Ishmael is broadened, both in terms of the kinds of activities he performs and the gender associated with him.[5]

Though feminist readings of this sort continue to appear,[6] there has been a recent reappraisal of the optimism of its earliest advocates. Expanding on an early suggestion by Joan Kirkby,[7] Christine Caver raises serious questions about the desirability of the Ruthian ideal. She reminds us that Ruth's "freedom" involves both a rejection of embodiment and, eventually, a complete breakdown in communication. For these reasons and others, she is less inclined to see *Housekeeping* as a text that carves out new and positive space for feminine agency, as much as an indictment of the absence of such spaces.[8] As with Thelma and Louise, the choice to resist traditional female paths and the masculine forces that police them is, in some sense, suicidal. In this light, "*Housekeeping* offers a damning critique of contemporary social structures by suggesting that as a culture we have not evolved much since Gilman's unnamed narrator tore the wallpaper off the walls."[9]

In the place of early feminist readings, Caver argues that *Housekeeping* is best understood as a story about the destabilizing effects of trauma. She writes, "*Housekeeping* represents the power of traumatic experience to destroy not only language and the illusion of a coherent self capable of agency but also a person's place within a larger community."[10] By thinking of "gender as a participatory, but secondary, concern,"[11] Caver looks to radically expand the scope of Robinson's novel. *Housekeeping* does not just use female characters to say something about female experience, it uses female characters to say something about a particular kind of *human* experience.

Caver is surely correct in supposing that Robinson's novel is, on some level, concerned to investigate the lasting consequences of trauma. But it is also important to see that *Housekeeping*'s range is not limited to the merely diagnostic or social-scientific—Robinson is not seeking primarily to explore and understand a special class of people. Her goal is, instead, more existential: to show that human life as such is traumatic in ways that are not always realized. In this regard, we join others in holding that *Housekeeping* develops a "philosophy of life,"[12] or "way of living in the world."[13] Instead of only treating questions of gender or parental loss, Robinson addresses the perennial and pressing issue of how temporally vulnerable creatures—beings who live in the shadow of their own death—relate to life. Understood in this way, the particular trauma experienced by the Stone sisters—Ruth and Lucille—has the capacity to reveal something in our development from childhood to adulthood that tends to go unnoticed. The experience of death can have the effect of awakening a person to the tenuousness of their existence; it provokes them to take up particular methods of "housekeeping."

In this chapter, we argue that *Housekeeping*'s Ruth and Lucille offer two especially clear examples of what Friedrich Nietzsche calls life-denial. Their cases are illuminating because, while both reject life, they have completely different intuitions concerning how best to do so. Lucille, on the one hand, looks to forget past pain and future vulnerability through a program of social absorption. If time and change are the enemies, she ignores them through unreflective participation in the settled world of middle-class convention. Ruth, on the other hand, looks to nullify loss by divesting herself of anything that can be taken from her. If the ends of housekeeping are comfort and protection, then Ruth "keeps house" by abandoning it. She looks to entirely transcend the everyday concerns that consume her sister. What Lucille and Ruth have in common is that they both, albeit in their own way, disengage from the world in order to protect themselves from it: one ignores the reality of loss, while the other imagines she has nothing to lose.

In terms of the larger argument of this book, *Housekeeping* both stands outside the Gilead novels (existing in its own fictional universe) and articulates a guiding question that each, in its own way, attempts to answer: *Is it possible to love life without falsifying it?* The characters that populate the world of Gilead struggle not only to say "yes" where Ruth and Lucille say "no" but also to synthesize the sisters' respective one-sidedness: life-affirmation must involve a commitment both to finitude and transcendence. What, in Robinson's first novel, presents itself as two distinct paths of escape will, in the later novels, reveal itself as two essential components in genuine homemaking. For now, we turn our attention to developing the former.

1 Two Paths of Escape

Housekeeping's opening paragraph serves as a tidy summary of the novel's most important themes. After Ruth's punchy introduction, the next two lines casually rehearse a litany of unfortunate events:

> I grew up with my younger sister, Lucille, under the care of my grandmother, Mrs. Sylvia Foster, and when she died, of her sisters-in-law, Misses Lily and Nona Foster, and when they fled, of her daughter, Mrs. Sylvia Fisher. Through all these generations of elders we lived in one house, my grandmother's house, built for her by her husband, Edmund Foster, an employee of the railroad, who escaped this world years before I entered it. (*Housekeeping* 3)

Our narrator, Ruth, has experienced more than her share of hardship. Her primary caretaker (who we notice is *not* one of her parents) dies—or, as she puts it, "eschewed awakening" (*Housekeeping* 29)—and she and her sister are bequeathed to two distantly related aunts who, shortly after coming into their inheritance, flee the scene. The only source of continuity is the family house, built by Ruth's grandfather, a Mr. Edmund Foster who has the proud distinction of not simply dying but *escaping* the world. In the same paragraph, we are invited to see Edmund's gift—the house in which this intergenerational drama unfolds—as perhaps slightly less than generous; the other home mentioned, Edmund's childhood abode, is likened to a "human stronghold," albeit no more so "than a grave."[14] Apparently, *Housekeeping* will be a story about the complex dialectic between family and home, life and death. It seems, too, that some homes, though "strongholds" of a sort, may nourish more death than life, leaving their tenants longing for escape.

While *Housekeeping*'s opening paragraph invites the reader to imagine that Ruth is embarking on a story of one family's trauma, the rest of the book strongly suggests that the Fosters' tale has a deeper significance, insofar as it lays bare in all its poignancy the thoroughly human experience of building a home in the face of constant and inevitable loss. Ruth emphasizes the ubiquity of her experience by placing it in the company of biblical precedents.[15] She writes, "Cain murdered Abel, and blood cried out from the earth; the house fell on Job's children, and a voice was induced or provoked into speaking from a whirlwind; and Rachel mourned for her children; and King David for Absalom. The force behind the movement of time is a mourning that will not be comforted" (*Housekeeping* 192). While reference to figures as mythically significant as Cain and Abel already suggests that Ruth is doing much more than reflecting on an isolated personal tragedy, her claim that mourning is a key force in the movement of history makes it clear just how common she takes her experience to be. Loss of the sort described in the early pages of *Housekeeping* is less something that happens to a person than something that constitutes her: human stories are always stories of loss. As Ruth puts it, "Every spirit passing through the world fingers the tangible and mars the mutable, and finally has come to look and not to buy. So shoes are worn and hassocks are sat upon and finally everything is left where it was and the spirit passes on" (*Housekeeping* 73).

In between personal trauma and the grandly biblical, Ruth occasionally turns her attention to loss of a more domestic sort: "there were still the perils of adolescence, of marriage, of childbirth" (*Housekeeping* 36). The everydayness of such dangers is accented when Ruth explicitly connects them to the town of Fingerbone. Where Ruth is typically content to present the citizens of Fingerbone in less nuanced terms, in a striking passage near the end of the novel, she allows several housewives to speak in their own voices, and what they say is revealing. "Families are a sorrow, and that's the truth," one says; and another, "I lost my girl sixteen years ago in June and her face is before me now"; and someone else, "If you can keep them, that's bad enough, but if you lose them—" "The world is full of trouble. Yes it is" (*Housekeeping* 186).

These confessions are significant because they express a form of sympathy that Fingerbone is designed to suppress, that, as Ruth puts it, "every soul is put out of house" (*Housekeeping* 179). The foundational story of all Fingerbone households, of homes in general, is that the world is comprehensible and safe. This is how we eat. This is how we pray. This is how we dress. This is what we sing to our children before we put them to bed. Dad works these hours, Mom those. The garden goes here, the tree swing there. Here are the jobs we work and the uniforms we wear. These rules and rituals make sense of the world, and a world that makes sense is deeply comforting. In this respect, a good home functions as a kind of Eden: it is a place that nourishes in virtue of its uncomplicated purity.

Although Robinson invites us to question whether most people can, in good faith, genuinely cultivate such an uncomplicated relationship to "home," children often do just that. *Housekeeping*, thus, places the reader at an important crisis point. We watch two sets of children—first the Fosters and then the Stones—endure the first tear in the household fabric. When Edmund, the family patriarch, vanishes into the murk of Lake Fingerbone, the most significant casualty is the integrity of the Foster home. Ruth puts it this way:

> That event had troubled the very medium of their lives. Time and air and sunlight bore wave and wave of shock, until all the shock was spent, and time and space and light grew still again and nothing seemed to tremble, and nothing seemed to lean. The disaster had fallen out of sight, like the train itself, and if the calm that followed it was not greater than the calm that came before it, it had seemed so. And the dear ordinary had healed as seamlessly as an image on water. (*Housekeeping* 15)

While the last two lines make it sound as though the shock of Edmund's death has little lasting impact, this is belied by other descriptions of how the Fosters relate to the "dear ordinary." After Edmund's "escape" there are two important changes that take place. First, there is an increased sensitivity to the explicit importance of the house as a barrier erected to keep darkness at bay. Ruth says of her mother and aunts that "Even then in the bright kitchen with white curtains screening out the dark, their mother felt them leaning toward her, looking at her face and her hands" (*Housekeeping* 11). Second, and relatedly, this leaning away from the darkness and toward their mother comes with a level of self-consciousness that is entirely novel.[16] They lean in, "Not because they ... [are] afraid she would vanish as their father had done, but because his sudden vanishing had made them aware of her" (*Housekeeping* 12). As the precariousness of the home is revealed through the traumatic loss of its central members, it becomes possible to see its rites and assumptions in a new light. It is also possible to begin to wonder why the people who inhabit the home and perform its rituals—especially Mothers and Fathers—do what they do.

Ruth loses her own mother to suicide, and she discusses the strangeness of these rituals as she experiences them in the years that follow. She says of her grandmother Sylvia during this time:

> Though she seemed abstracted, I think that like one dreaming, she felt more than the urgency of present business, her attention heightened and at the same time baffled by an awareness that this present had already passed, and had had its consequence. Indeed, it must have seemed to her that she returned to relive this day because it was here that something had been lost or forgotten. She whited shoes and braided hair and fried chicken. (*Housekeeping* 24–5)

Sylvia struggles to understand where her housekeeping went wrong. With the loss of first a husband and then later a daughter, and now entrusted with the care of her grandchildren, she must confront a flaw in her approach. Ruth tells us that she goes about the habits of housekeeping, "as if she could find the chink ... in her serenely ordinary life" (*Housekeeping* 25). Behind these reenactments is the looming threat of Lake Fingerbone which serves as a symbol, most immediately, of death and, more importantly, death's sense-destroying power. Ruth reminds us, "At the foundation [of Fingerbone] is the old lake, which is smothered and nameless and altogether black" (*Housekeeping* 9). To be nameless in this way is to be utterly resistant to the pacifying effects of societal storytelling. The lake is an ever-present rebuke to the home. Everyone, going about their housekeeping, knows and yet refuses to acknowledge that "in the spring the old lake will return" (*Housekeeping* 5).

If *Housekeeping* is a meditation on the construction and loss of home, then we might expect it to devote serious attention to the ways in which human beings respond to such crises. Near the end of its opening paragraph (recall Ruth's early litany of loss), there is a curious shift from the theme of displacement to a discussion of Edmund's interest in painting. Ruth focuses on one painting in particular, a large one with a "bell-shaped mountain" in the foreground. Edmund populated the mountain with a dense forest of trees, "each of which stood out at right angles to the ground . . . [and] bore bright fruit, and showy birds nested in the boughs, and every fruit and bird was plump with the warp in the earth." Ruth tells us she never could decide, "Whether the genius of this painting was ignorance or fancy." Later, Ruth returns to the topic of Edmund's paintings and tells us that they always reminded her of heaven (*Housekeeping* 149). These two asides suggest a promising approach to the larger idea of the novel. If heaven is a place where the fractures in Eden have been repaired, all wrongs made right, then Ruth's musings about the source of Edmund's "genius" may have special significance. The human endeavor to repair the scars and cracks that blight our respective homes is achieved (or at the very least attempted) with the help of two basic strategies: ignorance and imagination.

Though we know relatively little about Edmund (he makes his escape before the main action of the novel develops), we get some glimpses into his life that hint at how his artistic impulses play out in the everyday. Ruth writes,

> the silent Methodist Edmund who wore a necktie and suspenders even to hunt wildflowers . . . Edmund was like that, a little. The rising of the spring stirred a serious, mystical excitement in him, and made him forgetful of her [Sylvia]. He would pick up eggshells, a bird's wing, a jawbone, the ashy fragment of a wasp's nest. . . . This is death in my hand, this is ruin in my breast pocket where I keep my reading glasses.

At such times he was as forgetful of her as he was of his suspenders and his Methodism. (*Housekeeping* 17)

This passage showcases two aspects of Edmund's character set against one another: a rule-governed formality and an attraction to "ruin." While the latter is characterized by an interest in objects of "death," we know that Edmund's springtime walks are organized around the search for wildflowers. These wildflowers are ecstatically adorned and, rather importantly, entirely resistant to domestication; you cannot replant them without killing them. Although, admittedly, this passage provides only a hint, one might think that Edmund's strictly structured life—his "methodical" Protestantism—involves a kind of ignorance, while his flirtations with death are a manifestation of imagination. The former involves ignorance because it depends on maintaining precisely the sort of disregard for nuance and ambiguity associated with housekeeping more generally. Max Weber tells us in *The Protestant Ethic* that "The name [Methodist] already indicates what struck contemporaries as unique to its followers: the 'methodical' and systematic organization of life with the aim of attaining the *certitudo salutis*."[17] The strict and often baroque religious routines of sects like Methodism were formulated and embraced, at least in part, to pacify the doubts of the believer suffering under the anxious ambiguity of his own salvation. Thus, trust in these methods, just like trust in the rules and rites of housekeeping, requires one to elide a whole host of countervailing experiences and intuitions. As for the other connection, the one between "imagination" and Edmund's springtime wildflower hunts, it involves a departure from the strictly rule-governed. Just as Edmund's morbid desire for ruin functions as a release from the organizing rituals of the everyday, the imagination—with its powers of abstraction, association, and play—loosens the mind's grip on the concrete, particular, and literal. If a person were to design a house under the direction of these two competing principles, we should expect a bizarre hodgepodge. As Ruth says of Edmund's own construction, there would be a desire "to build things that might be considered permanent. But . . . [also terminate] rather oddly in a hatch or trapdoor" (*Housekeeping* 47).

Using the two poles of Edmund's art as the key for the novel invites us to place *Housekeeping*'s only significant male character in a dubious role. While Edmund's itch for the unconstrained openness of the West immediately reminds us of the conventional tropes of the "American Adam," his most important similarity to the biblical namesake may reside in the corruption of his bequest. Edmund's two approaches to life—one centered on a strategy of ignorance, the other fancy—are passed on to his family and, thus, perpetuate a basic detachment from the world. Most of *Housekeeping* focuses on how Edmund's two principles are embodied in his granddaughters. By carefully tracing the subtle ways in which each principle gets played out, we will not only get a much richer picture of what each position entails but also see precisely how the success of each strategy depends on rejecting life in some significant respect. First, though, we need to look at the events that help set the sisters on these opposing trajectories. Already, in the time between the death of their mother and their eventual separation, we see important hints of what is to come.

2 The In-Between Time

Ruth tells us that the worst part of loss is not what it takes but what it leaves. Comparing human memory to water, she writes:

> And here we find our great affinity with water, for like reflections on water our thoughts will suffer no changing shock, no permanent displacement. They mock us with their seeming slightness. If they were more substantial—if they had weight and took up space—they would sink or be carried away in the general flux. But they persist, outside the brisk and ruinous energies of the world. (*Housekeeping* 163)

If her thoughts and memories could dissolve into Lake Fingerbone as readily as the train that took her grandfather, then overcoming loss would be simple. Forgetfulness can be every bit as blissful as ignorance. Unfortunately, though, she is left with the debris, the physical and mental jetsam of her mother's absence. Naturally, such debris—things like the wonderfully unlikely head of lettuce that buoys up from Edmund's wreck—depend entirely on a person's memories and imagination for their associative power. Ruth thinks of these leftovers as "relics." They are especially painful because, unlike "pure object[s] (*Housekeeping* 209)," which elicit no associative links, or everyday objects, which play a direct and uncomplicated role in the life of the household, relics remind us of something that has passed. They are vestiges of a bygone whole.[18]

Ruth describes the aftermath of loss as a kind of in-between zone where, because all one encounters are relics, it is impossible to make coherent sense of one's life. She alludes to this sense of limbo in her descriptions of ice-skating with Lucille. She writes,

> Usually we would skate along the edge of the swept ice, tracing its shape, and coming finally to its farthest edge, we would sit on the snow and look back at Fingerbone. . . . Indeed, where we were we could feel the reach of the lake far behind us, and far beyond us on either side, in a spacious silence that seemed to ring like glass. (*Housekeeping* 34)

If town and lake represent the two poles of intelligibility and inscrutability, then ice-skating already suggests an important flirtation with boundaries. While even some of the citizens of Fingerbone are attracted to such boundaries, Ruth and Lucille take it a step further. They remain alone at the edge of the skating surface, moving further and further out onto the lake. From the edge, sitting on the ungroomed snow, they feel the pull of the lake behind them and see the town of Fingerbone ahead. Ruth, foreshadowing her eventual path, tells us, "The town itself seemed a negligible thing from such a distance" (*Housekeeping* 34).

The first person who presents Lucille and Ruth a path back from the edge of the lake is their aunt Sylvie (their mother's sister). On a stormy evening, "with a quiet that seemed compounded of gentleness and stealth and self-effacement" (*Housekeeping* 45), Sylvie steps—wet-haired and with withered hands—back into the Foster home. After taking off her "shapeless and oversized" raincoat, she places a hand on

Ruth's head and proclaims, "You're Ruthie." She then turns to Lucille and, without placing her hand on her, states, "And you're Lucille." Both girls are named, but only one has been christened.

Sylvie's ascendance to the role of housekeeper is anything but subtle. Shortly after her return, the town of Fingerbone floods, leaving most of its homes literally displaced. Ruth writes, "at the end of three days [of rain and melt-off] the houses and hutches and barns and sheds of Fingerbone were like so many spilled and foundered arks" (*Housekeeping* 61). While this is going on, "Sylvie [sat alone] . . . on the vanity while Lucille and . . . [Ruth] played Monopoly on the bed" (*Housekeeping* 61–2). Not only does this three-day watery entombment announce a new domestic regime, its manner—a transgression of the bounds of home by the very elements it is designed to resist—perfectly foreshadows Sylvie's housekeeping method.

Where the citizens of Fingerbone labor to preserve a strict border between outside and in, darkness and light, Sylvie intentionally courts a confusion of the two spheres. Ruth notes,

> Thus finely did our house become attuned to the orchard and to the particularities of weather, even in the first days of Sylvie's housekeeping. Thus did she begin by littles and perhaps unawares to ready it for wasps and bats and barn swallows. Sylvie talked a great deal about housekeeping. (*Housekeeping* 85)

It is important to pay attention to the juxtaposition of these two apparently contradictory impulses, that Sylvie both readies the home for the inhabitation of "wasps and bats" and that she seems to care a "great deal about housekeeping." This suggests it is a mistake to see Sylvie as something other than a housekeeper, as perhaps a mere vagrant or someone who makes no domestic effort. Housekeeping is not about keeping out the elements as much as it is about providing protection, and Sylvie is ushering in a new example of what this can look like. Some people, call them traditional homemakers, look to protect the home by erecting impermeable barriers (Edmund's impulse "to build things that might be considered permanent"

(*Housekeeping* 47)). The rationale of this strategy is clear enough. Other people, nontraditional homemakers, look to protect their home by renouncing anything that can be taken from them, by refusing to consider anything capable of being taken from them as part of the home.[19] Both strategies seek to minimize the possibility of loss.

Though it will be a while before Ruth is formally educated in the way of Sylvie, soon after her aunt's return we see Lucille developing in reaction to her. Ruth characterizes these changes in terms of sexual maturity. She writes, "[Lucille's] tiny, child-nippled breasts filled her with shame and me with alarm. . . . While she became a small woman, I became a towering child. What twinges, what aches I felt, what gathering toward fecundity, what novel and inevitable rhythms, were the work of my strenuous imagining" (*Housekeeping* 97). On first pass, it is tempting to read this as merely a commentary on Lucille's developing body, that she—in contrast to Ruth—is growing up. This, however, misses the full import of Ruth's observation. Both girls are undergoing a "gathering toward fecundity." While Lucille's body is preparing to give birth to the next generation of Fingerbone and its rituals of ignorance, Ruth, too, is preparing to give birth, though of a more figurative kind. She will establish a household premised on an entirely distinct principle: imagination.

The natural differences between Ruth and Lucille come to a head when they are forced, on an otherwise innocuous outing, to make an impromptu camp on the shore of Lake Fingerbone. As the setting sun catches them unawares, the two sisters scramble to construct a makeshift shelter. "We dragged driftwood halfway out on the point. We used a big stone in its side as one wall, we made back and side walls of driftwood, and we left the third side open to the lake. . . . It was a low and slovenly structure, to all appearances random and accidental" (*Housekeeping* 114). After crawling into the small, womb-like hut, the girls fall asleep in fetal position, "heels against [their] buttocks." Soon, Ruth awakens and pushes her way through the roof "into darkness no less absolute." She continues,

> There was no moon. In fact, there appeared to be no sky. Apart from the steady shimmering of the lake and the rush of the woods, there were singular, isolated lake sounds, placeless and disembodied, and very near my ears, like sounds in a dream. . . . It was so dark that creatures came down to the water within a few feet of us. We could not see what they were. Lucille began to throw stones at them. "They're supposed to be able to smell us," she grumbled. For a while she sang "Mockingbird Hill," and then she sat down beside me in our ruined stronghold, never still, never accepting that all our human boundaries were overrun. (*Housekeeping* 115)

What Ruth says next is vital to understanding her development. She writes, "Lucille would tell this story differently. She would say I fell asleep, but I did not. I simply let the darkness in the sky become coextensive with the darkness in my skull and bowels and bones." Ruth immediately understands that something is at stake between her and her sister. She also senses that this act of surrender, giving in to the darkness, might be an answer to a question she is only now beginning to formulate. After opening herself to the communion of sky and skull, she continues:

> Everything that falls upon the eye is apparition, a sheet dropped over the world's true workings. The nerves and the brain are tricked, and one is left with dreams that these specters loose their hands from ours and walk away, the curve of the back and the swing of the coat so familiar as to imply that they should be permanent fixtures of the world, when in fact nothing is more perishable. Say that my mother was as tall as a man, and that she sometimes set me on her shoulders, so that I could splash my hands in the cold leaves above our heads. Say that my grandmother sang in her throat while she sat on her bed and we laced up her big black shoes. Such details are merely accidental. Who could know but us? . . . [W]hy must we be left with the flotsam, among the small, unnoticed, unvalued clutter that was all that remained when they vanished, that only catastrophe made notable? Darkness is the only solvent. . . . it seemed to me that there need not be relic, remnant, margin, residue, memento,

bequest, memory, thought, track, or trace, if only the darkness could be perfect and permanent. (*Housekeeping* 116)

Ruth confronts the absurdity of her plight, that *memories*—mere images seeded by the collusion of nerve and brain—are the source of her pain. She sees now that "Darkness is the only solvent." Finally, an intimation of a path that leads away from the scene of the accident; this is what her imagination has been stretching toward.

The next morning, on their return walk, Ruth comments, "It doesn't seem to get any lighter." Lucille, sensing the significance of the claim, insists, "It will" (*Housekeeping* 117). When they finally reach home, Sylvie welcomes them with a smile and serves them "Brimstone tea," a concoction of coffee and condensed milk. As Ruth sips, sleep overcomes her, making "one sensation of the heat in [her] palms and the sugar on [her] tongue." She thinks, "this is all death is," and begins to "hope for oblivion" (*Housekeeping* 118–19). When Ruth awakens, having rolled out of her chair, Sylvie greets her knowingly, "Sleep is best when you're *really* tired. . . . [y]ou don't just sleep. You die." Meanwhile, upstairs and far removed from this initiation ceremony, Lucille is setting her hair in curlers. She too has dreamed of death, though not as a pleasant passing into oblivion: Sylvie was trying to suffocate her. While Lucille admits that she initially experiences the prospect of death as "sort of nice," the dream has clearly put her on the defensive. She resists Sylvie in the only way that makes sense, a change in outfit for herself and an aggressive assault on the knots and tangles in Ruth's hair. At Lucille's firm behest, the two head to the drugstore in order to browse fashion magazines and purchase sewing supplies. While there, Lucille notices Ruth's distraction. "You're going to leave," she says. When Ruth responds, "I just want to go home," Lucille finally states the obvious: "That's *Sylvie*'s house." Of course, this isn't news to Ruth; when Ruth tells Lucille that she wants to go home, she is precisely announcing her allegiance to Sylvie, that only her aunt can teach her how to make the darkness from the beach absolute. Here, then, is where the sisters must make their opposition explicit. Ruth writes:

It seemed to me then that Lucille would busy herself forever, nudging, pushing, coaxing, as if she could supply the will I lacked, to pull myself into some seemly shape and slip across the wide frontiers into that other world, where it seemed to me then I could never go. For it seemed to me that nothing I had lost, or might lose, could be found there, or, to put it another way, it seemed that something I had lost might be found in Sylvie's house.

The "other world" or "Syvlie's house," ignorance or imagination: the sisters take their first steps apart.

3 Lucille and the Way of Ignorance

Ruth tells us that Lucille "was of the common persuasion. Time that had not come yet—an anomaly in itself—had the fiercest reality for her" (*Housekeeping* 93). She continues, "Lucille saw in everything its potential for invidious change. She wanted worsted mittens, brown oxfords, red rubber boots" (*Housekeeping* 93). Here, we get our first distinguishing feature of the so-called "common persuasion." Their anxiety about the future leads them to cultivate loss-resistant lives. Ruth's reference to "oxfords" and "worsted mittens" is naturally intended to express Lucille's need to protect her possessions from deterioration and loss. But, of course, it is in the nature of this attitude of Lucille that it will focus on rather conventional objects, the value of which lies not in what they are but in their sturdy usefulness. This basic strategy depends on a kind of collective ignorance: forgetfulness of the basic truth that Fingerbone is founded upon the ravages of the lake.

We see this forgetfulness played out in Lucille's description of her mother, especially the latter's death. She was "orderly, vigorous, and sensible, a widow . . . who was killed in an accident . . . [she] had accelerated too much and lost control of [the car]" (*Housekeeping* 110). In response to this blatant mistelling, Ruth interrogates Lucille. She asks, "Then why had she left us at our grandmother's, with all our things? And why had she driven her car off the road to the middle of the meadow?

And why had she given the boys who helped her not just her money but her purse?" (*Housekeeping* 110). While reality occasionally forces Lucille's hand, she manages to ignore the most important feature of her past: that her mother killed herself. Suicide, unlike a mere accident, threatens to radically challenge the self-understanding of those it leaves behind by suggesting that one's shared life—the collective home—was anything but. Obviously, Lucille has to edit the strict history of her life. The first step to conquering the future is vanquishing the past, and the latter becomes an all-encompassing project.

The first step in maintaining ignorance is complete and utter social absorption. One of *Housekeeping*'s central claims, and one that Ruth comes to appreciate as the novel progresses, is that loneliness breeds (or perhaps simply *is*) a kind of ironic detachment from one's immediate situation. While later we will investigate the upside of loneliness (the features that make it attractive for someone like Ruth), it is obvious why Lucille is wary of it: when a person exists at the margins of a social world its norms and practices lose their grip and begin to feel arbitrary. Where someone absorbed by the social acknowledges strict moral lines, the passing transient sees mere manners (*Housekeeping* 178). In order to reassert the authority of the former, one must reject everything that threatens to individuate.

Lucille begins the process of socialization by internalizing the voices of various Fingerbone exemplars, the "sleek and well-tended girls at school." One girl in particular plays an especially key role in this regard. Ruth writes, "Lucille has a familiar, Rosette Browne, whom she feared and admired, and through whose eyes she continually imagined she saw" (*Housekeeping* 103). Rosette is invited into Lucille's psyche where she is given a tour of the family home and asked to compile a list of reforms. The next step is to absorb Rosette's critical glance so that there becomes no real difference between the two. Rosette's gaze becomes Lucille's.

The merging of the two consciousnesses is developed in a passage where Ruth reads Lucille's diary. Ruth justifies the intrusion with the assumption that she will find nothing that Lucille wouldn't have shared in "better times." Naturally, this does not mean Ruth does not expect to encounter something personal, just that Lucille used to be open about such things. Given these expectations, the contents of the diary disappoint. Ruth writes, "I found . . . lists of exercises she had done and pages she had read. She had copied from somewhere a table grace, which had an aristocratic sound, being brief and crisp and not excessively reverent" (*Housekeeping* 133). This laundry list of prosaic duties (just as easily prescribed by the local Methodist minister) is entirely devoid—and proudly so—of any individuality. This is especially shocking since the genre, diary writing, being by nature hyperpersonal, explicitly encourages it. The diary is the one place where even *convention* demands revelation. Additionally, the litany of Lucille's exercises and prayers seem designed to explicitly suppress "reverence." While, presumably, Lucille adopts this tone in order to avoid offence when in mixed company, its irony is revealing. As Robinson writes elsewhere, reverence is appropriate in contexts of uncertainty. When something is revered, it's because it transcends our ability to understand it, and this, for Lucille and her kind, is always threatening.[20]

We see how language shapes and sustains domestic narratives in an earlier passage where Lucille recruits Ruth for a sewing project. Since this excursion into the domestic is among the girls' first, they need their grandfather's old dictionary to navigate the instructions (full of common, though for them, foreign words like "pinking shears"). In search of the definition, Ruth opens to P and explains what she finds. "At that place there were five dried pansies—one yellow, one blue-black, one mahogany, one violet, one parchment. . . . At Q I found a sprig of Queen Anne's lace. . . . At R I found a variety of roses" (*Housekeeping* 126). In response to Ruth's discovery, Lucille takes the dictionary "by each end of its spine and [shakes] it." Ruth describes the carnage: "Scores of flowers and petals fell and drifted from between the pages. Lucille kept shaking until nothing more came, and then she handed the dictionary back to me."

"Pinking shears," she said.
"What will we do with these flowers?"

"Put them in the stove."
"Why do that?"
"What are they good for?"

This passage draws us back to a tension we noticed in Edmund that is now being visited upon his granddaughters. Recall that during Edmund's sabbaticals from Fingerbone he took to the surrounding hills in search of wildflowers. Their presence in the dictionary gives rise to polarized reactions from the two sisters, and those reactions hint at the kind of significance they bestow on language. If wildflowers symbolize imagination and escape, the dictionary, at least as Lucille uses it,[21] serves as an especially effective symbol of the common persuasion. The advantage (and limitation) of a dictionary is that it purports to explain in literal terms. Pinking shears are, as the *OED* states, "Shears with a serrated blade, used to cut a zigzag edge in fabric to prevent it fraying." While fine enough in its context, a dictionary definition, if presented as the standard for all speech, invites a truncated view of language, one that dampens the rich and diverse allusions that radiate from language in its natural setting. This means that a dictionary, much like a brief aristocratic prayer, mitigates reverence. A person who sees through the eyes of Dickinson, as opposed to Webster, lives in a world where the ordinary always stands to become transfigured.

Lucille treats the dictionary and the definitions it provides as mere tools. She ends the back-and-forth with Ruth by asking, "What are [the flowers] good for?" In a world constructed to avoid reverence, objects are reduced to utensils. They do not suggest or mean or allude; they simply assist in tasks. This comes across beautifully in the almost comical particularity of the object under discussion: "pinking shears." Not only are they straightforwardly utilitarian and domestic, they are straight-jacketed by specificity. These are not just any shears, which could be used to cut anything one fancied. These are for *pinking*. *This* is how you use them. Under such conditions the ordinary remains safely battened down. As Ruth will later acknowledge, "It was absurd to think that things were held in place, are held in place, by a web of words"

(*Housekeeping* 200). Ruth likens this "web" to a "distorting mirror" that squashes and stretches.

Of course, the joke, so far as Ruth is concerned, consists in Fingerbone's refusal to acknowledge the signs of loss that litter their lives. Referring to the "other world," Ruth writes,

> I had seen two of the apple trees in my grandmother's orchard die where they stood. One spring there were no leaves, but they stood there as if expectantly, their limbs almost to the ground, miming their perished fruitfulness. Every winter the orchard is flooded with snow, and every spring the waters are parted, death is undone, and every Lazarus rises, except these two.... It seemed to me that what perished need not also be lost.... Sylvie, I knew, felt the life of perished things. (*Housekeeping* 123–4)

This passage highlights why Lucille's approach cannot satisfy Ruth. Ruth cannot help but notice the trees that do not revive in the spring. But since Lucille's world must ignore these relics—in fact, is constituted by this ignorance—it also abandons the possibility of resurrection. This means that Ruth has to reside elsewhere; she must turn from the way of ignorance, with its "scrolled couch[es]" and "bookcases full of almanacs," toward Sylvie's house (*Housekeeping* 158–9). Only Sylvie can teach her how to walk among the "perished things."

4 Ruth and the Way of Imagination

From the moment of Sylvie's return, a special bond develops between her and Ruth. This kinship remains mostly latent until the two sisters return from their night on the lake. As we saw, in a kind of first communion (though with a pointedly pagan twist), Sylvie serves Ruth "Brimstone tea" and initiates her onto the path of "oblivion" ("Sleep is best when you're *really* tired.... [y]ou don't just sleep. You die."). Ruth frames her relationship with her aunt quite explicitly as one of pupil to educator (*Housekeeping* 202) and, having cut ties with Lucille and the other world, prepares to give Sylvie her full attention.

The first and most important step in Ruth's education is the reverse of Lucille's: an expansion of loneliness. But loneliness is more than just separation from other people. For Sylvie, it involves a sense of isolation that extends even to the world of immediate perception. When Sylvie turns out all the lights in the house, she doesn't just prevent the girls from seeing the clutter gathering in the kitchen, she directs their gaze inward, attuning their "finer senses" (*Housekeeping* 101). While the darkness allows them to hear and smell things they could not otherwise detect, it also encourages them toward introspection. As they come into immediate contact with their own consciousness—made to feel their personality—their isolation is underscored. As Ruth becomes more and more accustomed to the dark, she begins to regard even her own body as an impediment. "It seemed to me that I made no impact on the world, and that in exchange I was privileged to watch it unawares. But my allusion to this feeling of ghostliness sounded peculiar, and sweat started all over my body, convicting me on the spot of gross corporeality" (*Housekeeping* 106).

During her kitchen table flirtation with oblivion, Ruth dreams of her mother. She later explains the feeling the dream induces, offering us a glimpse of how imagination figures in Sylvie's redemptive strategy. She writes:

> In my dream I had waited for her confidently, as I had all those years ago when she left us in the porch. Such confidence was like a sense of imminent presence, a palpable displacement, the movement in the air before the wind comes. Or so it seemed. Yet twice I had been disappointed, if that was the word. Perhaps I had been deceived. If appearance is only a trick of the nerves, and apparition is only a lesser trick of the nerves, a less perfect illusion, then this expectation, this sense of a presence unperceived, was not particularly illusory as things in this world go. (*Housekeeping* 122)

Here we see two things that Ruth's imagination offers. First, and most importantly, it revives the dead by re-creating a feeling of "presence." Second, it constitutes, or so Ruth reasons, a less "deceptive" presence because of its relative modesty. If everyday sense perception presents us with convincing "illusions"—appearances so vivid we consistently take them to be mind-independent—then the more transparent "illusions" of the imagination are all the more credible. Importantly, they are also more substantial than the banal and worldly illusions that captivate her sister. "By so much was my dream less false than Lucille's. And it is probably as well to be undeceived, though perhaps it is not" (*Housekeeping* 122). These considerations are meant to license Ruth's inward turn. If she cannot literally see her mother and, further, the things she can see are themselves a fiction of sorts, then why wouldn't she embrace the dreamworld?

In perhaps the most significant passage of the novel, we see these two components—loneliness and the activity of the imagination—come together. Sylvie has taken Ruth into the hills outside Fingerbone for her final lesson. Sylvie leaves Ruth alone near the wreckage of an abandoned homestead in order to meet the children who haunt the woods. Ruth writes:

> I knew why Sylvie felt there were children in the woods. I felt so, too, though I did not think so. I sat on the log pelting my shoe, because I knew that if I turned however quickly to look behind me the consciousness behind me would not still be there, and would only come closer when I turned away again. Even if it spoke just at my ear, as it seemed often at the point of doing, when I turned there would be nothing there. In that way it was persistent and teasing and ungentle, the way half-wild, lonely children are. This was something Lucille and I together would ignore, and I had been avoiding the shore all that fall, because when I was by myself and obviously lonely, too, the teasing would be much more difficult to disregard. Having a sister or a friend is like sitting at night in a lighted house. Those outside can watch you if they want, but you need not see them. You simply say, "Here are the perimeters of our attention. If you prowl around under the windows till the crickets go silent, we will pull the shades. If you wish us to suffer your envious curiosity, you must permit us not to notice it." Anyone with one solid human bond is that smug, and it is the smugness as much as the comfort and safety that lonely people covet and admire.

> I had been, so to speak, turned out of house now long enough to have observed this in myself. Now there was neither threshold nor sill between me and these cold, solitary children who almost breathed against my cheek and almost touched my hair (*Housekeeping* 154).

By turning her back to the children, Ruth is invited to feel for their presence. She realizes now why she has to be alone, that even one human bond is enough to steel a person against the ghost world. "Loneliness," as Ruth will go on to say, "is an absolute discovery" (*Housekeeping* 157); "by abandoning me [Sylvie] had assumed the power to bestow such a richness of grace."[22] Ruth now wears Sylvie's "coat like beatitude."

Under the protection of her new mantel, Ruth's ecstasy reaches an apotheosis. She exclaims,

> Let them come unhouse me of this flesh, and pry this house apart. It was no shelter now, it only kept me here alone, and I would rather be with them, if only to see them, even if they turned away from me. If I could see my mother, it would not have to be her eyes, her hair. . . . She was a music I no longer heard, that rang in my mind, itself and nothing else, lost to all sense, but not perished, not perished. (*Housekeeping* 159)

In addition to being a kind of climax to her tutorial, this passage returns to the motivation that brought Ruth to Sylvie's house to begin with: the resurrection of her mother. In turning away from the physical, her body and its crudities, she has become attuned to an interior music, the imminent presence of her mother, that she now plays on loop. She has made herself into a ghost (been "unhoused") in order to live with ghosts.[23]

This communion with the dead involves more than just conjuring vivid memories. Ruth, the true heir of Ishmael, uses her prodigious allusive capacity to overlay the imaginative onto the real, the dead on the living. As they return to Fingerbone by boat, under the cover of nightfall, Ruth observes, "the faceless shape in front of me could as well be Helen herself as Sylvie. I spoke to her by the name Sylvie, and she did not answer. Then how was one to know? And if she were Helen in my sight, how could she not be Helen in fact?" (*Housekeeping* 166–7).

Given the opportunity afforded by the darkness, Ruth allows the music of her mother to fill Sylvie's silhouette. Ruth notices she can achieve the same with her disappeared father. She writes, "I can't even remember what he was like, I mean when he was alive. But ever since, it's Papa here and Papa there, and dreams" (*Housekeeping* 186).

The ability to use memory and imagination to resurrect the dead is the great ambition and achievement of Sylvie's house. Consider again how Ruth frames her early predicament, "Memory is the sense of loss, and loss pulls us after it.... There is so little to remember of anyone—an anecdote, a conversation at table. But every memory is turned over and over again, every word, however chance, written in the heart in the hope that memory will fulfill itself, and become flesh, and that the wanderers will find a way home" (*Housekeeping* 194–5). Before meeting Sylvie this turning "over and over again" was experienced as a torment, like a fragment of a song that can't be placed or completed. After her time with Sylvie, the repetition of memory takes on restorative significance. Instead of a skipping record, she now has a repeating one; she has the resources to summon her mother on demand or, more accurately, to be summoned herself, as Ruth puts it, "to walk under water" (*Housekeeping* 175). "[M]emory is the seat not only of prophecy but of miracle as well" (*Housekeeping* 196).

After their fateful trip to the abandoned homestead, Ruth and Sylvie return to Fingerbone and, under the threat of legal separation, pretend to play by Fingerbone's rules. When it becomes clear that they won't be able to satisfy the authorities, they set fire to the house. As Sylvie and Ruth escape across the bridge that marked the beginning of their family tragedy, Ruth imagines the house burning, "the sovereign ease with which it burst its tomb, broke up its grave" (*Housekeeping* 211). Even the house must be "unhoused," being, like Edmund's childhood home, more sepulcher than haven.

Though Ruth and Sylvie have certainly escaped from something, it's not obvious that they now rest in peace. The final pages of *Housekeeping* are, rather ironically, obsessed with what they have left behind, obsessed with the living, with Lucille. Ruth imagines Lucille back in the reconstructed family home, "waiting there in a fury of righteousness, cleansing and polishing, all these years." She continues:

> Sylvie and I have stood outside her window a thousand times, and we have thrown the side door open when she was upstairs changing beds, and we have brought in leaves, and flung the curtains and tipped the bud vase, and somehow left the house again before she could run downstairs, leaving behind us a strong smell of lake water. (*Housekeeping* 218)

Changing the scenery, she next imagines Lucille "in Boston, at a table in a restaurant, waiting for a friend." Ruth describes the absence that hovers around Lucille as she sits alone: everyone who isn't there gathers in tightly. Ruth imagines Lucille feels this absence and is bothered by it. She tells us that "[Lucille's] water glass has left two-thirds of a ring on the table, and she works at completing the circle with her thumbnail." The incomplete circle is, of course, Ruth's way of suggesting that Lucille has not solved any of her problems. The way of Fingerbone does not restore the lost.

5 Conclusion

Lucille's failure, the failure of ignorance, is made apparent to the reader only by proxy, only by means of the imagination of Ruth. Ruth's life is essentially haunted by these imaginings—while in the world of the living she was haunted by the dead; now, after having been initiated into the world of the dead by Sylvie, Ruth is haunted by her imaginings of those still living. Her fixation on Lucille's waywardness in the end perhaps blinds her from her own. And so, it is natural for the reader to wonder: Is Ruth's solution to the problem, one posed to the sisters by their mother's abandonment, any more successful than Lucille's?

When Sylvie and Ruth first come upon the abandoned homestead in the woods to look for the ghostly children, the dawn is only just beginning to break, and Ruth notices that the house is "all white with the brine of frost" (*Housekeeping* 151). While she agrees with Sylvie that the place is pretty, she is mystified that anyone could have wanted to live there. Sylvie insists again that it is beautiful, and especially so in the daylight. But Ruth is overwhelmed by the early morning cold, and insists on leaving the place to find somewhere warmer to sit and eat something. When they return at noon, she does indeed find the scene "much changed." The noontime sunlight had transfigured it, and in particular that frost, which had "before seemed barren and parched as salt," but from which the light had "coaxed a flowering" (*Housekeeping* 152). The vision draws out from Ruth a particularly extravagant imagining:

> Imagine a Carthage sown with salt, and all the sowers gone, and the seeds lain however long in the earth, till there rose finally in vegetable profusion leaves and trees of rime and brine. What flowering would there be in such a garden? Light would force each salt calyx to open in prisms, and to fruit heavily with bright globes of water—peaches and grapes are little more than that, and where the world was salt there would be greater need of slaking. For need can blossom into all the compensations it requires. To crave and to have are as like as a thing and its shadow. For when does a berry break upon the tongue as sweetly as when one longs to taste it, and when is the taste refracted into so many hues and savors of ripeness and earth, and when do our senses know any thing so utterly as when we lack it? And here again is a foreshadowing—the world will be made whole. For to wish for a hand on one's hair is all but to feel it. So whatever we may lose, very craving gives it back to us again. Though we dream and hardly know it, longing, like an angel, fosters us, smooths our hair, and brings us wild strawberries. (152–3)

Sowing with salt is supposed to be an act of destruction, not just of living things but of the potential for future life.[24] And so it is certainly strange to see Ruth using it here as a symbol of life, and ultimately the source of hopeful thoughts about its redemption and consummation. These thoughts, given birth by the bizarre imagery of fruiting salt, are perhaps as close to Robinson's own religious views as anything explicitly stated in the text.[25] What is inspiring in them, and what makes them most alien from the thinking of Lucille, is the element of hope, of the thought that what is out of joint in the world will one day be made good, and that it is not human labor that will bring it about, but, in a sense, merely the fact that we desire it. It is, in short, a fundamental belief in the goodness of life.

But what is the "life" that Ruth believes in, longs for? Sown salt is an image of death and absence (the sowers are all "gone"), and her imaginings never stray very far from the thought of her mother who is dead and gone. Her images of satisfied craving, of consummated desire, are of the taste of wild strawberries and the feel of an angel's hand "fostering" her and caressing her hair. Both lead straight back to her mother Helen, whose surname is of course Foster, and who had been found sitting on her car eating wild strawberries immediately before committing suicide (*Housekeeping* 23).[26] The figure of Helen lies behind yet another image of salt, this time in an allusion to the story of the wife of Lot, who is turned into a pillar of salt upon having looked back on God's destruction of Sodom and Gomorrah (Gen. 19:26). Ruth imagines that, if there were snow close to the house, she would build a statue of a woman, who she calls "Lot's wife," and who Sylvie's imagined spectral children, such "wild and orphan things," could decorate and love as "more than mother" (*Housekeeping* 153).

Ruth's life, like Lucille's, is scarred and shaped by the loss of her mother. The loss spurs Lucille into a life of protection from the future possibility of traumatic loss, and thus from real engagement with the world around her. This is made most clear in her attempt to evade the truth that her mother really did commit suicide. Ruth's own way of coping with the loss is more honest, and in its own way far bolder: she submits herself utterly to the loss, and hopes and believes that it will be made good. But the cold and spectral images she uses to sustain that hope are dangerous; they perhaps contain the seeds of a more thoroughgoing embrace and affirmation of life, but also invite her to long for the death that is necessary to reunite with her mother. But her need, like that of Sylvie's children, is in fact for something "more than mother," something to which her admittedly prodigious imaginative resources are still not quite adequate.

Notes

1. Melville (2002, 188).
2. Melville (2002, 57).
3. "New American Eve" is Maureen Ryan's label for Ruth. See Ryan (1991). For other early feminist readings see Kirkby (1986), Mallon (1989), and Ravits (1989). For a more recent version of this narrative see Crisu (2016).
4. The full title of Ravits's (1989) essay is "Extending the American Range: Marilynne Robinson's *Housekeeping*."
5. Robinson herself does not seem to have intended this. In a 1994 interview, she suggests that she did indeed "think of creating a world that had the feeling of . . . femaleness about it," but that this was due to her own highly "unusual" experience of matriarchal families growing up in the American West (Schaub 1994, 233). She adds as well that she does not take the perspective of Ishmael (or Melville) to be limited by his gender; she says that she had been told that she was "pointedly excluded as a woman from *Moby-Dick*, that this was a world that meant to exclude me and did exclude me, but I never felt that was true" (1994, 234).
6. See, e.g., Crisu (2016).
7. Kirkby (1986).
8. Caver (1996).
9. Caver (1996, 116). Framing the issue in terms of "life after art," Kirkby concludes the same: "Perhaps there is life after art but we cannot yet imagine the forms it will take" (1986, 106).
10. Caver (1996, 111).
11. This is Galehouse's description, which fits Caver's interpretation rather nicely. The fuller quote reads, "What *Housekeeping* actually depicts is a different way of living in the world, with gender as a participatory, but secondary, concern" (2000, 123).
12. Hartshorne (1990, 52).
13. Galehouse (2000, 123).
14. Later in the novel, the Fingerbone house is explicitly likened to a grave. See p. 211.
15. Of course, Robinson does the same when she names her central character after a famous biblical exile.

16 Sylvia Foster understands her duty to her children in explicitly these terms. See p. 19.
17 Weber (2011, 146).
18 Thomas Gardner makes a similar point, claiming that "Ruth's sense that the ordinary is no more than a relic, cut off from what matters, can be understood as a version of Dickinson's insistence on the flimsiness of the apparently-stable givens of our the [sic] the world" (2001, 18).
19 Karl Ove Knausgaard makes this point when discussing the painter Edvard Munch's manner of dealing with early and traumatic loss. Knausgaard writes: "[With all of these losses] one ends up with a child, a teenager and a grown man who is so afraid of losing that he deals with it by simply not acquiring" (2017, 12).
20 See Robinson (2008).
21 Of course, one needn't take such a utilitarian approach even to a dictionary. One might treat it, too, with a kind of reverence, insofar as it is a repository of language, and thus a kind of representation of a repository of things. Dictionaries too can excite the imagination. Perhaps Edmund himself thought of his dictionary in some such way; after all, he chooses to put his precious wildflowers there.
22 This last line, while most immediately referring to the embrace Sylvie offers upon her return, clearly also alludes to the revelation of loneliness.
23 Gardner draws attention to this as well. See (2001, 27).
24 The legend to which Ruth refers is that of Scipio Aemilianus Africanus, the Roman general who was said to have sown the soil of Carthage with salt after having conquered the great city to end the Third Punic War. See also Judg. 9:45.
25 Indeed, one commentator has even gone so far as to claim that this passage, and Ruth's other imaginings beginning with "imagine that" or "say that" in the text are in fact something like creedal statements, cast in the form of "imperative hypotheses," around which the novel is constructed. See Anthony Domestico (2014).
26 These connections are also noted, and given a more psychoanalytical interpretation, in Donnelly (2017).

3

Gilead

More Beauty than Our Eyes Can Bear

In *Gilead* (2004), we find a novelist who seems to have radically changed course. It is not just a shift in tone—the movement from Fingerbone's gothic chill to Gilead's radiant warmth—but also a shift in outlook. *Housekeeping* depicts a world that rejects all attempts at reconciliation: life is not to be loved but painfully endured. In stark contrast, *Gilead*'s John Ames (the novel's fictional author) is by all appearances hopelessly in love with existence. What from the lips of Ruth or Sylvie might function as a cry of exasperation—"Ah, this life, this world"—is for Ames an expression of spontaneous delight (*Gilead* 9). Each day dawns as though the first, crowning even the humblest corners of the world with a shimmering light that invites fuller participation. As the seventy-six-year-old readies himself for death, he declares, without the slightest hint of bitterness, "Oh, I will miss the world!" (*Gilead* 115).[1]

Significantly, Ames seems to share in many of Ruth's tragic experiences. He is born into a home already mourning the deaths of two brothers and a sister; later, he is scarred by the delivery-room losses of a young wife and newborn daughter. This, Ames tells us, inaugurates "the dark time" in his life, a period of painful loneliness (*Gilead* 44). That the loneliness does not become absolute, and eventually blossoms into the joy that characterizes *Gilead*, is part of the central mystery this chapter looks to explore. Assuming that the differences between Fingerbone and Gilead cannot be reduced to mere coincidence, the reader has a vested interest in discovering what enables Ames to affirm life, especially a tragic one, with such relentless zeal.

One obvious place to start is with Ames's faith. When he begins writing the notes that will become his "begats" (reflections for his six-year-old son Robert "Robby" Ames), he has served as a Congregationalist pastor for over half a century. In that time, his life has been devoted both to serving the families that attend his small church and to writing volumes and volumes of carefully crafted sermons, enough to put him "up there with Augustine and Calvin for quantity" (*Gilead* 19). These reflections, as impressive in their magnitude as they are humble in their hiddenness, have slowly worked their way into the threads of his soul. Every moment of every day is lived as though in the presence of the sacred.

Reflecting on the work of Ludwig Feuerbach—the *enfant terrible* of nineteenth-century atheism—Ames writes,

> he is about as good on the joyful aspects of religion as anybody, and he loves the world. Of course he thinks religion could just stand out of the way and let joy exist pure and undisguised. That is his one error, and it is significant. But he is marvelous on the subject of joy, and also on its religious expressions. (*Gilead* 24)

These lines are remarkable for a few reasons. First, Ames explicitly associates joy and life-affirmation—Feuerbach knows joy and "loves the world." Second, he makes a strong claim about the connection between religion and joy. He does not just say that a joyful life *can* be religious; he claims that religion plays a necessary role in joy—it *can't* just stand out of the way. Finally, Ames admits that Feuerbach is "marvelous on the subject of joy." On the heels of his previous claim, Ames seems to suggest that Feuerbach might himself be religious. Joy requires religion; Feuerbach is well acquainted with joy. Therefore, Feuerbach is religious.

These remarks about religion offer a promising starting place in interrogating Ames's love of life, but they also present their own difficulties. Most pressingly, one might worry that any account of the religious life that includes sworn atheists among its members will be far too thin to justify any meaningful connection between faith and joy. In other words, Ames's strong claim about religion may be offset by a weak understanding of what counts as religious.

But Ames's account of the truly religious life is not vacuous, or purely secular. There are, in fact, two ways in which religion plays a role in life-affirmation. The first we've just discussed: experiences of joy are viewed as straightforwardly religious. Anytime a person experiences joy, whether during the fourth movement of Beethoven's 9th or while watching their children run through the sprinklers, they are responding to an implicit sense that the moment is set apart. The second, while related to the first, is considerably more substantial. Though it is possible for anyone in principle to experience joy, some ways of living more readily invite it because they intentionally train attention on the sacred. These lives are religious in a more traditional sense. They may include certain metaphysical beliefs (in the existence of God or the nonreducibility of human consciousness or the existence of an afterlife) and, most importantly for Ames, involve a living liturgy. They encourage a person to engage in rituals and activities that train their perception of divinity. For Ames, this training revolves around the sacraments: traditional rites like baptism and marriage, and even practices like keeping the sabbath. The sacraments, broadly construed, are essential to the larger story because they, first, function as beacons of the sacred and, second, transfer this sense to other experiences they exemplify: the bread of Eucharist to the dinner table, baptism to late-April rain showers, and the sabbath to a Wednesday morning sunrise.[2] Through this process the world becomes slowly saturated with a sense of wonder and mystery, which in turn feeds joy. This is what emboldens Ames to claim that Feuerbach is mistaken about the uselessness of religion. Not only is joy a fundamentally religious experience but a religious life is uniquely structured to put a person in the way of it.

This chapter is dedicated, first, to explaining more fully the ways in which Ames takes religion and joy to be connected and then, second, showing how this theoretical understanding is affirmed practically in his own life. The first task will require a close consideration of Ames's treatment of Feuerbach.[3] Ames regards interaction with the great atheists to be a precondition of his pastoral vocation, and he spends a significant portion of his reflections directly addressing their challenges.

Feuerbach's mistake lies in his refusal to grant that some things are not made to man's measure. This philosophical anthropocentrism threatens to strangle the kind of life that cultivates joy but also, and more personally, directly belies Feuerbach's own immediate experience of the world.

However, Ames's direct interactions with Feuerbach cannot be the final word. As Ames himself acknowledges, argumentation is always insufficient. If a person is to change their mind, they must receive a "vision." One of the great virtues of Robinson's novel is its commitment to achieving precisely this end, and exploring how it does this is the chapter's second main task. While Ames repeatedly tells his son that he prays he too will someday receive a vision, we see—as his confessions unfold—that Ames is in fact providing such a vision through his writing. Most importantly, Ames shows his son (and the reader) that the movement from right perception of the world to love of life is immediate. This drama unfolds in real time as Ames, through his own reflection, comes to see that his earthly vocation is far from finished—he is being invited to even deeper love. He must, he eventually realizes, extend his vision to encompass the novel's prodigal son, Ames's godson and namesake, John ("Jack") Ames Boughton. Ames's ability to vanquish his own "covetise" and bless Jack is the fulfillment of his "argument" with Feuerbach. A truly religious life is always and inevitably "drawn back into the world" (*Gilead* 238).

1 Ames's Relationship to Feuerbach

German philosopher Ludwig Feuerbach was considered, in his own context and time, *the* great voice of European atheism. A student of Hegel and an inspiration for Marx, his most famous work, *The Essence of Christianity* (1841), quickly gained an international readership assisted by the early interest of a young British writer named Marian Evans. Known to most as "George Eliot," Evans published the first English translation of the work in 1854, and it is this text that would have been found in John Ames's personal library. The book makes its way to the backwaters of Iowa through an unlikely channel: Ames's elder brother. Edward Ames, John's senior by nearly a decade, is described as fiercely intelligent. After graduating from college with a degree in ancient languages, he moves to Göttingen to continue his studies and eventually returns "with a walking stick and a huge mustache. Herr Doktor" (*Gilead* 25). He has "published a slender book in German, a monograph of some kind on Feuerbach" (*Gilead* 25). The family reunion is tumultuous and short-lived. When asked to pray over dinner, Edward refuses, mouthing the words of St. Paul: "When I was a child, I thought as a child. Now that I am become a man, I have put away childish things" (*Gilead* 26). As a parting gesture, "thinking to shock [Ames] out of [his] uncritical piety," Edward gifts his teenage brother with a copy of Feuerbach's *Essence* (*Gilead* 24).

The gift makes a significant impact on Ames, though not in the way Edward anticipates. Ames's first reference to Feuerbach lauds the great atheist as a true companion in faith, and he invites Robby to take special notice of his discussion of the sacraments. After quoting a passage that speaks of the "beautiful, profound natural significance [of Baptism]," Ames follows with the claim we just considered:

> Feuerbach is . . . about as good on the joyful aspects of religion as anybody, and he loves the world. Of course he thinks religion could just stand out of the way and let joy exist pure and undisguised. That is his one error, and it is significant. But he is marvelous on the subject of joy, and also on its religious expressions. (*Gilead* 24)

Clearly, Ames thinks that anyone who is "marvelous on the subject of joy" is friendly to faith. To understand why, we need to investigate Feuerbach's "one" and "significant" "error."

In a later passage, during a discussion of worship, Ames returns to the topic of Feuerbach. He writes, "right worship of God is essential because it forms the mind to a right understanding of God. God is set apart—He is One, He is not to be imagined as a thing among things (idolatry—this is what Feuerbach failed to grasp). His name is set apart.

It is sacred" (*Gilead* 138). This passage connects directly to Ames's earlier reference to Feuerbach's "one error," which is here discussed in terms of "idolatry." Feuerbach fails to acknowledge that God is set apart, that divinity utterly transcends categories of everyday experience. It is also here that Ames explicitly associates this mistake with a failure to acknowledge sacredness.[4]

These comments help make sense of the earlier passage where Ames connects religion with joy. There, recall, he wrote: "[Feuerbach] thinks religion could just stand out of the way and let joy exist pure and undisguised." Assuming that Ames is consistent in maintaining that there is really just "one error" to be criticized, we can now read this early passage in the light of the later one. By "religion" we see that Ames means "the sacred," that which is set apart. Feuerbach believes this idea of God's transcendence is both philosophically and, more importantly, existentially problematic; it distracts from the true wonder of the immanent world. This last claim is the real focus of Ames's criticism. In direct contrast to Feuerbach, he claims that transcendence—that is, maintaining a sense of the world's intrinsic mystery—plays a necessary role in one's love and appreciation of life.

Ames tells his son that one should always avoid defensiveness when engaging figures like Feuerbach. He writes, "In the matter of belief, I have always found that defenses have the same irrelevance about them as the criticisms they are meant to answer" (*Gilead* 178). He adds, "So my advice is this—don't look for proofs. Don't bother with them at all. They are never sufficient to the question, and they're always a little impertinent, I think, because they claim for God a place within our conceptual grasp" (*Gilead* 179). Despite this reluctance, Ames still feels a duty to avoid naivety, trying his best "never to say anything Edward would have found callow" (*Gilead* 154). Using Edward ("Herr Doktor") as a stand-in for Feuerbach, Ames rehearses an analogy meant to challenge the latter's core conclusion.

He begins by restating Feuerbach's position: "Feuerbach doesn't imagine the possibility of an existence beyond this one, by which I mean a reality embracing this one but exceeding it" (*Gilead* 143).

Ames is referencing the first chapter of *The Essence of Christianity*, wherein Feuerbach offers the most concentrated presentation of his projection theory. There, he argues that for something to be meaningfully regarded as existing it must be an object of possible experience. And since God is, by definition, *not* an object of possible experience, then God cannot, for all intents and purposes, be said to exist. Ames takes Feuerbach's point to really just concern "the awkwardness of language" (*Gilead* 143). Since language sets the limits of what can be meaningfully said, one shouldn't, and in some sense *can't*, discuss what lies beyond it. To be beyond language is to be nonexistent, to be so much cosmic noise.

Obviously, Ames thinks Feuerbach's conclusion does not follow, and he attempts to show this with an analogy to his cat, Soapy. He writes:

> [T]his world embraces and exceeds Soapy's understanding of it. Soapy might be a victim of ideological conflict right along with the rest of us, if things get out of hand. She would no doubt make some feline appraisal of the situation, which would have nothing to do with the Dictatorship of the Proletariat or the Manhattan Project. The inadequacy of her concepts would have nothing to do with the reality of the situation. (*Gilead* 143)

In the same way that the world quite clearly "embraces and exceeds Soapy's understanding of it," Ames thinks it also embraces and exceeds human understanding. Human interpretations of the world no more exhaust the limits of existence than do Soapy's feline ones. Ames admits that this is "a drastic way of putting it, and not a very precise one." He continues,

> I don't wish to suggest a reality that is simply an enlarged or extrapolated version of this reality. If you think how a thing we call a stone differs from a thing we call a dream—the degrees of unlikeness within the reality we know are very extreme, and what I wish to suggest is a much more absolute unlikeness, with which we exist, though our human circumstance creates in us a radically limited and peculiar notion of what existence is. (*Gilead* 143)

If Ames is right to suppose that argumentative "defenses" are irrelevant at best and impertinent at worst, we probably should not place too much stock in either the aptness of the analogy or Ames's hopes for it. Certainly, if Edward himself had entertained it, he would have found much to criticize. To begin with, Ames's argument seems to miss the real punch of Feuerbach's point. Feuerbach doesn't look to establish God's nonexistence but rather the irrelevance of that existence *for us*. Edward would have granted that in the same way a larger human world embraces and exceeds Soapy's, there might be a larger divine world that does the same for the human. But just as human ideologies can only ever be so much nonsense to a cat, any reality that exceeds human categories cannot play a meaningful role in a human life.

Thus the importance of Ames's argument is found less in its strict validity than in its indication of his broader position. Ames knows that the only thing that can convert Edward is a performative refutation—a direct encounter with the sacred. It is worth noting that, in this regard, Ames is in the company of another Herr Doktor who, for his own part, was also an admiring, yet critical, student of Feuerbach: the great Protestant theologian Karl Barth. In addition to being one of Ames's intellectual and spiritual touchstones, Barth begins his academic career at the same German university (in Göttingen) where Edward studied decades before, and inaugurates his transition to a professorship in Münster with a 1926 lecture on the wisdom and folly of Feuerbach, claiming that modern theologians are "the true children of *his* century." He writes:

> By the same token, the suspicion has been aroused that in its most highly human idealism, Christian theology's "God," or its otherworldliness, may be a human illusion in the face of which it is well to remain true to the earth. With this thoroughly sound reminder, necessary for a knowledge of the real God, Feuerbach . . . was and is really stronger than the great majority of modern and most recent theologians.[5]

In the closing lines of the lecture, Barth's prose elevates. His words anticipate and clarify Ames's position:

> One had better look out if one picks up the only weapon that will take care of Feuerbach. No one may strike him with it unless he has himself been hit by it. The weapon is no mere argument which one exploits in apologetics, it should rather be a ground on which one can stand, and with fear and trembling allow to speak for itself. Whether or not we stand on this ground will be tested by our answer to this question: are we capable of admitting to Feuerbach that he is entirely right in his interpretation of religion insofar as it relates not only to religion as an experience of evil and mortal man, but also to the "high," the "ponderable," and even the "Christian" religion of this man?[6]

Barth admits that Feuerbach's point is, within its own limits, "entirely right." It is almost always the case that human beings think about God in *idolatrous* terms: as a thing among things, a mere enlargement of their everyday experience. This reminder makes Feuerbach, in his own way, a valuable companion—he plays the prophet in a call to repentance. At the same time, Barth continues, it is still possible to "lay claim to [God's] truth, His Certainty, His Salvation." Like a nail piercing through human flesh, God is revealed through "*grace* and *only* as grace." Barth ends, "So long as this nail is not firmly in, so long as the talk about 'God in man' is not cut out at the roots, we have no cause to criticize Feuerbach, but are with him 'the true children of *his* century.'"[7] Like Ames, Barth insists "no mere argument" "will take care of Feuerbach." A vision of grace is the only means by which a person can come to see God and, thus also, the folly of Feuerbach's position. However, as Barth's reference to "fear and trembling" indicates, this grace is not cheap.

Ames hints that Edward has in fact received such a vision. During Edward's short return-stay in Gilead, young Ames makes a habit of "slipping away" to spend time with his brother. On one of these clandestine trips, he brings along a baseball and a couple of mitts for a game of catch. On a side street, and careful at first of his clothes, Edward begins to zing the ball into Ames's glove. After throwing a stinger, Edward laughs with pleasure—he is recovering his arm. The street is dusty and the day hot, and the two brothers soon grow thirsty. Edward asks for a glass of water and, upon receiving it, pours it over his head, water cascading "off that big mustache of his like rain off a roof." As he stands there, with dripping mustache and plastered hair, he quotes Psalm 133:

> Behold, how good and how pleasant it is,
> For brethren to dwell together in unity!
> It is like the precious oil upon the head,
> That ran down upon the beard;
> Even Aaron's beard;
> That came down upon the skirt of his garments
> Like the dew of Hermon,
> That cometh down upon the mountains of Zion.

Ames reflects, "It meant [Edward] knew everything I knew, every single word. Perhaps he was telling me that he knew everything I knew and he was not persuaded by it." More significantly, Ames adds, "after that day I did feel pretty much at ease about the state of his soul. Though of course I am not competent to judge" (*Gilead* 64). Strictly speaking, it is Ames who receives the vision. He sees that God's radiance no more excludes his older brother—the cane-wielding, Feuerbach-reading, Herr Doktor—than it does Moses's brother (the oil runs down "Even Aaron's beard"). To say that he is at ease about the state of Edward's soul is simply to grant that his brother acknowledges the sacred. So much so that he is occasionally taken up in reveries of worship, spontaneous baptisms that call for the benediction of scripture. Edward stands as a direct refutation of the idea that religion is necessary for joy. Like his philosophical mentor, he explicitly rejects faith and looks to actively convert others—Ames included—to atheism. At the same time, he is capable of ecstatic outbursts of joy, so beautiful in their intensity that they put to rest all pious concern. However, instead of denying the connection between religion and joy, Ames offers another explanation.

A few pages after his "Soapy analogy," he returns to the topic of Feuerbach as he discusses "two insidious notions, from the point of view of Christianity in the modern world." The first, which he attributes explicitly to Feuerbach, is the idea "that religion and religious experience are illusions of some sort" (*Gilead* 145). Recalling that Ames includes experiences of joy as religious, and that Edward is no stranger to them, we have to assume that the "insidiousness" is a product of how Feuerbach and others *interpret* these experiences. While they certainly do not dispute that people experience awe and beauty and joy, because of their general dismissal of transcendence they are forced to see a certain aspect of those experiences as illusory. In contrast, Ames seems incapable of prying joy and transcendence apart. We see this early in his reflections as he recounts a memory from a "morning a few years ago":

> There was a young couple strolling along half a block ahead of me. The sun had come up brilliantly after a heavy rain, and the trees were glistening and very wet. On some impulse, plain exuberance, I suppose, the fellow jumped up and caught hold of a branch, and a storm of luminous water came pouring down on the two of them, and they laughed and took off running, the girl sweeping water off her hair and her dress as if she were a little bit disgusted, but she wasn't. (*Gilead* 27–8)

Ames adds, "It was a beautiful thing to see, like something from a myth." This joyful memory causes Ames to reflect on the "excessiveness" of experience. He writes:

> I almost wish I could have written that the sun just shone and the tree just glistened, and the water just poured out of it and the girl just laughed. . . . People talk that way when they want to call attention to a thing existing in excess of itself, so to speak, a sort of purity or lavishness, at any rate something ordinary in kind but exceptional in degree. . . . There is something real signified by that word "just" that proper language won't acknowledge. . . . (*Gilead* 28)

Here, Ames argues, in his own indirect way, that at the level of felt experience joy includes precisely what Feuerbach denies: that one has made contact with something that exceeds all possible attempts to understand it. Joy betokens a kind of lavish encounter with existence, a squandering and overflowing of life. If Feuerbach's thought can be summarized in the idea that all things are made to human measure, then joy is a direct challenge. It draws attention to the way in which things "ordinary in kind" can be "exceptional in degree." Like the feeling of the disciples who witness Christ's transfiguration, joy fills a person with the impulse to build an altar and spend an eternity in inexhaustible appreciation. Ames expresses this impulse when, in response to his memory, he says, "I wish I had paid more attention to it" (*Gilead* 28).

If experiences of awe and beauty and joy really do include the content that Ames attributes to them, then we can finally appreciate what is so insidious about Feuerbach's position. It leads someone to mistrust their best experiences. This is problematic for a few reasons. First, it indicates a kind of dishonesty—a rejection of evidence that supports a religious interpretation of life. Second, and more importantly, it undermines the intensity of the very experiences that ground life-affirmation. If joy gives rise to the impulse to praise precisely because it hints at the supersensible, then a way of thinking that begins by rejecting the transcendent is bound to either stifle the impulse to praise or, worse, choke it off completely. A person like Edward is forced to reject in everyday life that which he acknowledges when gripped by joy: God is in this place! Though both Feuerbach and Ames are concerned by this kind of practical dissonance, they address it in opposite ways. Where Feuerbach proposes to atheize joy in order to bring it into conformity with the everyday, Ames aspires to introduce divinity into ordinary life in order to bring it into conformity with moments of joy. This aspiration to live a religious life is perhaps the most important casualty of Feuerbach's view. Refusing to acknowledge the religious content of joy means that it is all the less likely to inspire a religious way of life. Religious life, however, is precisely constructed to train a person to be hyper-receptive to joy. Such a life runs on a feedback loop where experiences of joy feed rituals of attention which lead back again to experience.

2 The Role of Religion

As Ames frames his "debate" with Feuerbach, their disagreement is practical: it is an issue of whether religion impedes joy. Earlier, we explored how Ames resists this conclusion in his explicit interactions with Feuerbach's philosophy. He links joy to the sacred and the sacred to religion. While these reflections are not without merit, Ames would be the first to admit they are, in themselves, quite limited. Arguments do not change people; visions change people. Marilynne Robinson seems to be in full agreement and allows Ames to say just enough about the mechanisms of transformation to draw the reader's attention elsewhere. The reader is invited to consider how Ames's reflections on the relationship between religion and joy are manifested in the way he lives. Working both through Ames's artful narrative and the unexpected ways in which his Christianity draws him deeper and deeper into the world even as he approaches death, Robinson answers Feuerbach in terms that present the religious life at its strongest.

Much of Ames's writing is dedicated to recording memories, both of the distant past (his boyhood and early life) and present day (the lunch menu or some escapade with the family cat). Occasionally, though, Ames looks to impart a specific message of fatherly wisdom, and about midway through the book he turns to discuss the importance of the Bible's Ten Commandments. What he says is crucial for understanding the way in which religious practice relates to life-affirmation.

Ames begins by reflecting on the command to honor one's father and mother. While Ames uses the opportunity to express confidence that Robby has "been particularly aware" of it, he is more interested in a theological puzzle this command presents—one that, as we will see, allows him to return to the topic of Feuerbach's "idolatry." The puzzle concerns the Fifth Commandment's placement on the first tablet with the other injunctions to honor God. Upon first consideration, it seems a much more natural fit with the commands of the second tablet, the civil-social injunctions that inform right relationship with one's neighbor. Ames hypothesizes that the command to honor one's parents "belongs in the first tablet, among the laws that describe right worship, because right worship is right perception . . . and here the Scripture commands right perception of people you have real and deep knowledge of" (*Gilead* 135–6). Noting that this might seem to place undue burden on children, Ames is quick to point out that "it is the consistent example of parents in the Bible that they honor their children" (*Gilead* 136).

After a brief interlude, Ames goes on to discuss why right worship (the command to "honor") is so vital. He says it leads to right understanding, and explains how this works in the cases of God (the first three commandments), the sabbath (the Fourth), and parents (the Fifth):

> God is set apart—He is One, He is not to be imagined as a thing among things (idolatry—this is what Feuerbach failed to grasp). His name is set apart. It is sacred.... Then the Sabbath is set apart from other days, for the enjoyment of time and duration, perhaps, over and above the creatures who inhabit time. Because "the beginning," which might be called the seed of time, is the condition for all the creation that follows. Then mother and father are set apart, you see. (*Gilead* 138–9)

What each case of honor achieves is recognition of holiness, not just of the particular entities in question (God, sabbath, parents), but of a much larger class of things they exemplify. Ames explains: "Every day is holy, but the Sabbath is set apart so that the holiness of time can be experienced. Every human being is worthy of honor, but the conscious discipline of honor is learned from this setting apart of the mother and father" (*Gilead* 139). Acknowledging the special difficulty the latter command poses, Ames concludes:

> the rewards of obedience are great, because at the root of real honor is always the sense of the sacredness of the person who is its object. In the particular instance of your mother, I know that if you are attentive to her in this way, you will find a very great loveliness in her. When you love someone to the degree you love her, you see her as God sees her, and that is an instruction in the nature of God and humankind and of Being itself. That is why the Fifth Commandment belongs on the first tablet. I have persuaded myself of it. (*Gilead* 139)

It is important to see how these reflections on the commandments connect Ames's earlier discussion of joy with the more particular commitments of his faith. The commandments, especially those that call for worship, encourage joy because they invite a person to attend to the sacredness of life. Despite focusing this attention on very specific things—God, His name, the sabbath, parents—Ames insists that all of creation receives the blessing. When, for instance, a single day is set apart, the effect is not just to acknowledge that particular slice of time, but to notice the holiness of time in general. The same holds true for the call to honor one's parents. Through this command a child is forced to look past the myriad ways in which his parents, being human, are "cranky or stingy or ignorant or over-bearing" in order to see them as beautiful (*Gilead* 139). This beauty has no more to do with their status as parents than the sacredness of the sabbath has to do with any features particular to Sunday. Parents are beautiful because they are *human*, and it is for this reason that the call to attend to them is just as much an invitation to see the sacred in everyone else. Honoring specific things is training in honoring all things.

The commandments are by no means the only place where Ames's Christianity invites him to honor and attend to the world. The sacraments function in the same way. This is communicated in especially clear terms in Ames's thoughts about baptism. He tells the story of a time when he and some childhood friends baptize a litter of "dusty little barn cats," "moistening their brows" and "repeating the full Trinitarian formula" (*Gilead* 22). Ames reflects, "I still remember how those warm little brows felt under the palm of my hand. Everyone has petted a cat, but to touch one like that, with the pure intention of blessing it, is a very different thing. It stays in the mind" (*Gilead* 23). Ames then finishes with a more general point about the nature of blessing:

> There is a reality in blessing, which I take baptism to be, primarily. It doesn't enhance sacredness, but it acknowledges it, and there is a power in that. I have felt it pass through me, so to speak. The sensation is of really knowing a creature, I mean really feeling its mysterious life and your own mysterious life at the same time. (*Gilead* 23)

Having just considered Ames's view of the commandments, it is clear he thinks baptism serves a similar purpose. Like the call to honor one's parents, baptism requires a person to focus and acknowledge the reality of another being. Baptism doesn't impart sacredness. It doesn't bestow dignity or worth or beauty. It creates space where they can be properly seen—ideally by all who bear witness to it, but especially by the minister. This is why Ames encourages Robby to consider a pastoral vocation: "Not that you have to be a minister to confer blessing. You are simply much more likely to find yourself in that position" (*Gilead* 23).

A final way in which Ames's faith trains attention on the world is through participation in the stories of scripture and the lives of the saints. To take just two significant examples, consider first the New Testament parable of the Prodigal Son. Jesus uses the story in order to illustrate the extravagance of God's love for human beings, but also the kind of love humans ought to extend to each other. The story, like most parables, is intended to be typological; it invites the listener to place herself in the role of one (or several) of the characters and through this imaginative projection see and feel something she has either forgotten or never known. In the particular case of the Prodigal Son, the parent's call to honor his children is extended to all people in general, but especially the wayward and downtrodden, those who have precisely betrayed a trust in the past. This story, like many of the stories in the Bible, is a call to attention: Look and see the prodigals among you. They are your sons and daughters. They are holy!

A second kind of participation is present in the invitation to imitate the lives of the saints. For Ames, the most important example of this is one he never directly mentions, but nevertheless clearly informs his entire literary project. As Ames surely knows, the practice of writing one's "begats" has a hallowed place in the Christian tradition and is exemplified in Augustine's fourth-century *Confessions*. *The Confessions* is important for Ames not just because it commends the practice of spiritual autobiography but because of the specific reason for this commendation. In Book X, after narrating the story of his passage to grace, Augustine claims a special place for memory in the human ascent to God and truth. He writes:

[B]y the act of thought we are, as it were, collecting together things which the memory did contain, though in a disorganized and scattered way, and by giving them our close attention we are arranging for them to be as it were stored up ready to hand in that same memory where previously they lay hidden, neglected, and dispensed, so that now they will readily come forward to the mind that has become familiar with them.[8]

With passages like this in mind, commentators emphasize the centrality of memory and imagination in the larger context of *The Confessions*: "For to ascend to God by means of memory is to ascend to God by means of memory rightly ordered by imagination in accordance with truth. Truth cannot come forward in memory until the things stored there are arranged by 'close attention.'" "Indeed, to some extent imagination is identified with the act of confession itself.... Conversion thus becomes a function of imagination, the ordering of memory."[9]

Ames obviously shares Augustine's view of the revelatory capacity of memory.[10] This becomes apparent in the way he discusses an especially important experience from his early childhood, a day when the larger Gilead community gathers to clear away the remains of a church fire. Though it's raining, Ames recalls the mood as one of quiet joy, "like a camp meeting and picnic" (*Gilead* 94). The women let down their hair and the men work in the liquid-ash, pulling down the remains of the building and burying the ruined Bibles and hymnals in careful graves. In the midst of all this, Ames's father brings him "some biscuit that had soot on it from his hands" (*Gilead* 95). He writes:

I remember my father down on his heels in the rain, water dripping from is hat, feeding me biscuit from his scorched hand, with that old blackened wreck of a church behind him and steam rising where the rain fell on embers, the rain falling in gusts and the women singing "The Old Rugged Cross" ... I mention it again because it seems to me much of my life was comprehended in that moment.... I remember it as communion, and I believe that's what it was. (*Gilead* 96)

This moment is significant for several reasons. First, it serves as a foundational vision. Ames tells Robby that "much of [his] life was comprehended in the moment" (*Gilead* 96). This idea of "being comprehended" is reminiscent of Ames's earlier discussion where, taking exception to Feuerbach, he expresses belief in a world that "embraces and exceeds" understanding. In the memory of that day, Ames receives a clear glimpse of something larger his life participates in. This is confirmed as Ames adds, "I can't tell you what that day in the rain has meant to me. I can't tell myself what it has meant to me. But I know how many things it put altogether beyond question" (*Gilead* 96). What it puts beyond question is the reality of religion, which is to say the sacredness of life and the holiness of everyday experience. The "day in the rain" is an anchor point not just for Ames's faith but for his entire existence.

A second thing to notice is that the memory of that day reverberates constantly into the present.[11] Ames writes, "Whenever I have held a Bible in my hands, I have remembered the day they buried those ruined Bibles under the tree in the rain, and it is somehow sanctified by that memory" (*Gilead* 96). Every time he opens a Bible he feels—in some small measure—the blessing of that day reincarnated. At the same time, the significance of these aftershocks is not strictly nostalgic, as though the present is valuable only because it mirrors the past. Like the first five commandments or the sacraments, a foundational vision draws attention to one's current experience in such a way that its unique value can be seen and acknowledged.

Third, Ames's story reveals the way in which it is *memory*, and not immediate experience, that provides the vision. Though Ames recalls that day in the rain as one in which he receives communion, it is apparent that this is realized in hindsight. Ames writes,

> I remember that day in my childhood when I lay under the wagon with the other little children, watching them pull down the ruins of that Baptist church, and my father brought me a piece of biscuit for my lunch, and I crawled out and knelt with him there, in the rain. I remember it as if he broke the bread and put a bit of it in my mouth, though I know he didn't. (*Gilead* 102)

The last sentence is especially illuminating because it suggests that the significance Ames currently attaches to the memory is something he arrives at later. It takes years of reflection and further experience to come to a place where he can finally see that day as including the sanctification of communion. While this may make it sound as though he is merely making up the memory—fabricating details after the fact—Ames invites the language of discovery. Present experience casts new light on the past so that unnoticed details and unavailable interpretations are thrown into relief.

This idea of memory as a source of endless insight is made explicit when Ames, reflecting back on that day, tells Robby: "My point here is that you never do know the actual nature even of your own experience. Or perhaps it has no fixed and certain nature" (*Gilead* 95). Ames's point isn't that there is no fact of the matter regarding what occurs in the past but rather that an interpretation of any given moment is limited in important ways by the concerns, past and present, that are brought to it. This is part of what Ames means when he says, "I can't tell you what [that day] . . . meant to me." This is not an admission that the day lacked significance, but rather that it contained so much meaning it would take a thousand lifetimes to unpack. It is this that connects Ames to Augustine. Both regard the process of searching one's memory as a way not merely to reflect on one's path of salvation but to move one further down it. The present shines on the past so that its light can be reflected into the future.

3 Ames's Living Vision

The task now is to describe, in some small way, how Ames's actual narrative achieves this Augustinian effect. The first half of *Gilead* seems to function as a direct application of the first five commandments: it is an homage to existence. "Each morning," Ames confesses, "I'm like Adam waking up in Eden, amazed at the cleverness of my hands and at the brilliance pouring into my mind through my eyes" (*Gilead* 67). The scenery, both familiar and astonishing, is so saturated with beauty that Ames begins to lose grip on what properly qualifies. He reflects, "I really can't tell what's beautiful anymore" (*Gilead* 5).

This sense of wonder is apparent in an early passage wherein Ames describes two grease-stained mechanics he meets on the street. Ames knows the men as "decent rascally young fellows who have to be joking all the time," and, as he walks by, hears them "passing remarks back and forth the way they do and laughing that wicked way they have." He reflects, "it seemed beautiful to me. It is an amazing thing to watch people laugh, the way it sort of takes over them." Ames appreciates the scene in a way that is free of moralizing—it is striking that he combines "decent" and "rascally" without a hint of irony. As the men watch him approach, Ames is dismayed to hear the joking stop, and thinks to tell them that he likes to laugh as much as anyone, ruefully noting that people want preachers to be "a little bit apart" (*Gilead* 5).

Ames sometimes characterizes these moments of beauty as revelations of "existence." The first time the term appears is when it is used to describe his son, Robby:

> There's a shimmer on a child's hair, in the sunlight. There are rainbow colors in it, tiny, soft beams of just the same colors you can see in the dew sometimes. They're in the petals of flowers, and they're on a child's skin. Your hair is straight and dark, and your skin is very fair. I suppose you're not prettier than most children. You're just a nice-looking boy, a bit slight, well scrubbed and well mannered. All that is fine, but it's your existence I love you for, mainly. Existence seems to me now the most remarkable thing that could ever be imagined. (*Gilead* 52–3)

Ames admits that if it were just a matter of adding up all the stray details of his son's life—his dark hair or even his manners—there may not be much to recommend. Yet Ames, with the careful eye of a father, senses that such appraisals inevitably leave something out. As Ames says later, "We participate in Being without remainder. No breath, no thought, no wart or whisker, is not as sunk in Being as it could be.

And yet no one can say what Being is." He continues, "you can assert the existence of something—Being—having not the slightest notion of what it is" (*Gilead* 178).

This feeling of knowing and not-knowing—the sense that Robby is both fully comprehended and a complete mystery—is what Ames calls the "most remarkable thing," and it is fittingly the source of one of *Gilead*'s most ecstatic hymns, Ames's ode to joy.[12] In a kind of prelude, Ames writes, "I have been thinking about existence lately," and then begins to describe the "row of big oaks by the war memorial" and the autumn a few years back when they "dropped their acorns thick as hell." "It was a very clear night, or morning, very still, and then there was such energy in the things transpiring among those trees, like a storm, like travail," he continues. "I stood there a little out of range, and I thought, It is all still new to me. I have lived my life on the prairie and a line of oak trees can still astonish me" (*Gilead* 56–7). Then, inhabiting the storm's energy, Ames bursts forth:

> I feel sometimes as if I were a child who opens its eyes on the world once and sees amazing things it will never know any names for and then has to close its eyes again. I know this is all mere apparition compared to what awaits us, but it is only lovelier for that. There is a human beauty in it. And I can't believe that, when we have all been changed and put on incorruptibility, we will forget our fantastic condition of mortality and impermanence, the great bright dream of procreating and perishing that meant the whole world to us. In eternity this world will be Troy, I believe, and all that has passed here will be the epic of the universe, the ballad they sing in the streets. Because I don't imagine any reality putting this one in the shade entirely, and I think piety forbids me to try. (*Gilead* 57)

The "human beauty" Ames finds in this life does not carry with it an implicit "mere." The things that might be regarded as "corruptible," because they are finite and limited—sex and death, especially—Ames sees as "fantastic," as a "great bright dream." Ames can think of no better way to do justice to that great bright dream than to compare it to the creation of Homer, that grand dreamer and poet of *"golden nature,"* as Nietzsche had called him (GM III:25). The next life will not be a place where this life is forgotten, and still less a place to look on in finally fulfilled revenge at those who have wronged us. It will be a perspective from which we can look back at our lives with a mood befitting its value. It is the same perspective which moved Homer to invent the gods and sing the story of Greek heroism, and moved his fellow Greeks to sing it in the streets for centuries after—not moral satisfaction, not righteous condemnation, but love, gratitude, and glory. This life, Ames says, has "meant the whole world to us," so much so that only an eternity of celebration and remembrance could be equal to it.

One gets the feeling that if not for the interruptions of life, Ames's paean to love and death, "our fantastic condition," would continue unabated. However, as providence would have it, it is finally disrupted by the unexpected return of Jack Boughton, Ames's godson and namesake. For Ames, the timing of this unwelcome homecoming could not be worse, as his confessions must now expand to include his present anxieties. As we will see, Ames's attempts to navigate this change in fortune constitute the most important lesson he leaves his son.

4 Drawn Back into Life

Jack Boughton's return is foreshadowed early in the novel when Ames mentions a conversation with Jack's sister, Glory. "She told me Jack might be coming home, too." Given what we later discover—that Jack is actually Ames's namesake—what Ames says next is revealing. He continues, "It actually took me a minute to think who that was" (*Gilead* 18). Presumably it takes a special kind of disregard for someone with a memory as richly endowed as Ames's to forget his godson. This is the first hint that not all is right between the two men.

When Jack finally arrives on scene, he greets Ames with the apparently innocuous exclamation, "You're looking wonderful, Papa!" Ames senses a challenge behind these words, thinking "after so many years, the first words out of his mouth would have to be prevarication" (*Gilead* 92). As the reader is left to puzzle out what could really be going on, Ames weighs the wisdom of a full confession, the urgency of which seems to expand in proportion to his family's growing affection for Jack—Robby has taken to playing catch with him, while Lila seems especially sensitive to his feelings. Finally, after Lila seems to rebuke her husband for what she sees as his own lack of sensitivity toward Jack, Ames writes, "I believe it will put my mind at ease to tell you straightforwardly what is at issue here" (*Gilead* 155).

Jack is a dishonorable man. Though there are a host of minor and not so minor offenses that blemish his youth—lies and thefts and mean pranks—the culmination of Jack's depravity comes later. "About twenty years ago, while he was still in college at any rate, he became involved with a young girl, and the involvement produced a child" (*Gilead* 156). Ames admits that this "sort of thing happens" and is not, in itself, remarkable. "In this instance, however, there were aggravating circumstances"—the girl was quite young and her "family situation was desolate, even squalid" (*Gilead* 156). To make matters worse, Jack took no responsibility for the infant, leaving it to his own parents and sister to offer outside care, which was mostly refused by the girl's family. Eventually, the child died; she cut her foot and it became infected. During all this time, Ames imagines Jack back at college in St Louis, "under a tree somewhere, reading Huxley or Carlyle," completely unconcerned about the situation at home (*Gilead* 157). From this moment on, Jack, out of shame or sheer malice, is estranged from Gilead. For the next two decades, to his family's great sorrow, the details of his existence—with the exception of a few stray sightings—become the subject of speculation and rumor. The Boughtons's beloved son and brother is lost.

Almost immediately after relating the details of Jack's story, Ames mentions that Lila has been reading through his old sermons and has set a few aside for consideration: "I found a couple of my sermons under the Bible on the night table, which I take to mean that your mother recommends them to my attention. . . . She says that I should use some of them, to spare myself effort that I might otherwise spend writing to you [Robby]." Ames comments on one of them, a sermon on forgiveness from June 1947.

> [I]t makes the point that, in Scripture, the one sufficient reason for the forgiveness of debt is simply the existence of debt. And it goes on to compare this to divine grace, and to the Prodigal Son and his restoration to his place in his father's house, though he neither asks to be restored as son nor even repents of the grief he has caused his father. (*Gilead* 161)

It does not take an especially perceptive reader to see that Ames is being invited (by both his wife and fate) to forgive Jack. What's slightly less apparent is why forgiveness is in order. Though Jack surely harmed his own family, it is not as though he has directly hurt Ames, a few childhood pranks aside. This question, as well as the source of some of Ames's anxiety, is addressed just a few pages later when Ames, dredging his subconscious, admits, "That one man should lose his child and the next man should just squander his fatherhood as if it were nothing— well, that does not mean that the second man has transgressed the first." He ends, "I don't forgive him. I wouldn't know where to begin" (*Gilead* 164). Despite this apparent resolution, Ames cannot let the issue go, and the next day, when Jack comes over to play catch with Robby, he writes, "I believe I will just step outside and see what he has on his mind. I know there is something" (*Gilead* 164). This last thought—"I know there is something"—applies just as much to himself as to Jack. Ames senses that his earlier claim to not "know where to begin" was less the end of a debate than the beginning of a spiritual inquiry. He is hiding something.

Prompted to self-interrogate, Ames begins, apparently at random, to explore his relationship to Jack. This brings him back to the beginning, the day so many years before when he performed Jack's baptism. What he recalls is significant:

> The child's name was to be Theodore Dwight Weld. I thought that was an excellent name. . . . But then when I asked Boughton, "By what

name do you wish this child to be called?" he said, "John Ames." I was so surprised that he said the name again, with the tears running down his face.... If I had had even an hour to reflect, I believe my feelings would have been quite different. As it was, my heart froze in me and I thought, This is not my child—which I truly had never thought of any child before. (*Gilead* 188)

Ames continues to explore the reason for his reaction and arrives at this significant admission:

I'll tell you a perfectly foolish thing. I have thought from time to time that the child felt how coldly I went about his christening, how far my thoughts were from blessing him. Now, that's just magical thinking. That is superstition. I'm ashamed to have said such a thing. But I'm trying to be honest. And I do feel a burden of guilt toward that child, that man, my namesake. I have never been able to warm to him, never. (*Gilead* 188)

This icy baptism is especially significant given what Ames elsewhere says about the purpose and joy of administering the sacrament. He writes, "I've always loved to baptize people," and later, "whenever I take a child into my arms to be baptized, I am, so to speak, comprehended in the experience more fully, having seen more of life, knowing better what it means to affirm the sacredness of the human creature. I believe there are visions that come to us only in memory, in retrospect" (*Gilead* 63, 91). That this "vision" was absent in Jack's case is all the more problematic given Ames's status as godparent and namesake—"the father of his soul." Ames is reminded of this in a later conversation when Jack, referring to the fact that Ames followed his own father into the ministry, remarks, "It's an enviable thing, to be able to receive your identity from your father" (Gilead 168). Though ostensibly a claim about the Ames family, or perhaps the way in which Jack's own biological father failed to pass on his pastoral vocation, Ames has reason to interpret the comment as a claim about his own failure to pass something on to Jack. He could not bless him, and this led to legitimate guilt.

Ames's guilt is not, however, a product of the failed baptism as much as the *reason* for its failure. Ames hints that "covetise" clouded his vision, and then goes on to describe it in terms that make its significance immediately apparent: "[covetise] is not so much desiring someone else's virtue or happiness as rejecting it, taking offense at the beauty of it" (*Gilead* 229). In his earlier discussion of the Ten Commandments, Ames was frank about his open struggle with the Tenth—Thou shalt not covet—especially after the death of his first wife and daughter.

> I have been candid with you about my suffering a good deal at the spectacle of all the marriages, all the households overflowing with children, especially Boughton's—not because I wanted them, but because I wanted my own. I believe the sin of covetise is that pang of resentment you may feel when even the people you love best have what you want and don't have. From the point of view of loving your neighbor as yourself (Leviticus 19:18), there is nothing that makes a person's fallenness more undeniable than covetise—you feel it right in your heart, in your bones. In that way it is instructive. I have never really succeeded in obeying that Commandment. (*Gilead* 134)

As Ames writes these words to Robby, the direct source of his envy seems to have been addressed. Now he has his own son, his own domestic bliss. While Robby is clearly part of the solution to Ames's covetise problem, it is not at all in the manner suggested. Ames knows that covetise is not extinguished by acquiring what your neighbor possesses but rather through an encounter with the sacred which announces that the world is not at all something to be owned. Robby helps Ames to confront his covetise not by satisfying the urge to acquire what the Boughtons have but by focusing Ames's attention in such a way that he is all but forced to recognize his son's existence and thereby the beautiful mystery of all human beings. In this way we see that the first five commandments, the injunctions to honor, are designed to equip a person to satisfy the last five—the injunctions to love one's neighbor. Becoming Robby's father prepares Ames to become Jack's.[13]

    This realization is all the more pressing because Jack's return to Gilead reveals that Ames's covetise is far from dead. As his confessions unfold, it slowly becomes clear that his current anxiety is grounded in a suspicion that Jack might replace him in the lives of Lila and Robby.

After all the years of dark loneliness, Ames finally receives a family, the very thing which he had envied in his happy neighbors. Now, on the verge of death, he rebels against the thought that Jack might simply step into his fortune. The day after Ames reflects on Jack's "failed" baptism, wishing that he "could christen him again" in order to "feel that sacredness," he finally makes his worry explicit (*Gilead* 189). He writes, "How should I deal with these fears I have, that Jack Boughton will do you and your mother harm, just because he can, just for the sly unanswerable meanness of it?" He continues, "if he harmed you in the slightest way, I'm afraid theology would fail me" (*Gilead* 190). For a man as devout as Ames, to identify an apparently unforgivable sin in this way is also to identify a place where grace must extend.

That evening, as Ames sits with Lila on the front porch, enjoying what "might be the last mild night" of the year, Jack visits (*Gilead* 195). They exchange pleasantries, and between moments of small talk, Ames imagines how things would be if Jack were his son and "had come home weary from whatever life he had, and was sitting there still and at seeming peace in that peaceful night." Ames admits,

> There was a considerable satisfaction in that thought. The idea of grace had been so much on my mind, grace as a sort of ecstatic fire that takes things down to essentials. There in the dark and the quiet I felt I could forget all the tedious particulars and just feel the presence of his mortal and immortal being. And a sensation came over me, a sort of lovely fear. (*Gilead* 197)

Later that night, as Ames lies awake, he thinks back on the conversation and begins to pity Jack, thinking, "I wish I could put my hand on his brow and calm away all the guilt and regret that is exaggerated or misplaced, or beyond rectification in the terms of this world. Then I could see what I'm actually dealing with." Ames ends, "I believe I am beginning to see where the grace is for me in this" (*Gilead* 201).

Here, Ames pauses to apologize to Robby. He writes:

> I have been looking through these pages, and I realize that for some time I have mainly been worrying to myself, when my intention from

the beginning was to speak to you. I meant to leave you a reasonably candid testament to my better self, and it seems to me now that what you must see here is just an old man struggling with the difficulty of understanding what it is he's struggling with. (*Gilead* 202)

Ames begins his reflections with the thought that his life is more or less over, and that he can simply pass its record on to posterity. However, as he looks back, he has been drawn deeper and deeper into its wonder. The world honors those who pay attention to it, and its visions of glory give rise to invitations of grace—to receive and to give, the two sides of "the great gift." "To be forgiven is only half [of it].... The other half is that we also can forgive, restore, and liberate, and therefore we can feel the will of God enacted through us, which is the great restoration of ourselves to ourselves" (*Gilead* 161). Ames feels anew the fullness of the blessing that has been visited upon him. He thinks of his young wife, Lila—a gift in old age. "How soft her voice is. That there should be such a voice in the whole world, and then that I should be the one to hear it, seemed to me then and seems to me now an unfathomable grace" (*Gilead* 209). Feeling the gratuity of it all, Ames's heart moves from Lila to Jack, preparing to embrace his godson.

> If I were to put my hand on her brow and bless her purely, as if I were indeed and altogether a minister of the Lord, I would hope just such an experience for her as that one of mine. Oh, I know she is fond of me, and very loyal. But I could hope that sometime the Song of Songs would startle her, as if it spoke from her own heart. I cannot really make myself believe that her feelings could have been at all like mine. And why do I worry so much over this Jack Boughton? Love is holy because it is like grace—the worthiness of its object is never really what matters. I might well be leaving her to a greater happiness than I have given her, even granting every difficulty. Sometimes I think I have seen the beginnings of it in her. If the Lord is letting me momentarily be witness to a grace He intends for her, I should find in this a great kindness toward myself. (*Gilead* 209)

Ames's confessions have led to this moment of revelation. When a person encounters the glory of God—in the trees, in the rain, in a son and wife—

the meanness of envy melts away. The world cannot be owned, and thank God for that, because therein lies the secret of its beauty. It is always too much for us; at best, we are its stewards and admirers, keepers of a gift that must be shared. Ames sees this now. Jack may be a dishonorable man, but so are we all, too often blind to the constant light. Ames's one task is to love, and there is no "justice" or "proportion" in that, "and there need not be, because in any specific instance it is only a glimpse or parable of an embracing, incomprehensible reality. It makes no sense at all because it is the eternal breaking in on the temporal" (*Gilead* 238).

In the closing pages of the novel a great secret is revealed: Ames learns that "Jack Boughton has a wife and a child" (*Gilead* 217). This is why Jack has returned, to see if there is a place in Gilead for his mixed-race family. As Jack prepares to leave, sensing that Iowa is no longer the progressive bastion once lauded as "the shining star of radicalism," Ames meets him one last time (*Gilead* 176). Ames has brought along a parting gift: his copy of Feuerbach's *The Essence of Christianity*. He has dog-eared page 20—"Only that which is apart from my own being is capable of being doubted by me. How then can I doubt of God, who is my being? To doubt of God is to doubt myself" (*Gilead* 239). After giving the book to Jack, Ames asks if he can bless him and receives Jack's head into his outstretched hand. He recites a benediction from Numbers: "The Lord make His face to shine upon thee and be gracious unto thee: The Lord lift up His countenance upon thee, and give thee peace." As Jack remains bowed, he adds: "Lord, bless John Ames Boughton, this beloved son and brother and husband and father" (*Gilead* 241).

Ames writes, "I'd have gone through seminary and ordination and all the years intervening for that one moment" (*Gilead* 242).

5 Conclusion

As we have seen, Ames's confessions have served less to mark the end of his life than to call him back into it. They have reminded him that the world, while full of its share of heartache and loneliness and shame, can still—"wherever you turn your eyes"—"shine like transfiguration." "Only," Ames adds, "who could have the courage to see it?" (*Gilead* 245). On the next page, drawing his reflections to an end, Ames returns to the same idea:

> Theologians talk about a prevenient grace that precedes grace itself and allows us to accept it. I think there must also be a prevenient courage that allows us to be brave—that is, to acknowledge that there is more beauty than our eyes can bear, that precious things have been put into our hands and to do nothing to honor them is to do great harm. (*Gilead* 246)

It might seem out of place to emphasize courage (as Ames does twice) when admonishing someone to look and see. For Ames, though, they are inextricably connected. "There are two occasions," he writes, "when the sacred beauty of Creation becomes dazzlingly apparent, and they occur together. One is when we feel our mortal insufficiency to the world, and the other is when we feel the world's mortal insufficiency to us" (*Gilead* 245). Though he does not make it explicit, we might suppose that more than merely co-occurring these two feelings unfold in sequence. A person is first gifted with a vision of the grandeur of the world and ends with a vision of the grandeur of oneself—how bizarrely wonderful one must be to feel such "mortal insufficiency." Understood in this way, it becomes clear why courage is necessary. One must be prepared to be completely unseated, to vacate all their petty envies and rights of property, to be—as Ames was—drawn into the world. This is what it means to live religiously, and Ames's final words bear witness to it: "I love this town. I think sometimes of going into the ground here as a last wild gesture of love—I too will smolder away the time until the great and general incandescence" (*Gilead* 247).

Notes

1 Christopher Leise calls these outbursts "irruptions of aesthetic appreciation" and sees them as part of Robinson's larger strategy of reading the Calvinist Puritan tradition against itself (2009, 349).

2   Andrew Stout (2014) refers to this as Robinson's "sacramental vision" and sees it equally present in *Housekeeping* and *Gilead*. On our reading, Robinson introduces the language of sacramentality in *Gilead* as an answer to *Housekeeping*'s interest in "relics." A sacrament is a kind of redeemed relic.

3   For another approach to *Gilead* that emphasizes Ames's interaction with Feuerbach, see Justin Evans (2014). Evans argues that Feuerbach is at the center of *Gilead* because the latter is first and foremost a defense of subjectivity over and against "reductive atheism." While we fully agree that *Gilead* opposes reductive atheism, we also see Ames's interest in Feuerbach as going well beyond any goal he may have in defending "subjectivity." Feuerbach is not included in *Gilead* to make the general point that a person can change; he is present for exactly the reasons Ames draws attention to: he is fantastic on the joyful parts of life.

4   Haein Park (2010) makes a special point of emphasizing the importance Ames places on transcendence in response to those, for example, Leise (2009), who argue that Ames intentionally deemphasizes the concept.

5   Barth (1957, xxv).

6   Barth (1957, xxix).

7   Barth (1957, xxx).

8   Augustine (1963, Bk. X, Ch. 11).

9   Breyfogle (1994, 217).

10 Andrew Ploeg makes a similar point with an emphasis on Ames's continued attempts to speak truly. Just as Ames revisits his memories for revelatory insight, he continually looks for new and fitting ways to "express the divine" (Ploeg 2016, 7).

11 This insight is indebted to June Hadden Hobbs, who argues, quite persuasively, that among Ames's virtues is an ability to dynamically integrate the past into the present. She makes this point in terms of Ames's use of "typology." She writes, "Typology is a tool for giving significance to memorialized human events by describing them in terms of sacred symbols. It is also a way to show that the most significant events of the past recur, that the day of miracles—or at least of transcendent moments—is not past" (2010, 245).

12 In an interview with Rebecca Painter, Robinson expounds on this idea. She says, "The sense of mystery may itself be the great missing value. By that I don't mean a conjured mystery but an intrinsic one, the kind

that comes with a good long look at things, and people, as they are" (2009, 488).

13 Rebecca Painter (2010) argues that another important element in Ames's growing sympathy toward Jack is the memory of his own past prodigality. This seems right, especially as Ames begins to openly acknowledge his struggle with covetise.

4

O Sinner, Come *Home*

Marilynne Robinson's third novel, *Home* (2008), might naturally seem to be something of a step down from the dizzying existential heights of *Housekeeping* and *Gilead*. It takes up the world already created in *Gilead*, narrating many of the same events from a different perspective, while perhaps depriving it of some of the quiet, internal suspense that Ames's story had had. And, more remarkably, that different perspective is now far more diffuse. In *Home*, Robinson eschews the first-person perspective, which had so clearly centered her first novels on the striking voices of Ruth and Ames. This new third-person perspective gives us privileged access to the thoughts of one of its characters—Jack's younger sister Glory—but even then it does not really give us Glory's *voice*. It is certainly important that Glory's thoughts and feelings are the filter through which we experience the novel's events and as we shall see the crucial final pages of the novel concern her directly. But she is not so much at the center of this novel as Ruth and Ames were in theirs. Indeed, it is natural that much of the reason a reader of *Gilead* might have wanted to return to this fictional world would be to find out more about Jack, who had up until now existed mostly as a cipher for his namesake, Ames. Unfortunately for such a reader, Jack remains a cipher in *Home*, in which we see him viewed through the lens of a sister who is no more capable of puzzling out his inner thoughts than Ames is. *Home*'s goals do not really lie in revealing to us the secret of Jack, or even of tracking the development of a central character at all; its issues are more interpersonal and it is far more concerned to immerse us in the dynamics of the Boughton family, to call us to attend to the "home" in which they live.

The novel's title, like "Housekeeping," contains an ironic subtext. While reading the novel, one is naturally reminded of the words of the familiar Christian hymn, "Softly and Tenderly"[1]:

> Softly and tenderly Jesus is calling
> Calling for you and for me
> See on the portals He's waiting and watching
> Watching for you and for me

> Come home, come home
> Ye who are weary come home
> Earnestly, tenderly Jesus is calling
> Calling, "O sinner, come home."

This desire to "come home" lies deep in the human race, but it is also complicated. Part of the complication is the fact that the desire is likely less about the return to a place than it is about a return to a time, and the particular feelings present in that stage of our development as human beings. It is the desire to flee the inevitable but often crushing realities of adult life—its arduous but inescapable responsibilities, our consciousness of the wrong turnings we've made in life, the missed opportunities that are gone forever—and to go back to a time when all of this was shouldered for us by someone else, or at any rate still yet to concern us. A good part of the effectiveness of the hymn lies in the fact that it is precisely weariness that often brings on the desire.

The issue of home is one that Ames grapples with in *Gilead*, too, though his relationship to it is less fraught. Unlike the Boughton children, as we shall see, and also unlike the rest of his family, Ames stays and lives his entire life in his hometown. The luminosity of his prose in *Gilead* lends an air of confirmation to his decision and a "hominess" to the novel as a whole. Ames's romanticization of the place in which he has lived his whole life is seductive, even if the careful reader will still notice that Gilead, Iowa, is far from an idyllic utopia. *Home*, focusing as it does on the troubled homecoming of Glory and Jack Boughton, does much to undermine the romantic impression of this hometown and of the version(s) of Christianity that find their home here. The Boughton home is in many ways a hostile place for Glory and Jack, a place that is more the cause of their weariness than a prospect for its relief.

As we shall see, a large part of the problem is how much the Boughton family leaves unsaid in their interactions with each other. This is especially true of their relations to poor Jack, whose problems no one (not even Jack himself) understands nor knows how to solve. The Boughtons' secretiveness and reticence, which Glory perhaps too charitably calls their "tact and discretion," create problems that Robert Boughton, their father, tries and fails to solve with appeals to lofty theological phrases about grace and forgiveness. In the first part of the chapter, we will trace this destructive dynamic, placing particular emphasis on its effects on Jack and his views about his own sinfulness and assured damnation. This background sets the stage for Jack's attempts to reach out to Ames, to which we turn in the next three parts of this chapter. Jack hopes Ames might be more capable of helping him than his father is, not only with his own moral and theological problems but perhaps even with the practical problem of where and how he, his young, Black wife Della, and their child can have a life together. The relationship between Jack and Ames is the subject of the two biggest plot intersections between *Gilead* and *Home*—a sermon that Ames gives on the subject of Hagar and Ishmael (and, more broadly, on the responsibilities of parents to children), and a conversation on the Boughton porch about the doctrine of predestination. Both of these are subjects of intense interest for Jack, who has abandoned one child from his past and does not know how to care for his current one, and who has felt all his life as if he has been headed inexorably for perdition. We learn in *Home* that these events are more complex and more personally troubling for Jack than Ames's letters in *Gilead* let on, and the event in *Gilead* that seems at least in part to redeem these failed communications—Ames's blessing of Jack at the bus stop—does not occur in the pages of *Home*. But though Jack does not come back to find the home he had hoped for in Gilead and decides instead to leave town again, the novel does not end in despair. The possibility of redemption in the Boughton home is present in the person of Glory, Jack's loving sister, who comes at the end of the novel to a new and life-affirming realization about her relationship to her childhood home, her brother, and his family. It is her decisions (and as we shall see, her imagination) which bring the novel to its complex and surprising close.

1 Secrets under the Boughton Rugs

We join the Boughtons at a troubled time. Robert Boughton, friend to John Ames and father of the six Boughton children, is nearing the end of his life. Though he was all of his life a vigorous man, he has become tired and frail in his old age, and Glory has returned to the family house in Gilead to help take care of him. Glory's feelings about returning are mixed, to say the least—though she keeps it a secret from her father, she has recently ended her relationship with a man to whom she was engaged and quit her job as a schoolteacher. Though she has a certain nostalgia for her childhood home, her return under these circumstances troubles her. Returning to stay, she says, turns her memory of the place "portentous," and she laments that the memory will "overrun its bounds" and "become present and possibly future too." Even more difficult for her is the dissonance between her attitude on this subject and that of her father, who is (perhaps understandably) all too eager to live in the past. Glory wryly notes that the Boughtons "kept everything," their house and its surrounding land, appearing to her exactly the same as it was when she and her siblings were children, and when the children got together again in Gilead, "[t]hey looked at photographs and went over the old times and laughed, and their father was well pleased" (*Home* 8). One gets the sense that all of them were well pleased... except for Glory and Jack. We learn, as the novel opens, that Jack has sent a letter to his father, announcing his imminent arrival after years of silence and absence, though not announcing a reason for it. So it comes to be that the two Boughton children who feel least at home in that house will be the ones to share it with Boughton as he lives out his last, tired days.

Boughton himself recognizes the importance of weariness in an early passage in the novel. Jack has just come home, some unspecified number of weeks after his letter, weeks of "trouble and disruption" (*Home* 28) for Glory, who must deal with her father's anticipation. When Jack finally comes and the table is set for his welcoming dinner, Boughton summons his powers to speak a blessing over the table, a speech he has dreamed of making many times in the years of Jack's absence:

> But when I think of what it is that brings us to our Father, it might be grief or sickness—trouble of some sort. Weariness. And then there we are, and it's a good thing at such times to know we have a Father, whose joy it is to welcome us home. It really is. Still, humanly speaking, there is that trouble, that sorrow, and a Father has to be aware of it. He can't help it. So there is a sadness even in great blessing, which can be a hard thing to understand. . . . Lord, put the veil of time and sorrow aside for us. Restore us to those we love. And restore the ones we love to us. We do long for them— (*Home* 41)

At this point in the speech, Jack interrupts his father to say, softly, "Amen." And well he might, since Jack also has loved ones to whom he hopes to be restored—his wife Della, and their son Robert. His father, of course, knows nothing about this. He takes the "Amen" as a sign from Jack that his speech, which had been running on for a while, ought to come to a close. It is a heartbreaking moment—Jack's "Amen" is an expression of affirmation and of a connection hoped for. He is weary with the troubles he has faced in the years he has been away, and he hopes for a father who might welcome him despite those troubles and help him to deal with them. He hopes, in fact, that there is some way he could live with his wife and their son in Gilead, where the attitudes of the locals (and the local authorities) might be less hostile than they had been in the South. But his father misunderstands this. This is due only in part to Boughton's lack of knowledge, though. We cannot expect him to understand *why* Jack wants to say "Amen" there, but his assumption about what it does mean is revealing—Jack is not someone from whom his father expects meaningful affirmation, or genuine connection. He is suspicious of his son, and interprets the "Amen" in light of this.

It doesn't take us long to learn from Glory's reminiscences that this suspicion and the barriers to communication it generates are common in the Boughton family. We are told that when she was a child, Glory confused the words "sacred" and "secret." The quiet and moralized restraint of the church setting, the idea that there are "words you must never say" and "things that will be explained to you when you are old enough to understand"—these things suggested to the young child's mind a deeper association between the two (*Home* 15).[2] She explains an early childhood memory that cemented the confusion: when she is still too young for school, she ventures into the orchard and finds Jack skipping class. Glory bursts into tears. Jack tells her, "Damnit, kid, grow up," and asks if she will get him in trouble. Though Glory generally has trouble keeping secrets and is taunted by her siblings for it, she keeps this one; indeed, "[i]t seemed to her she had learned honor then" (*Home* 15). She reflects now that this experience, formative though it was, perhaps cemented this conflation of sacred and secret in her, so that now she "loved tact and discretion better than she should," and that "in all this she may only have been a Boughton, after all" (*Home* 16).

And certainly, the Boughtons do love tact and discretion, in a way that far outstrips the importance of those values. (As Glory puts it, "Her family was slower to forgive a failure of discretion than they were to forgive most things actually prohibited in Scripture" (*Home* 247).) What is most characteristic about Boughton's reaction to Jack's "Amen" is not his interpretation of it as a sign that Jack wishes for the old codger to shut up and let them eat, but rather his perfectly tactful response to this perceived slight, an apparently compassionate apology for letting the food get cold. The effect of Boughton's discretion is clear, even if Boughton himself doesn't consciously intend it—he has proven himself apologetic and gentlemanly, even perhaps going a bit above and beyond his obligations in the moment, while the underlying issue of his suspicion of his son is brushed neatly under the rug.

The Boughton rugs conceal many such slights and suspicions, most of which are never dealt with openly. Another similar instance, which we can imagine was quite formative for Jack, is shown in a passage describing another scene from the childhood of Jack and Glory. This one concerns the Boughtons' land, which was large enough to cover two blocks and which remained largely unused by the Boughtons. Some unnamed neighbors, whom the Boughtons took to calling "the Trotskys" because of their agnosticism and political leanings, decided on their own to plant alfalfa on the unused portion. Boughton disapproved, mostly because they had not asked his permission. But he stayed quiet, perhaps because the Trotskys were "probably spoiling for an ethical argument" that Boughton "could not risk losing" (*Home* 9). The man, normally not particularly sociable, would make a big show of the planting, driving around a big tractor and yelling hello at passersby, knowing that it all reflected poorly on Boughton. Boughton's response to the whole affair is, in Glory's memory, freighted with religious significance. She notes that Mr. Trotsky was in fact *trespassing* on the Boughton land, and that this is precisely the sin that the Lord's Prayer lists as "the very act against which Christians leveraged the fate of their own souls, since they were, if they listened to their own prayers, obliged to forgive those who trespassed against them" (*Home* 10). But Boughton, though he doesn't outwardly condemn, doesn't really forgive either; he is vexed by the whole situation and sees the display as "holding him up to public embarrassment," as if he was supposed to be answering for "the history of religious hypocrisy."

What brings the matter to a head, we are told, is that one day the children, *sans* Jack, in a fit of "joyless and determined" mischief, decide to play a game of fox and geese in the alfalfa field, destroying it as they run around and realizing as they destroy it that they are satisfying a kind of "craving for retaliation" in themselves. When they return home, coated in the evidence of their crime, their father's face shows a "slight satisfaction," since he recognizes it as an "opportunity to demonstrate Christian humility in such an unambiguous form that the neighbor could feel it only as a rebuke." This reaction is, unfortunately, characteristic of Boughton.[3] He is eager to do the Christian thing, and indeed all the more eager when it is difficult to do so, but the eagerness is in part born of a desire for revenge. Boughton's Christianity is not insincere but one senses that he does not see, because he does not care to see, the other motivations that feed what appears to him to be his moral courage.

Boughton pushes his children out the door to apologize to the Trotskys. Jack joins them on the way, "as if penance must always include him" (*Home* 11). The dutiful Teddy apologizes, while Mrs. Trotsky shames them for destroying the field. When Teddy pushes back, insisting that the field, after all, belongs to the Boughtons, she snaps back, saying that their "priest" father "earns his money from the ignorance of the people" and tells "foolish lies." The children are stunned to hear their father spoken of in this way, all except Jack, who laughs. The woman shifts to insulting Jack, who already has a history of misdeeds: "The boy thief, the boy drunkard. While your father tells the people how to live! He deserves you!" (*Home* 12). When the children report back about the failed apology, Jack mentions this point to his father:

> "She was really mean. She even said you deserved me."
> Her father's eyes stung. He said, "Did she say that? Well now, that was kind of her. I will be sure to thank her. I hope I do deserve you, Jack. All of you, of course." That tireless tenderness of his, and Jack's unreadable quiet in the face of it. (*Home* 13)

Glory's reference to Boughton's "tireless tenderness" is revealing: she speaks of it not with affection, as one might expect, but with something approaching exasperation, so that Jack's "unreadable quiet" seems to us somehow an appropriate response to Boughton's display. And it is not hard to see why. Boughton's reaction is, on the surface, the right one, and even a creative one: he redirects the harsh insult of Mrs. Trotsky, which clearly stings him as well as Jack, into a charitable Christian comment about the value of all human beings and of his son in particular. One can easily imagine him being satisfied with the result. But the response is nonetheless an evasion, as Jack's reaction shows—

Boughton could have said these reassuring words (and in the end does say them) about any of his children, or indeed about anyone at all close to him, but Mrs. Trotsky's insult could not have been aimed at anyone but Jack. Boughton's high-minded, universal response doesn't touch the *particular* offense directed at Jack, who knows that there is a sense in which "deserving" him is not a good thing, at least in the eyes of many. Because Boughton doesn't address that, Jack is left to wonder whether his father perhaps thinks so too. But since what Boughton does say is at a surface level so morally unassailable, there is nothing really that Jack can say in response, and so he has no resources to deal with his problem. He is left to believe that there is something wrong with him, that his father sees but does not know how to address other than with pious generality.

2 Gilead and Home—Ames's Sermon on Hagar and Ishmael

Readers of *Gilead* no doubt will wonder how the person of John Ames is related to all of this. Ames is of course not a member of the Boughton family, though he has been a keen observer of it over the years. And the version of Christianity he espouses would, it seems, have much to say to someone in Jack's predicament. *Home* is written in large part out of a motivation on Robinson's part to continue, deepen, and complicate what was begun in *Gilead*. This becomes especially evident in two crucial scenes, discussed at length but in different ways in both novels, in which Ames and Jack interact.

The first of these is a sermon, preached by Ames and heard by Jack, on the subject of Hagar and Ishmael. In *Gilead*, Ames's sermon on Hagar and Ishmael doesn't seem to proceed from any particularly important plot developments. Ames tells us that he is preaching on this passage of Genesis (21:14-21) not because of any external reasons but simply because it has been on his mind and he "found a great assurance in it" (*Gilead* 118). In the story, Hagar the slave-woman is sent away from Abraham, her master, because Abraham's wife, Sarah, is jealous of the son that Hagar has borne to Abraham, a son named Ishmael. Abraham sends the two away with only a little food and a skin of water, and before long Hagar has set her child down under a bush and walked away, thinking he will die and that she cannot bear to watch. But God tells her not to despair. He leads her to a nearby well, promising that he will make her son into a "great nation." Ames rehearses the theme of his upcoming sermon:

> it says that even if the mother can't find a way to provide for [the child], or herself, provision will be made. At that level, it is a story full of comfort. That is how life goes—we send our children into the wilderness. Some of them on the day they are born, it seems, for all the help we can give them. Some of them seem to be a kind of wilderness unto themselves. But there must be angels there, too, and springs of water. Even that wilderness, the very habitation of jackals, is the Lord's. (*Gilead* 118–19)

Ames is, in part, thinking of his own impending death and the fact that he will have to send his own young son, Robbie, "out in the wilderness," so to speak, far sooner than he would have preferred. But naturally more is on his mind, too. His mention of children who "seem to be a kind of wilderness unto themselves" evokes Jack, though he doesn't name him. And perhaps Jack is also conjured by that image of "jackals," those dangerous creatures who inhabit the wilderness into which Robbie will go. Jack has, it turns out, been coming by the Ames house of late, and Ames is anxious about it, worried that Jack's intentions with respect to his wife and child will be something other than honorable.

The anxiety of it keeps Ames awake at night, including the night before the sermon, and so Jack is very much on his mind when he goes to the church to preach. And Jack remains on his mind during the sermon since, much to Ames's surprise, he looks out onto his congregation to find Jack sitting in the pew. Ames initially speaks on the themes he had worked out in advance but quickly begins to go off script—he finds himself reflecting on why God would ask Abraham to sacrifice

Isaac and to send away Ishmael, since these two events seem to be the only times in Scripture when "a father is even apparently unkind to his child" (*Gilead* 129). He quotes Jesus's words from the Sermon on the Mount: "What man of you, if his son asked for bread, would give him a stone?" (*Gilead* 129–30; cf. Mt. 7:9). It is at this point that Ames notices Jack's reaction; he is "[w]hite as a sheet, and grinning" (*Gilead* 130). Obviously, Jack is understanding Ames's words to be directed at him personally, as a judgment on Jack's actions toward his abandoned child. Ames soldiers on nonetheless, suggesting that the apparent cruelty of what Abraham is asked to do is meant to show that children, even when they are victims of cruelty or violence, are still under the protection of God. But Ames worries (and tells us he has often worried) that this point can be misconstrued—that some might take it as a license to be cruel or violent or oppressive—and so he quotes Jesus's words again: "If anyone offend these little ones, it would be better for him if a millstone were put around his neck and he were cast into the sea" (*Gilead* 130; cf. Mt.18:6). Ames adds, tersely, "That is strong language, but there it is." In the pew, Jack's devastating grin widens.

Strong language indeed, and we could have guessed much of Jack's reaction just from the context in *Gilead*. *Home*'s account only deepens the devastation. Jack does not show up to Ames's church that day just to vex him. (Ames wonders: "I just don't know why he isn't worshipping with the Presbyterians" (*Gilead* 131).) Jack has actually been trying for a few Sundays to work up the courage to come and has been ingratiating himself to the Ames family, because he has cultivated certain hopes with respect to Ames.[4] In particular, he hopes that somehow he could marry and live with his Black wife Della in Iowa, since there are no laws against interracial marriage there. And, he hopes, perhaps Ames could do the marrying.[5] But the sermon stops Jack in his tracks. According to Jack, the theme of the sermon was "the disgraceful abandonment of children by their fathers. And the illustration was my humble self, sitting there beside his son with the eyes of Gilead upon me" (*Home* 206). Glory points out to him that Ames would not have known Jack was there and so would not have been thinking about Jack when he was writing it, but Jack recognizes that "[t]he old devil was extemporizing," and tells her, "anyway, I would have been on his mind while he was working on it" (*Home* 207).

Jack's reaction to the sermon is admittedly simplistic and self-centered. He has no inkling that the sermon might in any way have been about Ames's relationship to his own son. And Ames laments after the sermon is over that Jack "treats words as if they were actions. He doesn't listen to the *meaning* of words, the way other people do.... He decides whether they threaten him or injure him, and he reacts at that level" (*Gilead* 130–1). There is justice in Ames's remark. There is, of course, *more* in Ames's sermon than merely a condemnation of Jack; even Jack ruefully allows that "He didn't say 'Jack Boughton, the notorious sinner in the first pew. The gasoline-scented fellow'" (*Home* 207). The sermon's words apply to other father-son relationships too, including not only Ames-Robbie but also Boughton-Jack. But Ames oversimplifies as much as Jack does. Words *are* also actions, as a preacher like Ames knows as well as anyone. They are spoken not just to convey meaning but also to *do* things. Ames naturally *hopes*, as any pastor must, that his congregants will not just take his words theoretically but will try to apply them more or less directly to their lives. And he knows as well that his words, especially when he extemporizes, come in part from his anxieties about Jack: "I will concede that my extemporaneous remarks might have been influenced by his sitting there with that look on his face, right beside my wife and child" (*Gilead* 131). So while it is true that Ames did not show up at church that day with the intention of attacking Jack, it is not the case that that intention played no role in the words he said, and Jack's overreaction to those words is thus perfectly understandable. Ames admits later: "I conceal my motives from myself pretty effectively sometimes" (*Gilead* 147).

Jack's conversation with Glory about the sermon continues. He admits to her the hopes he had harbored about Ames marrying him and Della and the worries he had about his father understanding his situation. The attack from Ames has confirmed for him that these hopes were false ones and that his problems are as deep as he has always suspected. When Glory asks what she should tell their father about what has happened, he says, "Oh, let me think. Tell him my life is endless pain and difficulty for reasons that are no doubt apparent to anyone I pass on the street but obscure to me" (*Home* 211). It may seem that Jack takes this back immediately after—"And I do know why my life is the way it is, Glory. I was joking about that. I wouldn't want you to think I don't. I'm fresh from a sermon on the subject." But the sarcasm gives him away. Jack, it seems, would rather think that he is to blame for his misspent life than to have no explanation for it at all. That is the central problem of Jack's life: he is, or at least wants himself to be, responsible for the pain and difficulty of his life. But is he?

3 Jack on Sin, Forgiveness, and Self-Responsibility

Jack's religious outlook, as we've caught glimpses of it in *Gilead* and now in *Home*, is strange: he is a declared religious skeptic, but still feels as if he is damned. Glory tells him, "I don't really think you get to believe in perdition unless you believe in all the rest of it," to which Jack responds, "perdition is the one thing that always made sense to me. I mean, it has always seemed plausible. On the basis of my experience of it" (*Home* 119). Jack does not, we sense, have a clearly defined position on these matters, though not for lack of trying. He seems to want to hold together what is at best a tension-wracked combination of views—that Christianity is false, but that the doctrine of hell is true—but this desire is rooted in experiences that are undeniably real and overwhelming to him. No doubt, Jack spends most of his time feeling condemned. From a young age it is clear that Jack has some undefined problem and that others around him cannot help. Jack is a loner and commits misdeeds for reasons he doesn't understand. He is convinced, it seems, that others (including his family) *do* understand what's wrong with him and rightly condemn him for it. "I really am nothing," he says, "Nothing, with a body. I create a kind of displacement around myself as I pass through the world, which can fairly be called trouble. This is a mystery, I believe" (*Home* 288–9).⁶

Given his Christian background, one interpretation of this experience naturally presents itself: Jack is a sinner, in need of divine forgiveness and salvation. Ye who are weary, come home. And this is the way that his father interprets his situation, or at least claims to; like the old hymn, he is committed to the idea that salvation for Jack does lie in "coming home" to his father (both worldly and eternal). But Jack is skeptical of this response and for good reasons. As Boughton's response to Mrs. Trotsky's insult already makes clear, Jack finds that universal message alienating—it does not seem to be about *him*. He experiences Christian forgiveness as a sham, at least in his particular case. Though Jack's sins as a young boy were mostly petty, they escalate as he gets older; the crisis point is a brief affair with a poor young girl named Annie Wheeler, whom Jack impregnates and then abandons to deal with the child on her own. The child, born into squalid circumstances, dies from an infection at the age of three. She never sees her father. It is this act more than any other that comes to define Jack's problematic nature, and we've already seen Ames wrestling with the same problem in *Gilead*. In *Home*, we see more directly how the situation affected the Boughtons. "It was as though a great gulf had opened," Glory tells us, "Jack on the far side of it, beyond rescue or comfort" (*Home* 56). Most devastating to the young Glory is the effect it has on her father, who finds what Jack did indefensible and beyond his ability to forgive. Glory confronts Jack about this, asking, "what is Papa going to do?," to which Jack ruefully responds, "Do to me? Nothing, I mean, he's going to forgive me" (*Home* 57). But Jack does not mean those words, not really. What they translate to is: Papa is going to speak the words of Christian forgiveness to me, as he always does, but in his heart he will not really forgive and will go on being vexed and pained at my very existence. When Jack later tells Glory about his wife Della, he wryly notes that her minister-father thinks he is "damn near worthless—'damn near,' because he's professionally obligated to take a charitable view" (*Home* 107). One suspects that Jack thinks his father "forgives" him for similar reasons.

Jack's rejection of the Christian faith is not rooted in standard theological objections.[7] It is not even rooted in objections to Christian values, since he seems to accept that his actions deem him worthy of damnation. Rather, it comes from the loneliness and alienation occasioned in him by the invoking of traditional pieties about sin and forgiveness. He clearly suspects that the sin Christianity promises to save him from does not really include the very serious sins that *he* has committed. Perhaps one can wipe away the guilt of forgetting to turn in old library books, or even of underage drinking and thieving, with an airy theological phrase, but the same cannot be said for abandoning a child to die in squalor. Glory asks him at one point, "How could you think you were the only sinner in the family? We're Presbyterians!," to which Jack replies, "Yes, 'we have all sinned and fallen short.' . . . Talk is cheap." (*Home* 124) Elsewhere, Glory herself notes that in his sermons her father did "mention sin, but it was rarefied in his understanding of it, a matter of acts and omissions so commonplace that no one could ever be wholly innocent of them or especially alarmed by them, either—the uncharitable thought, the neglected courtesy" (*Home* 111). Jack's life obviously puts these Christian doctrines to the test in ways that the others' lives do not, and it seems to him that the universalism of the Christian message is employed in his case primarily to cover over his problems rather than really to address them. As such, Christianity cannot help but appear to Jack to be hypocritical. It claims to reckon with the sins of humankind but actually is only strong enough to deal with the socially respectable sins of quaint Midwesterners.

Jack is left, then, to deal with his problems on his own, a task for which he is, for the most part, woefully inadequate. But his struggles are, at the very least, honest ones. He tries conscientiously to avoid the hypocrisy with which the people in his life have tended to approach him and his problems, and at this he largely succeeds, for better or worse. When Glory, worried about her father's declining health and his complicated feelings toward his son, suggests to Jack that he might lie and tell his father that he has been reconciled to the faith, Jack refuses, on the grounds that honesty—or, more accurately, not being a hypocrite—is his "one scruple" (*Home* 144). And in fact this is true. Although Jack is willing to accept the epithet of "fraud," and does all manner of dishonest things, he does not lie and he does not shy away from admitting the things that he has done. But it is a cruel scruple, when practiced in isolation: it effectively places a barrier between Jack and any possibility of forgiveness, even from himself, since forgiveness is so connected to hypocrisy in his mind. Glory notes that Jack is very hard on himself, to which Jack responds, "Yes, I am. For all the good it does me" (*Home* 145).

For the most part, Boughton avoids mention of Jack's abandonment of Annie Wheeler and their child. But one night, before bed, he decides to break the silence. He suggests to Jack that he has come to a realization about the child, about something he'd always known but just hadn't admitted to himself: he, Boughton, was really the one at fault: "I should have baptized her. I have regretted many times I didn't do at least that much for her" (*Home* 152). There is good reason to worry that Boughton's declining mental health plays a role in his willingness to believe (or at any rate, to say) this—it's an absurd idea on its face. Glory reminds her father that Presbyterians do not believe in the necessity of baptism for salvation anyway. Jack is stunned not only at the point about baptism, which had of course never occurred to him, but also and more importantly at the idea that his father could have thought that what happened between himself and Annie was in any sense Boughton's fault. Jack, of course, blames himself entirely. It is an unfortunate moment for Boughton, who *is* at fault in this situation, though not in the way he thinks. In fact, he displays rather than confesses his fault in the scene. His fault lies not in having failed to perform some service but in failing to reckon honestly with what his son had done and to undergo a real process of forgiveness for it. Jack's response to Boughton's idea follows a pattern we now recognize as typical: he is forced to be impressed by the old man's ability to take on responsibility, while at the same time remaining vexed that the real problem in the situation has not been addressed. When Jack leaves to get some air, Glory follows him and the conversation continues:

"If I were an honest man I'd have told him I have never given a single thought to—any of that. Not one thought. Ever."

"Well."

"I mean, to whether or not she was baptized. I have thought about the rest of it, from time to time. I have." He laughed. "Never because I chose to."

She said, "That was all so long ago. You were young."

"No. I wasn't young. I don't believe I ever was young." Then he said, "Excuses scare me, Glory. They make me feel like I'm losing hold. I can't explain it. But please don't try to make excuses for me. I might start believing them sometime. I've known people like that." (*Home* 153–4)

We can see in Jack's resolute refusal to entertain excuses many of the central traits of his character, both positive and negative. Positively, of course, it's an expression of his commitment to avoiding hypocrisy: he will not portray himself as better than he takes himself to be and will not evade responsibility for his actions. But on the negative side, his rejection of all mitigating circumstances is pathological. His totalizing worry that any excuses will make him "lose hold" on himself threatens to make it impossible for him to understand himself properly. What Jack will lose hold on if he makes any excuses for himself is not personal responsibility as such but his conception of himself as a problem. Jack's unfortunate problem is that he confuses the two, or at least does not know how to pry them apart in his own particular case. This is why he "never was young"; that is, he never was able to think of himself as anything but a troublemaker fully responsible (indeed, damned) for his troublemaking. And though this self-conception obviously does him no good, at any rate it gives him some modicum of self-understanding, some way to diminish the mystery of why his life is the way that it is, of why he suffers so much.[8]

It is for this reason that Jack feels a kind of freeing sensation in the committing of a serious wrong—it confirms for him that everything is his fault, just as he suspected. In a later passage, he tells Glory of his complicated feelings after the incident with Annie:

That last time I spoke to [Boughton], before I left, I knew I had done something he couldn't forgive. He thought he could. He said he had, but he's a terrible liar. It shocked me that I could hurt him so badly. It scared me. It was what I expected, but it scared me. It was like stepping off a cliff. And it was a relief, too. I thought, It's finally happened, I knew it would. (*Home* 277)

Much of the mystery of Jack's character lies in that strange combination of emotions, fear and relief. Jack is relieved, since it brings to a seemingly definitive resolution the obscure relationship he bears to his father, and perhaps more importantly to himself: he is the committer of unforgivable sins. (For, if Robert Boughton cannot forgive him, then who could?) Of course, there is also fear, since now he actually *is* what he had once merely played at being, and what he is is obviously not something he wants to be.

4 Gilead and Home II: The Porch Conversation

And so, it seems inevitable that Jack would come to concern himself with the doctrine of predestination. Clearly the most important overlapping scene in *Gilead* and *Home* is a conversation about that very topic, a conversation Jack initiates with an abrupt request of Ames. It is repeated *verbatim* in both novels: "I'd like to know your views on the doctrine of predestination" (*Gilead* 149; *Home* 219). As we are told in *Home*, the conversation comes about due to the disastrous fallout of Ames's sermon on Hagar and Ishmael. Boughton had been hoping something good would come of Jack's going to church but instead got an "incomprehensible disappointment" (*Home* 212). In an effort to mend some fences, Jack finds an article, a sociological study of American religion, in the *Ladies Home Journal* that he thinks Ames and his father might enjoy arguing about. He has them both read it and meet up to discuss it.[9] Ames comes to the Boughton house to return the magazine, and, with Glory looking on, he and Boughton sit and talk on the porch, chuckling over some of the theological crudeness of the article. It is at this point that Jack comes out to join them and expresses agreement with what the article had said about race in particular—namely, that "the seriousness of American Christianity was called into question by our treatment of the Negro" (*Home* 217). Boughton repellently suggests that "we" have done well enough by Black people insofar as we have given them Christianity, but Jack presses Ames for his opinion. Ames, though he admits that he hasn't kept up with recent developments as much as he used to, says, "I have to agree with you [Jack]" (*Home* 217). Boughton's defensive response is that there is something wrongly judgmental in questioning the seriousness of people's Christianity in this way. The following back-and-forth is worth quoting at some length:

> Ames said, "Jack does have a point, though."
> "And I have a point, too. My point is that it's very easy to judge."
> That was meant to end the conversation, but Jack, who was studying the ice in his glass, said, "True. Remarkably easy in this case, it seems to me."
> "All the more reason to resist that impulse!"
> Jack laughed, and Ames looked at him, not quite reprovingly. Jack's gaze fell.
> Boughton said, "If there is one thing the faith teaches us clearly it is that we are all sinners and we owe each other pardon and grace. 'Honor everyone,' the Apostle says."
> "Yes, sir. I know the text. It's the application that confuses me a little."
> Ames said, "I think your father has shown us all a good many times how he applies that text." (*Home* 218)

As is often the case with conversations in Robinson's novels, there is a great deal of thematic compression to unpack here, since so much is left unsaid and the conversation becomes so personal so quickly. Jack is wanting to draw out a difference of opinions regarding race between Ames and Boughton, one that (though neither of the old men know this) concerns him personally. Ames is more concerned with Boughton's well-being and thus is not inclined to amplify that difference, even if he feels it, nor is he likely to let slights on Boughton's character pass. But of course, there is no way for Jack to express himself without slighting his father, for at least two reasons. One is that his father obviously still harbors some racist views, so that questioning the seriousness of racists' faith is also an implicit questioning of his father's faith. The other, as we've seen at length in this chapter, is that Jack can't help but hear Boughton's words about pardon and grace as empty, since his father has always failed to effectively extend true grace to Jack. When he says that the application of those doctrines confuses him, he means both that it is difficult to apply it to racists and also that it is confusing to see how it applies to himself. Ames's reproving response shows that he understands Jack's meaning but it also exasperates Jack, who throws up his hands in surrender. In initiating this conversation, Jack had been hoping to find like-mindedness in Ames, who is less racist and perhaps more sincerely forgiving than his father, but ends up effectively turning Ames against him, yet again.

Interestingly, Ames's account of the porch conversation in *Gilead* leaves out this part of the conversation concerning race. For all we would know from reading his account, the conversation with Jack effectively starts with his blunt request that Ames explain his views on predestination. It is perhaps important that it is at this moment, noted in both novels, that Lila arrives. Jack is visibly relieved to see her (as he typically is). Ames tries to engage her in the conversation, telling her that they had been discussing the fact that "the way people understand their religion is an accident of their birth" (*Home* 219). Though Lila does not respond to this, Jack does, using it as the springboard to ask about predestination. It's not a favorite subject of Ames and he answers evasively. The *Gilead* account focuses on why: he tells us it is his "least favorite topic of conversation in the entire world" (*Gilead* 149), since it tends to make people angry, and is in his view a mystery about which there isn't much that is productive to say. Ames feels that Jack is bringing up predestination not out of real theological curiosity but just to "devil" him and put him in a "false position." And Ames's account of the conversation is in fact drily theological—he notes Jack's seemingly theoretical question about whether there are people who "are simply born evil, live evil lives, and then go to hell" (*Gilead* 151). Ames's response is evasive, indeed circular: "Generally, a person's behavior is consistent with his nature. Which is only to say his behavior is consistent." Ames is frustrated with the fact that he has to talk in this indirect way, and Jack's comment that he is being "cagey" exasperates him further. Though Ames's defensiveness is understandable, it is nonetheless striking how theoretical his approach is. He even chafes at the idea that others get angry over this topic (since presumably they are thinking of how it applies to their lives). Ames, who has told us about Jack's tendency to treat words as actions rather than meaning-conveyors, must know that Jack is really asking about himself, but his account focuses entirely on Jack's devilment of pressing on insoluble questions. It is perhaps telling that Ames closes his account with reference to his atheist brother Edward and the fact that he has tried "never to say anything Edward would have found callow or naïve" (154). But he is not talking to Edward here, and one wonders if Ames often forgets this fact in theological conversation.

In *Gilead*, where all we have is Ames's perspective on the conversation, we may still be inclined to take his side. But we learn in *Home* that things are very different than they appeared in the earlier novel. In fact, once again, Ames's account of the conversation leaves a long stretch out (*Home* 220–5). Ames remembers Glory saying that she hates this conversation, and then leaving. But when she leaves, we learn, she continues to listen. She hears Jack ask about Ames's sermon but his question, of course, is really about the relationship of fathers to children. (Notably, Ames tells his son, Robbie, to clear off while they talk.) Jack asks if Ames believes "that a man might be punished by the suffering of his child. If a child might suffer to punish his father. For his sins. Or his unbelief" (*Home* 222). Glory thinks Jack is retaliating for the sermon, suggesting that Ames's own dead child might be a punishment for his own sins. Neither of the novels can tell us whether that is the case, though it is likely that Jack's question is mainly about his own dead child, not Ames's. He says, "you do hope a child will have a life. . . . And you hope he will be safe. You hope he'll learn more than—bitterness."

At this point Boughton breaks down, clearly applying all that is said to his own relationship to *his* son, Jack. He says, "Oh! I am a very sinful man!" and tells of the night when Jack was born and almost didn't live. Ames says, "Theology aside, Robert, if you are a sinful man, those words have no meaning at all" (*Home* 222). Boughton's response—"You don't really know me!"—is quickly brushed aside by Ames, who has known him all his life. But Boughton's claim is not merely false modesty, as we and Jack (but perhaps not Ames) well know. And indeed, we might well ask, why leave "theology aside" here? As Ames ought to know, even paragons of their community, even fathers who try to be loving, may well fall into grave sin. It is precisely these kinds of moments that are likely to confirm what Jack has long suspected, namely that universal claims about the sinfulness of man are not really sincerely meant by those who say them, and so the universal claims about forgiveness aren't either. Jack has in fact learned little more than bitterness, and though that is not uniquely Boughton's fault, he has played a crucial role in it. Ames is generally skeptical of the claim that the misfortunes children suffer "when their fathers aren't good men" are somehow a punishment from God, but when he says this, Boughton interjects, insisting that "we should have done much more" for Jack's dead daughter. Jack responds, "I really am a sinful man. Granting your terms . . . Granting my terms" (*Home* 224). He goes on: "And I don't know why I am. There's no pleasure in it. For me, at least. Not much, anyway." Jack tells Ames what a good reader already knows—that he worries so much about predestination because he thinks that he may himself be predestined to damnation, and that he worries about others being punished for someone else's sin because he feels "as though I spread a contagion of some kind" (*Home* 225). We ought to be reminded of Jack's pronouncement that he is "nothing, with a body," and that he creates a "displacement" (*Home* 289) around himself. From the Christian theological perspective, this is not the right way to think of Jack's problem, but Ames and Boughton do not exactly help Jack to conceive of it in any other way.

Again, remember that all of this is left out of Ames's account in *Gilead*. But why do the two accounts differ so much? Presumably it is not simply that Ames fails to recall the bits of the conversation that he leaves out. They are too important for him to have simply forgotten. It is important to remember that *Gilead* is addressed to someone—Ames is writing to his son, Robbie—while *Home*, with its focus on Glory, from the third-person perspective, is not. It is possible that Ames leaves these things out because they are not fit for Robbie to hear about, and one can imagine why he might think that. He does not want Robbie's mind to be darkened by these speculations about the relationship of the sins of fathers and children. But while this is obviously true of Robbie as a young child (it makes perfect sense that Ames sends his son away when the conversation happens), Robbie will not read the letters until much later, and elsewhere Ames does not shy away from very serious subject matter. Is he worried, to use Jack's words, that the father/son issues of the Ames and Boughton families will "spread" like a "contagion" to Robbie, too? Whatever his worries, it is clear that Ames does not want to reckon with the problems this part of the conversation raises, at least not at this point in his letters to his son.

Jack's problem—whether he is born predestined to hell, whether born sinners ever change—is still to be resolved. It is at this point that Lila enters the conversation. She asks about salvation: "If you can't change, there don't seem much point in it [i.e., salvation]." Jack alludes to the fact that he has been at tent revival meetings, though "only as an interested observer," where people are called to be saved "along some muddy riverbank in the middle of the night," and he and Lila enjoy reminiscing about a mutual past experience (*Home* 227). Ames is notably alienated by this allusion—he says in *Gilead*, after having done with his short description of the porch conversation, that he "was left wondering what [Jack] was referring to when he mentioned tent meetings," and well Ames might wonder, since he (wrongly, we must presume) remembers Jack saying, "I know you [i.e., Ames and Boughton] have attended tent meetings only as interested observers, but..." (*Gilead* 153). But Jack is reaching out to Lila here and senses in her question about salvation that she sees, in a way that Boughton and Ames do not, what Jack is *really* asking about. When it becomes clear that the conversation is not going anywhere, as Glory had predicted, Jack finally decides to let it go. But Lila will not let him. In *Home*, she is described at this point as "mustering herself,"[10] before she says, "A person can change. Everything can change" (*Home* 227). Jack responds, simply but with some emotion, "Why, thank you, Mrs. Ames. That's all I wanted to know" (*Home* 228). It might be better to say at this point that that is what Jack wanted to *hear*, and in particular what he wanted to hear from Ames. Lila senses this, since Ames tells us that she chides him for being so hard on Jack after the conversation is over: "He was only asking a question. . . . Maybe some people aren't so comfortable with themselves" (*Gilead* 154).

5 "The Lord Is Wonderful": Home Regained

Jack is certainly not comfortable with himself, and the events of *Home* do not really bring him any closer to being so. He is weary and a sinner; perhaps he would like to follow the advice of the old hymn and come home. But he is a misfit, a man who "never was young," the illegally married husband of a Black woman, and father of a mixed-race boy, and he has no place where his return would be welcomed. When he decides to leave Gilead again at the end of the novel and is saying goodbye to his father, Boughton pushes his handshake attempt away, saying, "Tired of it!" (*Home* 317). "Me, too. Bone tired," responds Jack. What, then, is achieved by *Home*, the novel, since it does not bring Jack home? We might feel, after finishing it, a bit like Glory does on the day she first meets Jack's first child, living in squalor and destined to die: "I do not understand one thing in this world. Not one" (*Gilead* 164).

Glory herself is in the midst of a not-altogether-satisfying homecoming. She is a comfort to Jack throughout, perhaps the only thing keeping him from doing something truly terrible and irreversible. Much of the dialogue between them involves Jack simply saying "Thank you" or "You're kind" to Glory, so much so that some readers might find it tiresome, but the repetition underscores how seldom Jack is on the receiving end of kindness and how often Glory is willing to give it. We learn in the novel that she has her own reasons for being a particular comfort for Jack. Like Jack, she has marital secrets that she keeps from her father: she has ended her relationship with her fiancée but tells her father that they went to the justice of the peace. In fact, the now ex-fiancée bears important similarities to Jack, a fact Jack himself notes and has a bit of good-natured fun with. When Glory tells him that they met at a choir rehearsal, where the man said that he heard the music and was reminded of the "sweetest moments of his childhood," Jack recognizes it as the kind of phrase a drifter like himself would have used to snare a nice young girl (*Home* 121). When Glory first describes the man, she makes a particular point of the fact that he kept a record, to the penny, of the debts he owed her, a record that Glory sees as evidence of a "horrible, vindictive little streak of honesty" (*Home* 22). We find Jack, later in the novel, keeping similarly close records of *his* debts to Glory and the family, though part of his motivation is to make sure he doesn't have enough money on him at any one time to tempt his alcoholism.

But the fiancée is a sign of something deeper, a kinship that Jack and Glory share. Glory remarks at one point that "if she had been a man she might have chosen the ministry," but that, "to their father's mind, the world's great work was the business of men" (*Home* 20). Boughton and his wife name their daughters Hope, Faith, Grace, and Glory— Glory wryly says to Jack, when he makes a pun on her name based on *The Paths of Glory* ("Your memoirs?"), that "[t]he girls in this family got named for theological abstractions and the boys got named for human beings" (*Home* 82). Glory has obviously herself been hurt by the dynamics of the Boughton family, even if her case is not as dire as Jack's. She too has felt as if there was not a natural place for her within it. Indeed, when she is young she feels a kind of "special bond" with him, because "[t]hey were the unexceptional children—slighted, overlooked" (*Home* 55). She immediately acknowledges that the statement was false, since Jack plainly was exceptional, but this is an evasion; he *is* slighted and overlooked, precisely because his exceptions are not achievements but failures. From a young age, Glory takes these failures personally. She says later in the novel that it was an "old habit" of hers to make "a kind of happiness for herself out of the thought that she could be his rescuer" (*Home* 248). The habit manifests itself at the time of Jack's abandonment of Annie Wheeler and their child—it is Glory of all the Boughton siblings who cares for the child, who indeed cannot understand why the rest of the family does not take the birth of the child for the joy that it is, and who tries the hardest to get Jack to come back and care for her. The same habit obviously manifests itself in the events of *Home*, since Glory works so hard and in her way so skillfully at doing what she can to reconcile Boughton and Jack, and Jack to his life.

At the close of the novel, after Jack has left, his wife, Della, comes to the Boughton house, with their son, Robert. Heartbreakingly, they have just missed Jack. Glory gives what consolation she can, reassuring Della that Jack's departure had nothing to do with her arrival and accepting Della's contact information. She notes Della looking at her, and at her surroundings, fondly and with something like recognition, perhaps from stories that Jack has told her. More than anything, Glory studies Robert: "Jack had a beautiful child, a beautiful son" (*Home* 322). She looks wildly around the house for a gift to give the young boy, settling on a framed picture of the nearby river from Jack's boyhood room. She finds that the boy plays baseball too, just like Jack, and Della proudly tells her that Robert "thinks he's going to be a preacher," just as Glory herself had wanted to be.

Glory's brief meeting with Jack's wife and child settles something firmly in her mind.[11] She remembers a moment in which Jack told her that, when he would wander off as a child, he was always closer to home than they had thought. Though Jack had always seemed so estranged from them, he really did love and yearn for his home. Glory has a realization, and a resolution:

> And how cruel it was that he loved the place anyway. His little boy touching the tree, just to touch it. The tree that sounded like the ocean. Dear Lord in heaven, she could never change anything. How could she know what he had sanctified to that child's mind with his stories, sad

stories that had made them laugh. I used to wish I lived here, he said. That I could just walk in the door like the rest of you did. (*Home* 323)

Glory has, at this point in the novel, been making her peace with the fact that she will have to remain in the house and help her father, and perhaps stay on even after he passes, to keep the house up for the family. Now that her engagement is over, there is not much else for her to do. What happens after Della's visit is that this reluctant but dutiful willingness becomes something else: a real commitment. Jack's relationship to their home, revealed in its full significance to her for the first time, allows her to realize that two of her problems—her need to "save" or at least help her brother and her troubled relationship to her childhood home—really have one solution: she must keep the old Boughton house. But why? Della and Robert leave without setting foot in the house, and for all she knows Jack, Della, and Robert may never return to it. But Glory muses on the possibilities:

> She knew it would have answered a longing of Jack's if he could even imagine that their spirits had passed through that strange old house. Just the thought of it might bring him back, and the place would seem changed, to him and to her. As if all that saving and keeping their father had done was providence indeed, and new love would transform all the old love and make its relics wonderful. (*Home* 323)

Paradoxically, Glory must keep the house the same in order that it be transformed. Her keeping would be a continuation of the work of her father, who had kept the house the same all these years, even after all the children had left it. That work was not exactly his but God's ("providence"). Boughton had done it to hold on to what was, for him but often not for his children, the mostly positive story of his flourishing family. But God was preparing a future, a future that only Glory can bring about, a future that would be the only way for her to "save" her brother, Jack. Della and Robert in that house, the "new" love transforming the "old," and the "relics" of the house, including that picture of the river—all are "made wonderful" where once they were only reminders of a painful past.

It is crucial to Glory's character and to the meaning of the novel as a whole that even just the imagination of this possibility is sufficient to make what had previously seemed to her ugly and burdensome—Glory as the new lord of the Boughton manor, keeper of the knickknacks—look positively beautiful. Glory's ability to see the house under this new description changes its nature. Those knickknacks are not mere knickknacks, nor are they (as they had been before) mere reminders of trouble and failed love. Now, what once were mere "relics" of the old, imperfect love of the Boughtons for each other are now made into something "wonderful," something which always had in it, against all odds, the seed of something better, something that could save Jack after all.[12] Glory's realization and the love of Jack that occasioned it and had been preparing itself in her all her life makes beautiful the action that before had been an onerous necessity.[13] The novel closes with her imagining Robert returning to the house as a young man—"[y]oung men are rarely cautious," she notes (*Home* 324). She imagines that he will have an accent and a politeness indicative of his Southern roots and a "tall man's slouch" evocative of his father. He will be "very kind to me," she says, because he is Southern, and because he is Jack's. Glory's imagining continues, and brings the novel to a close:

> He will be curious about the place, though his curiosity will not override his good manners. He will talk to me a little while, too shy to tell me why he has come, and then he will thank me and leave, walking backward a few steps, thinking, Yes, the barn is still there, yes, the lilacs, even the pot of petunias. This was my father's house. And I will think, He is young. He cannot know that my whole life has come down to this moment.
> That he has answered his father's prayers.
> The Lord is wonderful. (*Home* 324–5)

The boy's coming would be the culminating moment of her life, because it would be the moment when Jack's prayers are answered, and because Glory's housekeeping would have played a necessary role in the answering. In a sense, it doesn't matter whether what Glory imagines will actually happen. It is for this reason that talking merely of Glory's "hope," as one commentator has done, can be misleading.[14] It is true to say that Glory's decision (and the actions that will follow from it) is separated from any particular material outcome but the separation is at once more radical and less abstract than the talk of "hope" suggests. Glory is not just hoping for this particular thing that she imagines might happen; nor is she hoping that God will, in some way that she is content to leave unspecified, make good on her labors by having things turn out well in the end. Glory's imagining is not an expression of hope *for* some kind of redemption; it is itself redemptive.[15] Her imagining of this particular scenario redeems, because it gives a meaning to her actions that they would not otherwise have had. It is for this reason that the last line of the novel ("The Lord is wonderful") serves as such an effective ending. It is crucial that it is said straightforwardly, in the present tense, and so is not itself part of Glory's imagining. She does not say, "Then, the Lord would be wonderful," or "The Lord will show himself to be wonderful." The Lord *is* wonderful—Glory's life *now* has been made good. Her staying and keeping the Boughton home will be a blessing for Glory too, and not just an arduous sacrifice. Of course, it *will* involve a certain kind of sacrifice. She will have to give up much that had, up to now, given her life meaning, including her desire to have children of her own. But that sacrifice will have meaning, and indeed a meaning that is not unrelated to the meaning children would have had for Glory—it will be her way of redeeming the love of her family, doing her part to redress the wrongs that have up to now been endemic to it. She has succeeded, by means of her imagining, in making the necessity of her staying in the house into a beautiful reality. She has found a way to affirm her life, and through it the life of the Boughton home.[16]

We stand at the end of the events of *Gilead* and *Home*, then, with a new future on the horizon. The two pillars of the Gilead community, John Ames and Robert Boughton, will soon pass on. Glory and Lila will now be the lords of the Boughton and Ames homes. This future, and the hopes for it that the characters evidently harbor, suggests something important about the overall theological outlook of the *Gilead* novels, as we have followed them so far. It suggests that there is something missing in John Ames and Robert Boughton, whose overall outlooks still sometimes reflect the quaintness and backwardness of their hometown. Those outlooks render them mostly incapable of helping Jack (aside from Ames's blessing at the end of *Gilead*), a fact which casts doubt on their ability to really address the depths of human sin and despair.[17] It is the "home" that Gilead was to them that makes that hymn, "Softly and Tenderly," seem to Jack like a cruel joke, but the home it could be in the future might actually make good on the hymn's promises. That future is strongly suggested already in Glory's decision and is developed further in Robinson's next two novels, *Jack* and *Lila*.

Notes

1 Jack is reminded of it himself (cf. *Home* 316).
2 There seem to be no strong actual etymological relationships between the two words, aside from the fact that both are derived from words in Latin that can mean something like "set apart" (*sacrare* and *secretus* respectively).
3 Of course, in the novel it is *Glory* who is remembering the story and not her father but there is no reason to suspect the narration, since so much of the rest of the novel corroborates the point. It is perhaps best to interpret situations like this, in which Glory purports to be describing the inner workings of other family members' minds, not simply as Robinson's insufficient resolve in employing third-person but non-omniscient narration (how could Glory have known what he was thinking?) but as reports of what the family generally thought (and presumably mostly *knew*) about that family member's thoughts. It is noteworthy that Glory *doesn't* do this with Jack, since she and the rest of the family almost never know what he's thinking and feeling; if she does opine upon it, it is explicitly noted as speculation.
4 It should be noted here that hope is not an indulgence Jack often allows himself. He tells his father, "I think hope is the worst thing in the world. I really do. It makes a fool of you while it lasts. And then when it's gone, it's

like there's nothing left of you at all. Except . . . what you can't be rid of" (*Home* 275).

5   Aside from his checkered history with his father, Jack has race-related reasons for preferring Ames to his father. Right before Jack visits Ames's church, he talks with his father about the Montgomery protests, insisting they are nonviolent. Boughton responds: "But they provoke violence. It's all provocation" (*Home* 204). After a "long silence," Jack says, "This week I will go to church" (*Home* 205).

6   It is this effect that makes him "keep to myself," he says, and in the later novel that bears his name, Jack formulates his ethical goal in terms of finding a way to be "harmless," that is, to limit this displacing effect as much as is in his power.

7   In *Gilead*, Ames imagines Jack "under a tree somewhere, reading Huxley or Carlyle," while Ames and Jack's family deal with the fallout of Jack's abandonment of Annie Wheeler and their child (*Gilead* 159). In fact, as we later find out in *Jack*, he is reading poets who express his loneliness and outcast status (see Chapter 5).

8   Jack's situation carries strong Nietzschean overtones. Nietzsche is keen to emphasize that the human need for a meaning for suffering is stronger than the need not to suffer: "Man, the bravest animal and the one most accustomed to suffering, does *not* negate suffering in itself: he *wants* it, he even seeks it out, provided one shows him a *meaning* for it" (GM III:28). Nietzsche raises the point in the context of discussing the ascetic ideal (see the second section of Chapter 1) which, like Jack's self-conception, begins with the Christian conception of suffering as the fault of the (sinful) sufferer and inevitably leads to the more secular and purely life-denying idea that the only good thing to will is to be "nothing": "Man would much rather will *nothingness* than *not* will" (GM III). Jack's positive ideal, insofar as he can formulate one in the later novel *Jack* (see Chapter 5), is one of mere "harmlessness," that is, a hope that his will's effectiveness on the world will be minimized.

9   Cf. Lear (2012, 40–1) for some illuminating discussion of the actual, original article.

10 In *Gilead*, Ames does not notice any mustering. Blinded a bit by jealousy, he says only that Lila doesn't look at Jack, suggesting that her looking away is intentional (*Gilead* 153). Ames also does not seem to attach much

significance to what Lila says. The reader, and Ames, must await the events of Robinson's third Gilead novel, *Lila*, to learn what significance *she* attaches to them.

11 Like Ames's experience of the ashy biscuit (see Chapter 3), we might say that this experience puts some things "beyond question" for her.

12 On "relics," see as well our discussion of *Housekeeping* in Chapter 2.

13 Remember Nietzsche: "I want to learn more and more how to see what is necessary in things as what is beautiful in them—thus I will be one of those who make things beautiful. *Amor fati*: let that be my love from now on!" (GS 276). For discussion, see the end of Chapter 1, and the Conclusion.

14 "The inward attitude of hope, manifested within the imagination, is what Robinson ultimately wants to affirm, rather than any material outcome. Where the reader might see a domestic catastrophe, Glory persists in the hope that everything will be healed, that all suffering and abandonment and loss lead ultimately to peace, joy, refuge, home" (Engebretson 2017, 77).

15 Jennifer Holberg gets closer to the meaning of the passage: "[Glory] begins to understand how she is an essential part of the divine work of restoration, to a remedying of the world's brokenness" (Holberg 2010, 296).

16 This sounds grandiose enough, and it is important not to give her commitment more significance than it can bear. Engebretson suggests that, in welcoming an African American child to a Gilead home, Glory will also "redeem her community's unjust and violent racism" (Engebretson 2017, 77). If that was indeed Robinson's intention, there would be a good deal of justice in Briallen Hopper's claim that Glory's imaginings at the end of *Home* are just a "lovely liberal reverie," and that the "empathetic fantasies" it offers do not present "the best possible public Christianity for our age" (see Hopper 2014). But the claims of both seem to us to expect something different than the novel is trying to offer. One may of course hope that Glory's attitude toward Jack's son is a sign of hope for the future of race relations in Gilead, but her decision at the end of the novel doesn't really have any direct effects on this complicated sociopolitical reality and nothing Glory says really suggests that she is attempting to take on this problem.

17 Of course, one shouldn't lump Ames and Boughton together entirely. Boughton's failures, especially with respect to Jack, are more serious than Ames's, and the ideal to which Ames gave such memorable and inspiring voice in *Gilead* is one of life-affirmation. Whether Glory realizes it or not, her realization, and decision, at the end of *Home* continues in and deepens the spirit of that ideal. Lila will develop it still further in the novel that bears her name and in ways that will in part seek to address its shortcomings in Ames.

5

Jack

A Glorious Presence

Jack is the great mystery of the Gilead novels. He is the beloved son and brother of the Boughton family, the godson and namesake of John Ames, but also the inveterate prodigal, a drunk and a thief, someone who is—as his sister Glory points out—insufferably *strange*. In the previous novels, Jack's strangeness is the cipher that moves the plot forward: Why is he back in Gilead? Where has he been? Why can't he accept the love his family so longs to give him? Is he doomed, as his Presbyterian father worries, to perdition? As things stand after *Gilead* and *Home*, few answers have been given. Jack has been in St. Louis, he has a wife and son, and he is considering a return to Gilead—this is about as much as we know. As for Jack's spiritual alienation, both its source and entrenchment, the reader is left to speculate. Perhaps some people really are beyond hope.

Jack's inscrutability places an almost impossible pressure on Robinson's fifth and most recent novel, the eponymously titled *Jack* (2020). The reader is primed to finally solve the "puzzle" of Jack. But we are also aware that transparency raises its own problems—after all, one of the real literary virtues of the early novels is their insistent refusal to offer clean resolution. *Jack* is set in the 1940s, roughly a decade before the action of *Gilead* and *Home*, and in the thick of a Jim Crow–dominated St. Louis. This segregated setting plays an important role in the novel's plot, as Robinson focuses on the early years of Jack's relationship to Della Miles, the daughter of a Methodist minister, a school teacher, and—importantly—a Black woman. *Jack*, at its most basic, is the story of a star-crossed romance.

Most early readers of *Jack* agree on one thing. The novel disappoints.[1] This judgment is defended in various ways, but most come down to some version of the following: the relationship between Jack and Della is not compelling. Neither character is sufficiently nuanced in their attraction to the other. Jack does not appreciate Della's blackness as anything more than a material obstacle to their happiness,[2] and Della is altogether too accepting of Jack's many and various character flaws. In this chapter, we will focus on the latter accusation—Della's blind loyalty to Jack—as it relates directly to a possible criticism leveled against the concept of life-affirmation more generally. Life-affirmation, of the kind on display in characters like John Ames and Glory but also (we will argue) Della, is marked by a kind of unwavering love that, to some, appears distinctly *life-denying*.[3] Instead of being sensitive to the particular characteristics of the people and things it loves, such love often seems to look through them, grounding commitment in some nebulous feature, like a person's "existence" or "soul." At the same time, it misses their concrete features—the particular details that make them beautiful or, in Jack's case, a scoundrel. This kind of love, the argument goes, is life-denying because it is not actually directed toward the world; its foundation rests in some imagined, and usually religious, phantom that resides beyond the material world wherein human beings actually live out their lives. If this is where Robinsonian life-affirmation leads, then all the worse for it.

In response to this worry, we propose to take up a defense of the kind of loyalty Della shows Jack. Without disagreeing entirely with critics who lament Della's one-dimensionality,[4] we defend the kind of love she shows as being, at least at its best, genuinely life-affirming. There are several important components to this discussion. First, there is the question of whether Della's love is properly world-directed. Though she talks about loving Jack's soul as a thing with "no earthly qualities," does this mean his material character is irrelevant? Second, there is the related worry that, even if Della's love depends on appreciating Jack's particularity, it still bottoms out in something he shares with everyone else—a human soul. The question then becomes, Why Jack in particular?—especially since he is so obviously flawed. Where these first two issues focus on the object of Della's love, the last two concern its effects: namely, that it causes Della to withdraw from certain forms of world engagement and, finally, to settle into a kind of quietism that ignores otherwise pressing social concerns. This last issue touches a nerve, as the Gilead novels have come under criticism for over-romanticizing characters who, in their gushing love for a sun-drenched world, seem to overlook the glaring injustices in their own neighborhoods.[5]

1 Too Much to Lose

Jack begins in the closing moments of a disastrous first date. Jack is trying to walk Della home, though with little luck: "I'm not talking to you," she tells him (*Jack* 3). They are returning from a dinner, during the last half of which Jack disappears. Della thinks he lost his nerve. Seeing as how she is Black, he is white, and it is a segregated town, it adds up. She notices he slips away just as two white men approach. "I saw them, Jack," she says. "Those men. I'm not blind. And I'm not stupid" (*Jack* 5). Jack is relieved to correct Della's misimpression. He tells her that yes, he was avoiding the men, but only because he owed them money. Jack was sparing Della a good bit of trouble, both from the debt collectors and likely the police, or so he thinks. By the time the couple arrive at Della's doorstep, Jack manages to wheedle some exasperated sympathy from Della, who remarks, "I have never heard of a white man who got so little good out of being a white man" (*Jack* 7). The evening ends cordially enough, though not without Jack twice warning Della that associating with a bum like him could "cost [her] everything" (*Jack* 7, 8). He adds, just to make the point clear, "and there's no good I could ever do you" (*Jack* 8). Della seems all too ready to acknowledge the truth in this, and her parting goodbye is unambiguously final. She won't be fooled by Jack Boughton again.

Almost a year later, Jack and Della reunite in the unlikeliest of ways. Both are spending the night in Bellefontaine Cemetery. For Jack, this is by choice. He finds occasional respite sleeping among the dead and, on this particular evening, is "commemorating" a birthday—an occasion, he tells us, that calls for a melancholy mood.[6] Della's intentions are less clear. She hints that she might be doing research for a poem (*Jack* 21), but the reader later learns that Jack, the first time they meet, recommends the visit to her—"there is a tree there, a really huge old tree" (*Jack* 125). Whatever her reasons for making this particular trip, it is clear that Jack's appearance is an unwelcome surprise. As the conversation between the two slowly warms up, Della reminds Jack of where he stands: "You're really not very charming. You should know that by now. You might as well stop trying" (*Jack* 20). Having established that not much has changed in the intervening year, and with the cemetery gates now locked, the two agree to pass the time politely.

At one point, dutifully playing her part in passing the time as inoffensively as possible, Della brings up the topic of Shakespeare. (The couple have a history with *Hamlet*, it being one of two books Jack steals from Della's apartment the first time he visits.) "Did you ever wonder why no one except Hamlet seems sorry that the old King Hamlet is dead?" Della asks. She continues, "It seems as though there were stories behind the play we only get glimpses of. But nothing is done to hide them, either, I mean the gaps they leave" (*Jack* 29). Though Della will return to this idea later, it immediately prompts Jack to share a childhood memory, a time when his siblings performed their own version of the play. His kid-sister, Glory, was cast as Ophelia and with impressive seriousness rehearsed her death scene in the bathtub, convinced that someone—perhaps Gertrude?—must have witnessed it (*Jack* 30).

This family memory prompts Della to reflect on her own childhood, eventually leading to an important breakthrough in the conversation. She says, "My father never had much time to spend at home. He's sort of a leader in the community, I guess.... He always made us show him our homework and our report cards, but he says he has a thousand children to look after, and that's true" (*Jack* 30). Recalling his own father's peculiar family-work imbalance, Jack counters, "One time my father was late to a funeral because Teddy and I had a game that went into extra innings. The widow dressed him down a little, I guess. He told her and anyone who ever reminded him of it that it was an exceptional game. We almost won" (*Jack* 30). This story has a remarkable effect on Della. She stops and quietly exclaims, "Oh." Jack, as he so often does, interprets this as an expression of judgment and replies, "Let me guess. Your father's favorite daughter is wandering the night with a disreputable white man" (*Jack* 30). But Della says, "You shouldn't call yourself that. 'Disreputable'" (*Jack* 31). This marks a turn in Della's attitude toward Jack. Earlier in the conversation, the first time the topic of Jack's soul comes up, Della had responded coldly: "[Y]our soul is your business, Mr. Boughton. I'd be happy to talk about something else" (*Jack* 18). Now, apparently concerned to handle Jack's soul with more care, she begins to open up.

A few minutes later, Della returns to the topic. She says, almost to herself, "Maybe everything else is strange" (*Jack* 33). Jack is shocked to hear "a thing that his soul had said to him any number of times," and wondering what Della means, he asks her to repeat herself. After some initial reluctance, she answers with a thought that becomes, in many ways, the focus of the novel. She says, "It seems to me sometimes as though—if we were the only ones left after the world ended, and we made the rules—they might work just as well" (*Jack* 33). As Jack and Della consider what this new world might look like, their conversation has the initial feel of playful escapism; they can both pretend, even if for just a night, that the world that rejects them has passed away. On a closer look, though, it is apparent that Della has something else in mind. She says, "Sometimes I feel like we've just been living on hints. Seeing the world through a keyhole. That's how it would seem to us when we looked back" (*Jack* 60). Della is not inviting Jack to close his eyes to reality but rather to see more of it than he is typically allowed.

Among the things that Della invites Jack to notice is his unlikely beauty. It is a beauty Jack himself does not seem to appreciate—"I'm at my best unseen. The Prince of Darkness. The Prince of Absence" (*Jack* 48). This and other such confessions move Della to observe that Jack is living like someone who "has died already" (*Jack* 72). After Jack objects to this "disheartening" suggestion, Della replies, "I don't think it's disheartening. I think it's kind of—beautiful." She continues,

"Something happened that made you decide you'd had all the life you could stand. So you ended it there. Except you have to stay alive, for your father.... You don't feel like part of the world anymore. Maybe you're more like most people than you think" (*Jack* 73). Jack, a bit irritated, replies, "I can't quite persuade myself that I'm like most people. And I certainly can't persuade anyone else that I am." Della tries again, saying, "I think most people feel a difference between their real lives and the lives they have in the world. But they ignore their souls, or hide them, so they can keep things together, keep an ordinary life together. You don't do that. In your own way, you're kind of—pure" (*Jack* 73).[7] After Jack again refuses to accept that anyone could possibly think his life is beautiful, much less "pure," Della offers a startling answer: "Well, there's Jesus." Realizing the difficulty her statement poses for a self-proclaimed reprobate, Della explains.

> I really just meant that there is—anyone, any human being, and then that person's actual life, everything they didn't mean or couldn't say or wished for or grieved over. That's reality. So someone who would know the world that way, some spirit, seems kind of inevitable. I think. Why should so much reality, most of it, count for nothing? That's how it seems to me. (*Jack* 74)

Jack deflects: "That spirit would not always be impressed, depending on cases." Della shakes her head. "I just think there has to be a Jesus, to say 'beautiful' about things no one else would ever see. The precious things should be looked to, whatever becomes of the rest of it" (*Jack* 74).

Even if the cemetery conversation has not actually expanded Jack's "keyhole" view of himself, something has shifted in Della. Just before the quiet outburst, the "Oh" that seems to inaugurate her change in tone, she asks:

> Have you ever noticed that if you strike a match in a dark room, it seems to spread quite a lot of light. But if you strike one in a room that is already light, it seems to make no difference?... I just think it's interesting. If you add light to light, there should be more of it. As much more as if you add light to darkness. But I don't think there is. (*Jack* 24)

The darkness of the graveyard has, counterintuitively, allowed Della to see more of Jack. Later in the novel, as Della's loyalty to Jack is poised, as predicted, to "cost [her] everything," she tries to explain what exactly she saw that night. She says,

> But once in a lifetime, maybe, you look at a stranger and you see a soul, a glorious presence out of place in the world. And if you love God, every choice is made for you. There is no turning away. You've seen the mystery—you've seen what life is about. What it's for. And a soul has no earthly qualities, no history among the things of this world, no guilt or injury or failure. No more than a flame would have. There is nothing to be said about it except that it is a holy human soul. And it is a miracle when you recognize it. (*Jack* 208)

In addition to serving as an emotional climax, Della's paean to life might be thought to finally address one of the reader's more pressing questions—namely, "Why, Jack?—Why choose *him*?" By the end of the novel, some readers at least[8] are inclined to agree with Jack's earlier insistence that, for those who actually take the time to look, there is very little to see in the way of beauty. The remainder of the novel showcases not so much Jack's grand moral failings—though there are a few such scenes—but rather his spiritual and psychological neuroses. The contradiction between Jack's genuine desire to extend love and his habit of causing harm leaves him full of shame and guilt and self-loathing. Like a child, he is drawn to fragile things and, for reasons he does not entirely understand, they tend to break in his hands.

For Della, a person who has (as everyone reminds her) everything to lose and nothing to gain, it seems inconceivable, even unconscionable, that she would be with Jack. This confusion is compounded by passages like the one quoted earlier, in which the apparent ground of her loyalty is attributed to an encounter with Jack's soul. The problem has less to do with Della's sense that his soul is in some way a "glorious presence" than it does the apparent lack of any relation between that soul and the actual person Jack. Souls, Della says, have "no earthly qualities" and "no history among the things of this world." Thus, one worries that the ground of Della's loyalty and eventual love is a ghost, and not even one that particularly resembles Jack, the thin-haired Iowan with an affinity for poetry. This looks to be about as far from life-affirmation as one can get.

2 Loving a Soul without Qualities

For readers who appreciate Robinson's tendency to develop characters who affirm life at all costs, *Jack* may appear the odd novel out. Either for artistic reasons or philosophical ones, it simply does not reach the heights of the others, and may in fact signal a kind of return to the world-weariness we saw in *Housekeeping*. One obstacle to dividing up the corpus in this way—the world affirming on one side, world rejecting on the other—is that there are significant passages from the early Gilead novels that appear to recommend exactly the kind of love that seems problematic in *Jack*. *Gilead*'s John Ames, for instance, often expresses himself in terms that anticipate Della. He says he loves his son Robby's mere "existence," which can be likened to a "flame on a wick." It seems, then, that instead of writing off Della to celebrate characters like Ames or Glory, it may be worthwhile to clarify why the kind of love Della shows Jack is *not*, in fact, incompatible with life-affirmation of the kind displayed in the early novels.

We see Ames's kinship to Della on display most prominently in two scenes from *Gilead*. The first comes in a passage where Ames is reflecting on his many years spent simply listening to his parishioners. This "work," which he regards as the better part of his pastoral vocation, has put him in close contact with the "life" of his neighbors. He writes,

> By "life" I mean something like "energy" (as the scientists use the word) or "vitality," and also something very different. When people come to speak to me, whatever they say, I am struck by a kind of incandescence in them, the "I" whose predicate can be "love" or "fear" or "want," and whose object can be "someone" or "nothing" and it won't really

matter, because the loveliness is just in that presence, shaped around "I" like a flame on a wick, emanating itself in grief and guilt and joy and whatever else. (*Gilead* 44–5)

This passage has obvious connections to Della's discussion of the soul, and not just because her description, too, likens the soul to a flame. The more important similarity is the reason *why* Ames thinks the analogy is apt. Ames seems to distinguish between, on the one hand, the material-historical details of a person—the particular things they "love" or "fear" or "want"—and, on the other, their "presence," that which "emanates" from these details. Ames makes this point again in a later passage where he attempts to explain to Robby why he loves him. He writes,

There's a shimmer on a child's hair, in the sunlight. There are rainbow colors in it, tiny, soft beams of just the same colors you can see in the dew sometimes. They're in the petals of flowers, and they're on a child's skin. Your hair is straight and dark, and your skin is very fair. I suppose you're not prettier than most children. You're just a nice-looking boy, a bit slight, well scrubbed and well mannered. All that is fine, but it's your existence I love you for, mainly. Existence seems to me now the most remarkable thing that could ever be imagined. (*Gilead* 52–3)

What Ames here refers to as Robby's "existence" is related to what he earlier describes as a person's "life." Like the latter, "existence" seems both to fully express the essence of a person (what it means to be Robby in particular), while also transcending the particular idiosyncrasies of the person (Robby's "straight" and "dark" hair, his looks, and his "manners").

With Della's and Ames's remarks as a guide, we can isolate a few positive features of the Robinsonian "soul": (i) it is the ground of the deepest kind of connection one person can have to another; (ii) it is what makes someone the person they are; and (iii) it cannot be reduced to the individual characteristics of a person's life (their "earthly qualities"). These three traits (especially (ii) and (iii)) make the tension in Robinson's account apparent. She seems to think that people, like Robby or Jack, can be appreciated without also appreciating their specific characteristics. But what could it possibly mean for Ames to love Robby's existence without also loving him *for* his particular features? Ames's eye for such details (the joy he takes in "dragonfly blue" soap bubbles and the seriousness of his wife's face) gives us some hope that for Robinson, careful attention to the details of a person's life must nevertheless play an important role in appreciating their soul.

We see evidence for this in *Jack* too. As Della develops the idea of what it would mean to see a person as Christ does, it becomes clear that a person's earthly qualities are far from irrelevant. In the same passage where Della claims to have seen the "glorious presence" of Jack's soul, she also discusses Christ's refusal to judge. She says, "But since it's your soul I've seen, I know better than to think about you the way people do when they judge. The Lord says 'Judge not,' because when He looks at people, He just sees souls" (*Jack* 209). Apparently, Della sees (or at least has "seen") Jack in a way not so different from how she imagines Christ seeing him. This means not only that she sees no more "guilt" or "injury" or "failure" than she would in a flame but also—as we noticed in the opening cemetery scene—that she sees the little things in him. Recall that Della tells Jack "there has to be a Jesus, to say 'beautiful' about things no one else would ever see. The precious things should be looked to, whatever becomes of the rest of it" (*Jack* 74). By the "precious things," Della seems to have in mind precisely the details of a person that their soul purports to transcend, things as mundane as the color of Robby's hair or the scar under Jack's eye. This means that seeing someone properly—as Christ would and as Della does—involves both noticing those details and transcending them. But how?

In his recent book on the life and work of the painter Edvard Munch, Karl Ove Knausgaard begins with a reflection on Munch's *Cabbage Field* (1915). He writes:

> Sometimes it is impossible to say why and how a work of art achieves its effect. I can stand in front of a painting and become filled with emotions and thoughts, evidently transmitted by the painting, and yet it is impossible to trace those emotions and thoughts back to it and say, for example, that the sorrow came from the colours, or that the longing

came from the brushstrokes, or that the sudden insight that life will end lay in the motif.⁹

When Knausgaard contemplates Munch's *Cabbage Field* he has such an experience. He sees death, "as if the painting intended reconciliation with death, but a trace of something terrible remains." But, he wonders, how is this possible? After all, "Munch's painting doesn't really say anything, doesn't give form to anything other than cabbages, grain, trees and sky." The painting leaves the viewer with a deep sense of "emptiness," but there on the canvas there is just "Yellow and green, blue and orange."¹⁰

Knausgaard puts his finger on an attribute of paintings that human beings seem to share. If asked to say what *Cabbage Field* is "about," it would be missing the point to merely rattle off a list of its properties: cabbages and wheat, mountains and trees, yellow and green. These details may begin to give a sense of what the painting is like, but they no more capture its essence than hair color does a person's soul. Of course, Knausgaard admits that the details on the canvas are all one has to work with. But those same particulars, in other contexts, would fail to give rise to an identical impression. He writes, "Many have painted fields, many have painted dusk; without attaining what this painting so calmly radiates."¹¹ Munch's painting is both only its details and entirely distinct from its details—it is yellow and green, certainly, but also death and emptiness.

Della perhaps has something like this relationship in mind when she imagines what it means to come into contact with a person's soul. On this analogy, Christian vision is tantamount to aesthetic insight.¹² Della's Jesus sees all of the details of a person—the scars, the small tragedies, the hidden graces—and *in* these "precious things" makes contact with something that utterly transcends them: the beauty of a soul. When pressed to explain the ground of this beauty, one might cite particular details, but such an answer inevitably misses the point. It is not any one trait (or even a collection of particularly flattering traits) that makes a person beautiful but the way in which all these details, even the homely ones, exist together. Seeing the material details of a person is, thus, a first and necessary step in seeing their soul.

While nowhere in Robinson's fiction is a person's soul likened to the subject of a painting, in *Gilead* Ames offers a comparison that both makes a similar point and draws attention to an additional one. In the closing pages of Ames's reflections, he writes, "It has seemed to me sometimes as though the Lord breathes on this poor gray ember of Creation and it turns to radiance—for a moment or a year or the span of a life" (*Gilead* 245). Clearly, in this example, the material features of the coal are in service to the fiery "radiance" that can, in the right circumstances, shine forth. At the same time though, the glow of the ember does not eclipse these features as much as cause them to appear all the brighter. Here, we see again a kind of feedback loop that will be familiar to both the lover of art and, as in Della's case, the lover of human beings. An experience that begins in the small appreciation of the details—a brushstroke or scar— gives rise to a larger sense of a thing's beauty. The latter, however, only draws one's attention back again to the details.

Though the painting analogy may be able to motivate the thought that appreciating the earthly qualities of a person's life is, for Della and Ames, a necessary part of loving a "soul," it may also raise a new concern: namely, that all paintings (and analogously people) are basically, beneath all their idiosyncratic traits, the same. Where with any particular Munch painting, we might discern a unique subject (say, one of death or emptiness or unfulfilled longing), Della seems to speak of human souls as all having, more or less, the same effect on a person. They are all beautiful, and "if you love God," equally worthy of loyalty and sacrifice. In other words, we have yet to answer the original question we posed to Della: *Why Jack?*

3 Loving Every Soul Equally

Having initially worried that Della's loyalty to Jack was built on something entirely distinct from his actual person, we examined passages that suggest there is no necessary conflict between loving someone's immortal soul and appreciating the particular details of their life. We saw that Della looks to cultivate a Christ-like vision of Jack, and she suggests that this implies noticing both the precious little things and the anonymously eternal. We then turned to an aesthetic analogy to make sense of how this might be possible. All of this was mustered with the thought of motivating the idea that Della's love is, despite appearances, sensitive to the particulars of Jack's person. However, it now seems that even if that line of reasoning is basically valid, it may still be insufficient. As sensitive as Della's appreciation of Jack may be, she suggests that careful attention paid to any human being leads to exactly the same kind of loyalty. This suggests, then, that her response to the world is not seriously guided by the particular features she happens to notice: all people, no matter their idiosyncrasies, demand the same generic response. Here again, we might worry that this entails world indifference. When a person is genuinely attuned to life, they vary their responses according to its unique features.

In *Works of Love* (1847), Søren Kierkegaard addresses this same issue as he defends against a similar worry. Starting from a presupposition not so different from Della's—"if you love God"—he argues that a person has a duty to love their neighbor unconditionally and, anticipating some pharisaical quibbling, specifies that the neighbor is the person you see. This of course raises the worry we've brought to Della—What if the neighbor is not particularly lovable? In response, Kierkegaard has his reader imagine two "artists" who represent two ways of loving. The first artist says, "I have traveled much and seen much in the world, but I have sought in vain to find a person worth painting. I have found no face that was the perfect image of beauty to such a degree that I could decide to sketch it; in every face I have seen one or another little defect, and therefore I seek in vain." Kierkegaard then asks the reader, "Would this be a sign that this artist is a great artist?" Assuming not, he introduces the second artist who says,

> Well, I do not actually profess to be an artist; I have not traveled abroad either but stay at home with the little circle of people who

are closest to me, since I have not found one single face to be so insignificant or so faulted that I still could not discern a more beautiful side and discover something transfigured in it. That is why, without claiming to be an artist, I am happy in the art I practice and find it satisfying.

Kierkegaard now asks,

> Would this not be a sign that he [the second artist] is indeed the artist, he who by bringing a certain something with him found right on the spot what the well-traveled artist did not find anywhere in the world—perhaps because he did not bring a certain something with him! Therefore the second of the two would be the artist. Would it not really be sad if what is intended to beautify life could only be like a curse upon it, so that, instead of making life beautiful for us, "art" only fastidiously discovered that none of us is beautiful!

Kierkegaard finally makes the connection to love:

> Would it not be even sadder, as well as even more confused, if love, too, would be only a curse because its requirement could only make it obvious that none of us is worth loving, rather than that love would be known by the very fact that it is loving enough to be able to find something lovable in all of us, that is, loving enough to be able to love all of us![13]

Kierkegaard's example is helpful, but not because it offers a satisfying answer to the *why Jack* question. (Kierkegaard's answer is just as blunt as Della's: because you see him!) Instead, Kierkegaard motivates the idea that there is a special kind of person who, through the close care and attention she extends to the people around her, is able to see anyone as beautiful. Understood in this way, Kierkegaard suggests it is actually his first artist—the one who sees beauty only in the rare and exotic—who is insensitive to the world. It takes an especially attentive and aesthetically adept person to see something remarkable in the apparently homely. The true life-affirmer, Kierkegaard claims, loves life come what may, even in an Iowan backwater or in the company of Jack Boughton.[14]

The type of person Kierkegaard praises is not so different from the John Ames of *Gilead* or the Glory of *Home*. Arguably, their ability to marvel at the beauty of their modest, even difficult, lives is among the characteristics that most impresses the reader. This suggests that when it is depicted well, readers are more than able to appreciate the kind of prodigal love that seems initially questionable in Della. The difference between the two cases is that with Della, because of Robinson's narrative approach,[15] one rarely gets to see Jack through her eyes.

This issue of Della's motivational opacity nicely parallels a topic she is eager to discuss in the early cemetery scene: the curious behavior of the characters in *Hamlet*, which hints, she thinks, at the existence of some text-behind-the-text that gives the reader necessary, but missing, background information. In *Hamlet*, but perhaps also in *Jack*, the reader has to look closely for clues that indicate there is a larger story to tell. In Della's case, the hints are there, and they are illuminating.

To begin with, it is important to appreciate both Della's status as a poet and the particular poets she claims to love. According to Jack, poetry (and especially the work of William Carlos Williams) has the ability to infuse even the most pedestrian objects with fantastic significance. He says to Della, "When I'm down by the river—that bridge seems like some huge ancient thing that has just leapt out of the earth, all mass and clay and fossils, on its way somewhere—everything seems like a metaphor, you don't need to know for what. After you read that book [Williams's *Paterson*]" (*Jack* 115).

Later, Jack again suggests something similar as he prepares to meet Della's sister:

> He could be very nice to the sister-in-law, who was not herself very nice. He would put the little volume of Frost in his pocket—"I have been one acquainted with the night. / I have walked out in rain—and back in rain." An honest account of himself, yet somehow romantic. Poetry does that, another perjured witness. Maybe he liked poetry because it also could not help lying. Oh well. (*Jack* 235)

Jack's reference to a "perjured witness"—a phrase itself plagiarized from Shakespeare—introduces some ambiguity into the matter, but it is clear that the poet is again depicted as exercising an alternative form of vision. Likening the poet's gaze to that other "perjured witness," the so-called "eye of the beholder," Jack is content, this time at least, to be seen in a more favorable light than he deserves—or so he thinks. What he does not allow for is that the poet might actually be a truth-teller, that she is reporting back—as Della might say, through a "keyhole"— not on a world of her own making but on an aspect of the world already present and often overlooked. Yes, the poet may eventually be indicted for perjury, but only by the authorities of "common sense," that coterie of "high principle[d]" men who, Della tells us, talk about turning the other cheek on Sunday only to advise prudence on Monday (*Jack* 95, 248).

Della's own interest in poetry suggests she is more than prepared to see past the pretense of Monday morning common sense and actually "[w]elcome the stranger" (*Jack* 95). In fact, this theme—seeing the beautiful in the hidden and the lowly—is a recurrent motif in Paul Laurence Dunbar's *Oak and Ivy*, the other book (and a prized one) that Jack steals from Della after their first meeting. Two poems in particular seem important in this respect. The first, titled "A Career," gives voice to a poet-protagonist straining to be heard. The first stanza begins emphatically, "Break me my bounds, and let me fly / To regions vast of boundless sky"; and ends in triumph, "As planets have their satellites, / So round about me will I bind / The men who prize a master mind!" Aside from its defiant reference to commonplace "rules / That serve to lead the mind of fools!" the first, long stanza doesn't obviously recall any particular details of *Jack*, either the novel or its namesake. (In fact, the internal voice of Jack is considerably quieter and less torrentially ambitious.) However, there is a dramatic shift from the first stanza to the second. The latter, no longer in the voice of the protagonist, reads: "He lived a silent life alone, / And laid him down when it was done; / And at his head was placed a stone / On which was carved a name unknown!"[16] The ecstatic verve of the poem's first half is never consummated, as the poet lives and dies in silent obscurity. It is possible for there to be an utter and complete divide between one's inner life—

articulate, perceptive, painfully alive—and what other people finally notice. Dunbar himself, in a letter of thanks to the critic who introduces him to the reading world, gives the impression that he could have easily met the same fate. He writes, "I can tell you nothing about myself because there is nothing to tell. My whole life has been simple, obscure and uneventful. I have written my little pieces and sometimes recited them, but it seemed hardly by my own volition."[17] Della, a Black woman living in the South, knows all too well how complete the disguise of a "simple, obscure and uneventful life" can be. Her admiration for Dunbar, evident in her worn and cherished copy of *Oak and Ivy*, has—one can only assume—further sharpened her sense that there is almost always more than meets the eye.

A second Dunbar poem, "Life," seems specifically designed to illustrate poetry's "perjurious" capacity. It reads:

> A crust of bread and a corner to sleep in,
> A minute to smile and an hour to weep in,
> A pint of joy to a peck of trouble,
> And never a laugh but the moans come double;
>   And that is life!
>
> A crust and a corner that love makes precious,
> With a smile to warm and the tears to refresh us;
> And joy seems sweeter when cares come after,
> And a moan is the finest of foils for laughter;
>   And that is life![18]

Like the first poem, "Life" allows the reader to see the same scene from two different perspectives, but this time with redemption at the end. Things that to many will seem to justify the conclusion that life is more trouble than it's worth—hunger, poverty, sorrow—are recast as not just elements that can be compensated for but experiences that themselves lend an extra sweetness to life's small joys. What initially reads, in the first stanza, as an exclamation of woeful exhaustion—"And that is life!"—is altogether transformed in the final sentence of the poem where the same words call the reader to celebration.

When paired with "A Career," the final stanza of "Life" is all the more remarkable, as it creates room for grace where in the former despair looms. Perhaps it is precisely the stark anonymity that ends "A Career" that makes space for the poet to discover that a moan can be "the finest of foils for laughter." The poet who learns this lesson needn't fear "a silent life alone." More to the point, Della Miles—someone who has spent considerable time internalizing these lines of Dunbar—is exactly the kind of person who might consider such a life with Jack Boughton.

It is Della's apparent frustration with the kinds of people who tend not to extend charity to the likes of Jack that gives us another hint about her state of mind that night in the cemetery. In a later conversation with Jack, in which he again cautions her against further involvement, the question of Della's father is raised. He tells her, "I'm just saying what your father would say. Don't take in strays" (*Jack* 95). Della replies, "My father would never say that." At first, this seems to highlight a virtue in Della's father, but what Della says next casts it in a different light. She continues, "They [people like her father] always talk as though the world has ended. Turn the other cheek. Welcome the stranger. All right. Then they say, Well, you do have to exercise a little common sense" (*Jack* 95). It is important to notice that "talking as though the world has ended"—the drawn-out hypothetical entertained by Jack and Della in the darkness of Bellefontaine—is, in Della's mind, a way of talking like Jesus, of saying, "Turn the other cheek. Welcome the Stranger." That night in the cemetery Della was trying to develop a *Christian* vision. It turns out that while Della's father talks like Jesus, he doesn't live like him. He is, in other words, a hypocrite.

Jack calls people like Della's father "men of high principle" and adds that they make him—the self-proclaimed Prince of Darkness—"feel pretty harmless" (*Jack* 248). These men (in the Gilead books they are always men) are especially destructive because they purport to represent God's cause but understand it in narrow terms. In the case of Ames's grandfather, he claims Jesus literally appears and directly implores him to take up the cause of the enslaved in Kansas. When his own family fails to fall in line with this vision, Ames's grandfather is quick to remind them that they are a disappointment (*Gilead* 84). He makes Christ's specific invitation so totalizing and pursues it with such unchecked zeal that he is blinded to the damage he does to the people right in front of him. It is no surprise then that his own son, Ames's father, rejects the idea of visions altogether. Ames, for his own part, must (and does) find another way: an understanding of vision that resolves the tension between his grandfather and father.[19]

In the case of Della's father, there is a strict commitment to the politics of Black separatism. He tells Jack,

> My family and many of our friends have devoted ourselves to a certain way of life, one meant to develop self-sufficiency in the Negro race by the practice of separatism, so far as this is possible in society as it exists now. I know there are white people who are offended by separatism, but the alternatives also offend them. I'm not asking your opinion about this. My point is that my objection is not to you as an individual. (*Jack* 305)

The last line underscores the tragic irony of Bishop Miles's position. Presumably, this plan of action is designed to address actual injustice—something Christ surely deplores. At the same time, the bishop's inflexible commitment to this particular way of "loving his neighbor" requires him to, on principle, ignore "the stranger" even when he literally knocks on his front door. When Miles meets Jack in Memphis, he makes this crystal clear: "You can never be welcome here. I want you to understand that." Their conversation ends when he hands Jack an envelope of money, to which Jack responds, "Christian of you." Miles replies, revealing just how complete his blindness has become, "You should be very grateful that I am a Christian man" (*Jack* 306).

Della's disappointment in her father's hypocrisy, while obviously extending to the way he treats people like Jack, seems to begin much earlier. Recall Della's confession from the cemetery scene:

> My father never had much time to spend at home. He's sort of a leader in the community, I guess. He gets called away constantly. He spends

lots of time with lots of people, trying to sort things out for them. It comes with serving a big church in a city. Especially a colored church, I think. He always made us show him our homework and our report cards, but he says he has a thousand children to look after, and that's true. (*Jack* 30)

This early admission foreshadows the speech Bishop Miles will eventually deliver to Jack. One can even imagine the bishop reassuring young Della, perhaps on a night when one of his other "thousand children" demands his attention: "[M]y objection is not to you as an individual." While this may be true in theory, in practice—for Della and later Jack—the distinction, at best, fails to offer any real relief and, at worst, clarifies the deep and disturbing discord between "high-principled" Christianity and Jesus's radical call to notice the "precious things." One can only assume that Della's own sense of vocation has been deeply informed by this schism.

Having now followed two leads into her background, Della's openness toward Jack looks increasingly plausible. When we add to this the darkness of the cemetery scene, conditions that lend themselves not to fantasy but seeing differently,[20] Della's sympathy for Jack begins to take on a degree of inevitability. Though this does not answer the question of why Jack in particular,[21] it, at least, helps us imagine that Della might not be so different from characters in the Gilead world who have made similar decisions with less opprobrium. One such character is John Ames, and in *Gilead*, worrying about Lila's growing affection for Jack, he seems to anticipate Della's predicament. He writes, "It is one of the best traits of good people that they love where they pity. And this is truer of women than of men." Expressing the tension readers encounter in Della, he continues, "[T]hey get themselves drawn into situations that are harmful to them. I have seen this happen many, many times. I have always had trouble finding a way to caution against it. Since it is, in a word, Christlike" (*Gilead* 186–7).

While Ames seems to believe that the kind of sacrificial love Della offers Jack is commendable (or at least "Christlike"), some are less convinced. Taking Ames's own case as an example, Robinson has come under scrutiny for romanticizing characters who themselves wax poetic about the incandescence of the world while remaining blind to the social ills growing in their own backyard.[22] Ames's apparent ignorance (or worse, apathy) concerning the not-so-subtle racism in Gilead is cited as a prominent example. He never indicates that he is aware of the larger social significance of the fire at Gilead's Black church, and—even more concerning—seems to have had only a passing acquaintance with the congregation's pastor (*Gilead* 36–7). One recent critic, not altogether unsympathetic to Robinson's vision, puts the challenge this way:

> A question that the Gilead novels raise implacably, if quietly, is whether the vision of that sun shining on us all can rescue the church from the forgetfulness that has settled over everything, forgetfulness that enables an "intractable whiteness." Do you see God everywhere? Now what will you do?[23]

In closing, we should ask whether Della's vision of Jack obscures a larger responsibility to her community.

4 Conclusion

As we discussed in Chapter 4, one of the more memorable scenes in all the Gilead novels (and actually depicted in two of them) is the Sunday when Jack, back at home with his father and sister, gathers the courage to attend Ames's church. In *Home*, we discover this decision is weeks in the making and an event that Jack places considerable hope in. However, because it is Jack, his attempt at goodwill is fated to backfire; Ames delivers a sermon, extempore, that seems designed to expose Jack's many failings, most prominently the abandonment of his infant daughter.

In *Jack*, unbelievably, we see this happen twice more, as Jack befriends a Baptist minister (Reverend Hutchins) who then *seems* to deliver sermons especially aimed at Jack's faults. (This receives a comical twist in *Jack* as others in the congregation, quite visibly—with tears and sweat—draw similarly self-involved conclusions about the pastor's specific intentions.) The second of the two sermons is an exposition of Matthew 25,[24] Jesus's discourse on the "least of these," the fragile and vulnerable who are set apart as objects of special care. The pastor then turns to the unique responsibility of "teaching," which he calls a "sacred vocation, right up there with preaching and prophesying" (*Jack* 272). He emphasizes the added weight of educating Black children, noting, "It wasn't so long ago that a man had to anchor a raft in the middle of the Mississippi River to teach our children at the high-school level, because it was illegal to do that in Missouri and in Illinois." He then commends a particular high school where Della happens to teach. He says,

> Now we have Sumner High School, where this very sacred work goes on today. It is a rare thing among us to enjoy a real education, and it is a heavy burden on us that schooling is what we lack. So those among us who are teachers are like pearls and rubies, the best help we can find for our children. Our teachers must be honored and assisted in this sacred work— (*Jack* 272-3)

It is these last lines that capture Jack's attention. The pastor knows that Jack's involvement with Della threatens to jeopardize her work at the school, and that on the whole, this would be a grave loss for the community. Simply put, Jack—one measly, lost soul—isn't worth the price.

Of course, we know that Della could not disagree more. Instead, thinking back on what we have surmised about her, we can presume she sees her commitment to Jack less as duty-driven "sacred vocation" than a beautiful fulfillment of her life. As in Glory's case, it would be entirely mistaken to see Della's commitment to Jack as just another instance of "good Christian service." She doesn't move to St. Louis in order to pursue, as her Father might have encouraged, some grand social plan. Instead, Della looks, in a way that "men of high principle" will never understand, to share her humble fate with a few forlorn souls. When she meets such a soul, one of just a few she claims to have ever seen, she loves him by first extending her friendship and later her love.

In *Jack*, along with the other novels, Robinson uses characters like Bishop Miles to illustrate the way in which certain abstract, broad, and inflexible approaches to loving "the least of these" can lead to moral blindness. Nowhere is this tragedy more powerfully felt than in the case of Ames's grandfather, who claims to have received his vocation directly from Jesus. Having adopted "too narrow an idea of what a vision might be," and taking no small amount of personal pride in its execution, Ames Sr.'s life ends in bitterness and disappointment, estranged from his family and with "nowhere to spend his courage, no way to feel it in himself" (*Gilead* 91, 47). In his final estimate, Ames writes, "He may, so to speak, have been too dazzled by the great light of his experience to realize that an impressive sun shines on us all" (*Gilead* 91).

But perhaps the grandfather's blindness is no worse than the social indifference some readers find in Ames. A careful reading of *Gilead* just does not bear this out. The "hero" of that novel seems to only just come into himself in the waning pages of his testimony. Ames's reflections on the goodness of existence, culminating in the unforeseen blessing of fatherhood, lead finally to a deeper recognition of the ways in which he has failed to honor the great gift of life. Most conspicuously, this leads to reconciliation with Jack, but it also allows him to see that he has done too little to love the town of Gilead.[25] Among his concluding thoughts, we read:

> I woke up this morning thinking this town might as well be standing on the absolute floor of hell for all the truth there is in it, and the fault is mine as much as anyone's. . . . It seems to me now we never looked up from the trouble we had just getting by to put the obvious question, that is, to ask what it was the Lord was trying to make us understand. The word "preacher" comes from an old French word, prédicateur, which means prophet. And what is the purpose of a prophet except to find meaning in trouble? (*Gilead* 233)

This note of lament suggests that the development of a social conscience is, for Robinson, never separable from "seeing God everywhere." Where Robinson appears to depart from some of her contemporaries is in her repeated insistence that such a conscience must always remain accountable to the specific needs of specific people. One cannot, Robinson suggests, love the neighbor without loving a particular neighbor, and in order to do this one has to cultivate the eye of an artist, exercising, as Nietzsche says, patience with a thing's "appearance and expression, and kindheartedness about its oddity" (GS 334). Having done this, one is confronted with a "new and indescribable beauty," what Della calls a "glorious presence." Nietzsche believes the beauty of this vision is more than sufficient recompense for one's hospitality, and Della—noting the same—insists that such a vision means "every choice is made for you" (*Jack* 208).

Notes

1. See, for example: Garner (2020); Row (2020); and Libman (2020). The negative reviews of *Jack* are all the more remarkable given the near universal praise critics expressed for the other Gilead books.
2. Kisner (2020).
3. See, especially, Garner (2020).
4. See, especially, Libman (2020).
5. This criticism takes an especially pointed form in Douglas (2011). Row (2020) makes the same point in his review of *Jack*. He writes, "'Jack' is, like the other books in [Robinson's Gilead] series, an act of wishful or even magical thinking. It works as a story about individuals transcending their racialized world only by treating racism as a vague evil perpetuated offscreen, to be overcome by virtuous intentions."
6. We later discover that Jack has buried a picture of his deceased daughter in the cemetery. This seems to be the birthday he is "commemorating" (*Jack* 213).
7. It seems significant that Della prefaces the claim about purity with the modifier "[i]n your own way." Though she sometimes uses language that suggests she sees Jack's soul as a kind of undefiled flame, other passages—including this one—suggest her view is more complicated.
8. Kisner (2020) writes, "One begins to sympathize with Della's relatives in their frantic attempts to shield her from him. Their refusal to see Jack's

love for her as at all moral or redemptive furthers the uneasy sense that if one is to root for these two characters, one would root for them to part."
9 Knausgaard (2017, 1).
10 Knausgaard (2017, 2).
11 Ibid.
12 Ames, himself, embraces the aesthetic metaphor. He writes, "Calvin says somewhere that each of us is an actor on a stage and God is the audience. That metaphor has always interested me, because it makes us artists of our behavior, and the reaction of God to us might be thought of as aesthetic rather than morally judgmental in the ordinary sense" (*Gilead* 124).
13 Kierkegaard (1995, 158).
14 In her essay "Imagination and Community," Robinson defends a virtue she calls "imaginative love" that suggests deep agreement with Kierkegaard. She writes, "I think fiction may be, whatever else, an exercise in imaginative love, or sympathy, or identification" (*When I Was a Child* 21). By this, Robinson means not just that it nourishes a deep sympathy for those who venture to write it, but also that it trains one to attend to the unlikely loveliness of people they would never think to consider (22). This use of the moral imagination is, Robinson claims, "the thing most conducive to human health, individual and global" (26); it is "[d]emocracy, in its essence and genius" (27–8).
15 The book is narrated with free indirect discourse with special access to Jack's thoughts.
16 Dunbar (2004, 5).
17 Quoted in Martin (2004, xii).
18 Dunbar (2004, 8).
19 Andrew Stout makes this point nicely, referring to Ames's vision as "a way of seeing which is forged in an attempt to avoid the extremes of the preceding generations. Visions are not simply to be sought in a dramatic and unmediated way, as his grandfather insists, but neither are they to be rejected altogether, as his father appears to do" (2014, 585).
20 Della says the darkness makes Jack's "atmosphere" palpable (*Jack* 48). One also recalls Ames's claim that "Trees sound different at night, and they smell different, too" (*Gilead* 71).
21 Earlier in the chapter, we turned to Kierkegaard in order to argue that this question (*Why Jack?*) may be less relevant to the issue of Della's apparent

life-denial than initially suspected. Kierkegaard argues that it takes an especially *attentive* person to see beauty everywhere.

22 For discussions of this issue see Douglas (2011), Gonzalez (2021), Row (2020), and Spinks (2017).
23 Gonzalez (2021).
24 Both of the sermons reference Matthew 25.
25 Spinks (2017, 145), who is otherwise critical of Ames's racial "repression," makes this point as well. He writes, "[Ames's] encounters with Jack Boughton are expressly designed by Robinson to enact a type of 'rememory' of the past which compels him to confront the continuing trauma of African-American disenfranchisement."

6

Lila

More Life than We Can Bear

In *Gilead*, Reverend John Ames claims that one great advantage of his line of work is the invitation to see a soul close-up. In each of the Gilead novels this vision is described as the source of an unbreakable bond—seeing a person and loving a person are intimately connected. Through creative attention, Robinson looks to extend this experience to her readers, and, as the reader becomes immersed in this fictive world, they cannot help but feel deep reverence for Robinson's characters. This sense of respect is primarily rooted in each character's personality (or "existence"), but it also extends to their presentation of a particular way of life. Sometimes, as we have already seen with Ruth and Ames, these lives appear to be in tension with one another. Moving from one novel to the next, Robinson often seems keen to interrogate past models. She does so not through direct criticism of her characters but through a compelling presentation of existential alternatives. If there really are a "thousand thousand reasons to live this life," it would be a mistake to fixate on just one.

Robinson's fourth novel, *Lila*, is a prime example of this dialectical impulse. As readers have noted, it marks a return to the terrain of *Housekeeping*.[1] Both novels center on strong female characters struggling to make sense of their lives in the wake of personal tragedy, and both novels explore the ways in which the active cultivation of loneliness can shelter a person from further pain. In Chapter 2, we argued that this tactic, considered as an approach to life, is not existentially neutral— Ruth succeeds in protecting herself from harm by removing herself from the world. The implicit nihilism of this maneuver is made all the more apparent in contrast to the exuberant life-affirmation of John Ames. In this case, the beauty of Ames's approach to life really does seem to be grounded in something like the negation of Ruth's approach. This strict division, however, is overly simplistic, and Robinson looks to complicate it in the character of Lila. She does this in two important respects. First, she suggests that Ruth's isolation and loneliness do not have to be final; there are ways to address pain and loss that include continued openness to relationship. Second, she suggests that acute suffering, especially in the form of social rejection, may actually be preparation for the kind of love we see hints of in Ames. This doesn't just mean that someone like Ruth might one day see the world through Ames's eyes, as though her task is merely to become Ames. Robinson's claim is stronger: Ruth (and Lila) may be in a *better* position than Ames to cultivate the kind of love and life-affirmation displayed in *Gilead*. There are good reasons to think that the Ames of that text—a man who eventually extends grace to Jack—exists only because of Lila's prior intervention.

If *Lila* can be read as an interrogation of Ames, it must also include a critical appraisal of his Christianity. One of our primary claims is that Ames's faith, far from being an obstacle to his love of life, actively deepens it. This idea flies in the face of a prominent strand of German thought extending at least as far back as the Romantics and culminating in the incisive critiques of Nietzsche. This continental approach to Robinson's fiction is not just the brainchild of philosophy professors, it is explicitly invited by the texts themselves. In *Gilead*, one of Ames's main dialogue partners is his older brother Edward. Edward spends his college years in Germany and returns with an imposing mustache and a self-authored monograph on the philosophy of Ludwig Feuerbach. Taking it upon himself to enlighten his younger brother, Edward gifts young Ames with a copy of Feuerbach's *The Essence of Christianity*, a text that played a prominent role in converting a whole generation of European intellectuals to atheism. As we saw (in Chapter 3), the gift backfires. Ames comes to regard Feuerbach as a great companion in faith, "as good on the joyful aspects of religion as anybody."

In Chapter 1, we reviewed the main tenets of Feuerbach's "projection theory." Though this thesis is the source of *The Essence*'s atheistic renown, arguably it is far less destabilizing than the claims made in its penultimate chapter: "The Contradiction of Faith and Love." In this later chapter, Feuerbach argues that there is an irresolvable contradiction internal to faith itself. Christianity's emphasis on dogmatic purity—the idea that right belief is necessary for salvation—prevents it from plausibly claiming to be a religion of love. Faith is by nature exclusive; love is by nature universal. Though this thesis is far less original than the core claims of *The Essence*, Feuerbach makes a strong rhetorical case. Anticipating Nietzsche, he offers an ingenious analysis of the unseemly pleasure the believer takes in his *exclusive* election. Being favored by the divine is not enough; all others must be damned.

The exclusivity of Christianity and of Gilead are not separate issues, and Robinson sees that she must, even if only implicitly, return to Feuerbach. If, as Ames insists, Feuerbach is wrong to think that Christianity gets in the way of joy, then surely he must also be wrong in insisting that Christianity is incompatible with love. The testing ground for this experiment is Lila herself. How far can Christianity extend to include her in its narrative of redemption? This chapter looks to shine light on this issue by steadily developing the arc that spans Lila's early experiences of shame and loneliness to the eventual restoration she discovers in Gilead. We see this restoration confirmed in Lila's baptism, but locate this in an unlikely place: the moment she "washes it off." This reverse-baptism, we argue, is where Robinson locates the true *imitatio Christi*: a decision to court divine judgment for the sake of one's "brethren" and "kinsmen," as St. Paul puts it. Next, we explore the way in which the love that drives Lila to her reverse-baptism expands through her gradual embrace of Christian concepts, especially through the idea of resurrection. We also see how Ames, under pressure from Lila herself, recommends a biblical hermeneutic that emphasizes this-worldly praxis. As Ames puts it, "Thinking about hell doesn't help me live the way I should" (*Lila* 101). Lila agrees and, with this insight, is prepared to expand Ames's experience of grace.

1 Ruth's Homecoming

As we saw in Chapter 2, Robinson's first novel, *Housekeeping*, ends with Ruth and Sylvie setting the family home on fire and crossing the bridge that leads away from town. For both, home has become impossible. Experiences of personal loss, of a mother to suicide and a father in a train wreck, have been an education in sorrow. Traditional sources of domestic protection—family, home, community—seem to offer no help, as they themselves constitute the very material of tragedy. The only answer is to sever all ties to the world, to guard against pain and loneliness by making it absolute. With this as their last hope, Ruth and Sylvie embrace homelessness and spend the following years drifting from place to place. In the final pages of the novel, we see the fulfillment of their escape: Ruth is now a ghostly figure, haunting the living through her absence. Neither she nor the ones she has left behind are at rest.

In *Lila*, Robinson is not subtle in connecting her title character back to Ruth. At the opening of the novel, we find Lila, just "four or five," on a stoop, "hugging herself against the cold" (*Lila* 3). As she whimpers, there is a shout: "Shut that thing up or I'll do it!" Then someone appears: "Why you keep pounding at the screen door? Nobody gonna want you around if you act like that. And then the door closed again, and after a while night came." Later, a woman walking the path comes upon Lila in the dark. She takes Lila "up in her arms and [wraps] her into her shawl, and [says], 'Well, we got no place to go. Where we gonna go?'" Doll, herself displaced, adopts Lila as her own. The narrator tells us that she "may have been the loneliest woman in the world, and [Lila] the loneliest child." As if this unfortunate superlative wasn't enough to evoke *Housekeeping*'s forlorn pair, Lila later imagines her father riding a train off a cliff (*Lila* 204).

2 Shame, Mistrust, and Loneliness

As with her literary forebears, Lila's early life is one of shame, mistrust, and loneliness. Though Lila and Doll find a provisional community in a group of itinerant workers, even as a young child Lila knows they are different—"She asked Doll one time, What are we, then? and Doll had said, We're just folks. But Lila could tell that wasn't true, that there was more to it anyway. Why this shame?" (*Lila* 47). For Lila, in a reversal of *Gilead*'s exultant claim that "There is more beauty than our eyes can bear," rejection is the dominant theme: "There was more shame in life than she could bear" (*Lila* 57). She likens her shame to a "habit," the only thing she feels except when she is alone (*Lila* 86).

Robinson uses one image in particular to communicate Lila and Doll's shame: their "ugly" faces. Doll, especially, is marked by "ugliness," a description that even Lila embraces, though not without sympathy (*Lila* 47). As we later discover, Doll becomes dramatically scarred when she is struck in the face. "You know how I got this scar?" she asks Lila. "A girl just as crazy as you're getting to be heated up an iron skillet as hot as she could make it, and then when I come in the kitchen she hit me with it. Broke the bone in my cheek and who knows what all." This confession is a cloaked warning to stay away from the whorehouses, suggesting that Doll herself had spent time as a prostitute. The scarlet burn serves as a grotesquely public marker of Doll's felt inferiority: "People would try to figure out that mark. . . . It was an astonishment to them. They would stare at it before they realized what they were doing, and Doll would just stand there waiting till they were done, till they looked past her and spoke past her." Most of the time, the pillory is too much: "[Doll] always stayed back from the firelight even when the night was cold and even when there were no strangers there to see." Lila was the "only one she ever really trusted to look into her face" (*Lila* 106).

Lila's ugliness, while less dramatic, is no less engrained in her self-understanding. In the early pages of the novel, just after rescuing Lila from the stoop, Doll considers what to call her. The name "Lila" is suggested because it is a "pretty name"; "maybe she could turn out pretty" (*Lila* 10). As we later discover, this early hope—that she might turn out—seems less a product of the ambiguity of her child-features than a reaction to a blossoming homeliness. The freckled face that leads her grade-school teacher to wonder whether she might be "Norwegian" receives a considerably less gracious reception at the brothel where Lila—against Doll's warning—eventually arrives. "They put powder on her face to try to hide the freckles, and purple lipstick, and pink rouge." Noting the general hopelessness of the cause, the house manager (the "Mrs.") warns, "You ain't a pretty girl, but you might try smiling"; another offers, "Just pretend you're pretty so they can pretend you're pretty." Later, when Lila is in Gilead, Ames mentions the welcome effect of seeing her face for the first time. She interrupts, "Don't talk like that. I know about my face" (*Lila* 85).

These references to Doll's and Lila's faces are enough to reveal shame is a defining feature of their lives. Even still, Robinson takes the image further, introducing a deeper theological element. After reading a characteristically strange passage from the book of Ezekiel ("And they had the hands of a man under their wings on their four sides; and they four had their faces and their wings thus . . ."), Lila considers the significance of a face. She reflects,

> If you think about a human face, it can be something you don't want to look at, so sad or so hard or so kind. It can be something you want to hide, because it pretty well shows where you've been and what you can expect. And anybody at all can see it, but you can't. It just floats there in front of you. *It might as well be your soul*, for all you can do to protect it. (Emphasis added, *Lila* 82)

The association of the face with the soul will turn out to play an important role in Lila's eventual healing, but, until then, it serves to sharpen Lila's sense of rejection. Putting aside the mean and shallow taunts of the prostitutes, we see that even Doll fails to find anything remarkable in Lila's face, and this in spite of much attention. We read, for instance, "Doll touched the soap and tears off [Lila's] face with the hem of her apron" (*Lila* 7); and "She'd go scrubbing at her face with a wet rag" (*Lila* 4); and "she would put her face close up to the child's face, to stare at her" (*Lila* 12). All of this sets up a more telling interaction where Doll arranges a meeting with an old widower, looking to marry Lila into stability. After the introduction fails, and Lila is sent away with a silver dollar, Doll surveys the situation: "You shouldn'ta took it." And then she says, "He would've been good to you. That's what matters. You got to do the best you can, and be grateful for whatever comes of it." Finally: "after looking at her for a moment, mildly and sadly," Doll adds, "If there was just something about you." (*Lila* 115) This cuts deep. Doll has scrubbed, touched, and stared close up; still, there is nothing much to see. These last lines, especially, will not be easily forgotten. They add weight to everything that comes later, including Ames's innocent question, "maybe you could tell me a little about yourself?" (*Lila* 29).

The intense shame experienced by Lila and Doll leads naturally to deep mistrust. We see the seeds of this in the opening pages of the novel when, just after being rescued from the stoop, Lila fights against Doll's attempt to clean her. As the suds drip from her head, Lila screams that Doll "could rot in hell." Doll remarks, "Them's about the only words I ever heard her say" (*Lila* 7). Lila's early and visceral revulsion to the attention of others becomes more refined as she and Doll pick up with a band of itinerant workers. The pair mostly keep to themselves, with Lila refusing to leave Doll's side. Though something like camaraderie eventually develops between the members of the group, Doll knows their invitation extends only as far as their usefulness. As times grow lean and work scarce, Doll senses that the end is near. In her desperation, she leaves Lila to explore other options. Judging that Doll won't be returning, Doane, the group leader, decides that Lila is dead weight and promptly gets rid of her. They walk to a nearby town and leave her on the front steps of a church—Lila is abandoned on the stoop.

Doll eventually finds Lila, but the damage has been done. As Doll calls her from the church steps, Lila refuses to move. "She wanted to rest her head on a bosom more Doll's than Doll herself, to feel trust rise up in her like that sweet old surprise of being carried off in strong arms, wrapped in a gentleness worn all soft and perfect. 'No,' she said, and drew herself away" (*Lila* 54). With equal measures of irony and tragedy, Doll is the source both of Lila's image of protection ("the surprise of being carried off in strong arms") and her conviction that such protection is nowhere to be found.

This mistrust follows Lila to the brothel in St. Louis and, later, to the backwaters of Iowa where she meets John Ames. As she becomes attracted, in spite of herself, to the light and warmth of Ames and his church, she begins to regularly attend services and, with intense self-consciousness, talk to Ames. These first steps toward openness are in themselves remarkable, but they pale in comparison to her later decisions to accept baptism and suggest marriage out of nowhere. While we will have much to say about these two events when we turn to discuss Lila's restoration, for now it is important to notice how these steps by no means signal a clean break with her past. Even after baptism and marriage, trust remains an excruciating barrier.

As, outwardly, Lila seems to be settling into Gilead—attending church, making acquaintances, tending a garden—her anxiety is evident in her inner dialogue.

> [S]tuck in Gilead with no reason to be there and no place to stay, knowing he would never look at her that way again, if he ever really did even once. Staying on anyway because the thought of him was about the best thing she had. Well, she couldn't let that happen. Doll said, Men just don't feel like they sposed to stay by you. They ain't never your friends. Seems like you could trust 'em, they act like you could trust 'em, but you can't. Don't matter what they say. I seen it in my life a hundred times. She said, You got to look after your own self. When it comes down to it, you're going to be doing that anyway. (*Lila* 50)

This word of advice is dredged up from Lila's past not to warn her against a decision she is poised to make but to caution against entanglements already forming. She has let Ames into her life, and now she is going to be hurt. Having "nobody to trust" is framed as a positive achievement, as in the following escape-fantasy where the final words are uttered as a hopeful promise: "She could go to California, where there wouldn't be winter to worry about. Crops coming in all year long. . . . That was a nice thing to think about. She could do it on her own. Nobody to trust" (*Lila* 81–2). We misunderstand Lila if we think the last sentence is a shift in tone, from the happy thought of escape to the sad reality of isolation. Rather, depending on her mood, having "nobody to trust" is not a lament but a "nice thing to think about." On the other hand, we also witness moments when her mood shifts—as it inevitably must—and she feels the full, weary weight of constant mistrust. On the day of her baptism, she confesses to Ames:

> "I want you to marry me! I wish I didn't. It's just a misery for me."
> "For me, too, as it happens."
> "I can't trust you!"
> "I guess that's why I can't trust you."
> "Oh," she said, "that's a fact. I don't trust nobody. I can't stay nowhere. I can't get a minute of rest."
> "Well, if that's how it is, I guess you'd better put your head on my shoulder, after all." (*Lila* 89)

As with ugliness and shame, Robinson uses one image in particular to embody this sense of mistrust: Doll's knife. Apart from Lila, there is nothing that Doll guards with as much care. The knife is described as violently sharp, and Doll's attention to its edge grows in proportion to her insecurity:

> The scrawnier Doll got, the more time she'd spent on that knife, whetting it long after it was as sharp as it ever would be. Sometimes Lila would hear that sound, be waked by it, when Doll had trouble sleeping. Doll carried it open, tied to her leg, so there wouldn't be any problem in using it fast if she had to. (*Lila* 135)

The knife, like Doll's face, is an open secret. Its plain brutality immediately signals the shameful desperation of its owner. At the same time, desperation demands exposing the knife: "When Doll gave Lila her knife she said, 'It's only for scaring folks with. If you go cutting somebody it's going to be trouble no matter what the story is'" (*Lila* 97). Eventually, Doll will have to cut somebody and there *is* trouble. After killing a man, Doll walks out of the story and the knife becomes Lila's burden and bequeath.

Having passed from Doll's hands to Lila's, the knife takes on increased significance. Now, more than just a mark of desperation and shame, it is also an invitation to loyalty and a source of guilt. It is an invitation to loyalty because the knife was Doll's only and dearest possession. In Lila's hand, it is now an heirloom, a precious inheritance from a woman who was as close to family as Lila has come. The knife is also what Ruth of *Housekeeping* would call a "relic"—a leftover from a life recently lost. The relic reminds the living of their lost loved ones, but also the incompleteness of life without them. These objects haunt the present owner demanding, finally, either to be buried or reborn. As an instrument of murder, the knife is also an inheritance of guilt.

To further complicate matters, Lila suspects that the deceased may have been a blood-relative, perhaps even her father. Thus, in receiving the knife, Lila takes on some measure of responsibility for the death of a family member. This sense of guilt only compounds the knife's ambiguity, placing Lila in the twice impossible position of having to guard her shame with an object that only deepens her shame and show loyalty to an object that spilled family blood.

Lila's conflicted relationship to the knife is on display when she arrives at the St. Louis brothel and is asked by the "Mrs." to hand over any valuables. As Lila presents the knife, she thinks, "This is it. I'm here now. This is the life I'm going to have. Mrs. just looked at it lying there in her hand like it was an ugly thing" (*Lila* 191). Later, Lila reflects: "Now I gave her my knife, she's got it locked up, the one thing in the world I had that was mine. And she was glad that she'd given it up" (*Lila* 192). This exchange is poignant for a few reasons. First, Lila makes it clear that she indeed regards the knife as valuable: not only is it her prized possession, it is her only possession. Second, even though the knife is considered dear, she is "glad" to give it up in order to demonstrate her loyalty to the Mrs., the only person of sympathy in her life. At the same time, we know that this "sympathy" is merely nominal. The Mrs. cares for her "daughters" as a pimp for his prostitutes—she is incapable of any genuine affection. Third, we can appreciate why the Mrs.'s unworthiness might be overlooked: the knife is a terrific and ugly burden. Hence, the Mrs.'s both natural and insulting response—she "just looked at it . . . like it was an ugly thing" (*Lila* 191). The tragedy of this exchange is not lost on Lila, and she later imagines Doll asking after the knife: "But where's my knife? Why you let that woman have my knife?" Lila replies, "It's the only thing I had to give her" (*Lila* 197).

Shame leads to mistrust, and mistrust finally to loneliness. Of the three, loneliness is definitive: "[Lila'd] heard people say that a sad woman will have a sad child. A bitter woman will have an angry child. She used to think that if she could decide what it was she felt, as far back as she remembered, she could know that much, at least, about the woman who bore her. Loneliness" (*Lila* 105). As we've already seen, Lila's loneliness has two sides: "[it] was bad, but it was better than anything else she could think of" (Lila 27). Among its benefits is the passing relief it gives from shame. Our narrator tells us, "She sat . . . hidden in the dark, not because she thought anyone would be there but because she always liked the feeling that no one could see her even when she knew she was alone" (*Lila* 20). However, more than just a fleeting experience in the dark, Lila eventually comes to identify completely with her isolation: "it was always there, always the same" (*Lila* 34). When Lila arrives in Gilead, she moves into a small abandoned shack at the outskirts of town. The hovel symbolizes her inner isolation: "in that shack where she still lived because it was hard for her to be with people. It would be truer to say hid than lived, since about the only comfort she had in it was being by herself" (*Lila* 36).

Given the intensity of Lila's early sorrow, it is tempting to divide her life into two clean halves: the pre-Gilead years wherein despair is absolute and the Gilead years marked by restoration. While there is, of course, something roughly right about this division, it ignores the finer details of her story. When we look closer, we see several ways in which Lila's early years contain the seeds of recovery eventually nourished in Gilead.

3 Hints of a Life to Come

There are several significant ways in which we see Lila's later restoration anticipated in the years leading up to Gilead: the love and care she receives from Doll; an intimate introduction to the "strangeness" of existence; an appreciation for the promise of baptism; and, finally, an imagination for happiness.

First, as we've already seen, Doll is Lila's only real experience of love. Doll lifts her out of abandonment, holds her close, and guards her—as best she can—against any dangers. Even if Doll herself will eventually disappoint, her warm embrace becomes the image by which Lila understands and longs for love and safety.

Second, Lila is intimately familiar with what she calls the "strangeness of it all." In response to a letter from Ames in which he discusses the "meaning of existence," the narrator tells us: "She knew a little bit about existence. That was pretty well the only thing she knew about. . . . The evening and the morning, sleeping and waking. Hunger and loneliness and weariness and still wanting more of it. Existence" (74–5). The feeling of "wanting more" is significant here. Lila's early and intense destitution, both physical and spiritual, places her in a position where, by all accounts, she *ought* to despise life. But, she doesn't. In a way that strikes even Lila as inexplicable, she longs for more. She regards human existence—her own and Doll's and all their forlorn companions'—as, beyond all expectation and explanation, deeply wonderful. Thinking about her life before Gilead, she reflects:

> How could it be that none of it mattered? It was most of what happened. But if it did matter, how could the world go on the way it did when there were so many people living the same and worse? Poor was nothing, tired and hungry were nothing. But people only try to get by, and no respect for them at all, even the wind soiling them. No matter how proud and hard they were, the wind making their faces run with tears. That was existence, and why didn't it roar and wrench itself apart like the storm it must be, if so much of existence is all that bitterness and fear? (*Lila* 112)

It is precisely the outlandish juxtaposition between the harshness of their lives and the ability to be disrespected that gives rise to Lila's sense of wonder. Human beings are inappropriately majestic and bizarrely beautiful; this is what makes them such a "strange" fit for the world, "the wind making their faces run with tears" (*Lila* 112).

It is important to appreciate that this sense of gratuity is singularly intense in a state of deprivation. When Lila finally walks through the doors of Ames's church, the narrator tells us, "The candles surprised her. It might all have seemed so beautiful because she'd been missing a few meals. That can make things brighter somehow" (*Lila* 11). A similar thought resurfaces later—"But light made you blind in the dark and there might be something you really needed to see out there" (*Lila* 73). This last passage, while superficially a reference to safety (and a fitting homage to *Housekeeping*'s Ruth and Sylvie), expresses something much deeper: living away from the warmth and light of community bestows upon the hermit a sixth sense, an ability to see what others can't, especially in the dark. This is something Lila eventually brings to Gilead, and not, Robinson suggests, something easily cultivated therein.

A third seed of restoration is found in Lila's early exposure to the beauty of baptism. One of the most significant passages in *Gilead* is John Ames's description of an early scene from his childhood. A church steeple has been burned by lightning and the people of Gilead, both men and women, young and old, gather in the rain to pull it down. The mood is festive, like "a camp meeting," and the people begin to sing hymns: "Blessed Jesus" and "The Old Rugged Cross." In the middle of all this—the singing and the food and the work—Ames's father feeds him a biscuit with a smudge of ash (*Gilead* 94–5). Ames receives it as he would the Eucharist and, in doing so, forever seals in his memory the association of Christ and the beauty of that day. Ames will later describe this moment as a religious vision, and affirm it as the bedrock of his faith.

Lila receives her own vision which parallels many of the details of Ames's. As a young girl, she visits an actual camp meeting, hoping to sell apples to those gathered. As a "mild, clear evening" sets in, lights begin to dance in the trees. She remembers that "Men were hanging lamps ... along the big old oak branches that reached out over the stage ... and the banjos and fiddles that had come along in the crowd began to agree on a song, and the people began to sing it—Yes, we'll gather at the river, The beautiful, the beautiful river." Lila is spellbound, "watching the lanterns sway and the light and the shadows move and move through the trees, huge shadows and strange light under a blue evening sky." The scene ends with the preachers extending an invitation to baptism: "'The great gift of baptism which makes us clean and acceptable—' 'Amen!'" (*Lila* 64–5).

The camp meeting affects Lila deeply and she is especially struck by the singing of the hymn "Bringing in the Sheaves." "She had some ideas about salvation, and mercy, but the old man never once mentioned sheaves." The final verse of the hymn references Ps. 126:6 and reads:

> Going forth with weeping, sowing for the Master,
> Though the loss sustained our spirit often grieves;
> When our weeping's over, He will bid us welcome,
> We shall come rejoicing, bringing in the sheaves

Lila leaves the camp meeting with an image of joy and restoration. The beautiful river has begun to exert its pull.

A final anticipation of Gilead is found in a less likely place: the darkness of the movie theater. After Lila leaves the brothel, she finds a job as a cleaning lady that affords her a modest income and the anonymity she so deeply craves. During this time, she also routinely goes to the movies. These trips to the theater soon become something of an obsession:

> If [the movie] wasn't very good, it was still all there was in her mind for an hour or two, a week or two. She might look like some woman going about her work, sitting by her window, but she'd be remaking a story in her mind. . . . She kept the dancing and the weddings. But the best part was always to be sitting there in the dark, seeing what she had never seen anywhere before, and mostly believing it. (*Lila* 209)

Not only does the theater provide Lila a place where she can be with people without being an object of attention, it gives her an opportunity to see the lives of others close-up. These interactions, especially those that showcase human happiness—"the dancing and the weddings"—are Lila's favorites. It is here, in events that reverberate with the same joy of the camp meeting, that Lila finally encounters people participating in a happiness worthy of themselves. Though deprivation alerts Lila to the strange beauty of human existence, it doesn't convince her that this is how things ought to be. In fact, the opposite is true. Lila "mostly believes" in the happiness she sees on the screen because it seems a more natural fit than sorrow or loneliness. Humans are clearly better suited to dancing than begging or hiding in the dark.

Lila moves naturally from the images in the theater to imagined visions of joy for her loved ones:

> What to imagine for Doll. That she had never cut that old man. That she'd never held a knife or spat on a whetstone. That she was wearing a new shawl that was really the old one on the day whoever owned it first had bought it. She couldn't wish that scar away, or how Doll never forgot to hide her face from anyone but Lila. The ghost couldn't really be part of the dream. Lila would just be there, so close, seeing that tender, ugly face. Just her. Nobody else would even want a dream like that. (*Lila* 209)

The cinema certainly provokes Lila's imagination for happiness, but there is something unique in how she conceives it. She is content to stand outside of the restoration she imagines for others. Surely, there is something both admirable and sad about this—admirable, because it bespeaks of selfless love (Lila takes genuine joy in the happiness of others even when she receives no benefit); sad because her absence from this picture seems to be at least partially a product of continued shame, the thought that she herself might not be worthy of joy. Addressing this lingering sense of unworthiness will be among the chief tasks of Ames and Gilead.

4 The Return to Fingerbone

When Lila finally decides to leave St. Louis, she is driven most of the way to Gilead by a reluctant "Nazarene." During the long car ride, the woman confesses her duty to save Lila, saying, "We're a mission church. So I'm supposed to try to bring you to Jesus." The woman's evangelical zeal soon fades as it confronts Lila's cool reticence: "you strike me as a woman with a lot of bitterness in her soul. I don't mean any offense. I might just make things worse." Instead, she leaves Lila with this advice: "You might visit a couple of [churches]. Just look in the door" (*Lila* 214–15). In Gilead, Lila eventually takes the woman's advice, but for a less high-minded reason: "[S]he got caught in the rain that Sunday and stepped into the church, just to save her dress. And there was that old man, speaking above the sound of the rain against the windows. He looked at her, and looked away again. 'Blessed be the name of the Lord'" (*Lila* 27). The missionary has played an unlikely role in "bringing Lila to Jesus"; Lila will make a point to return to church. The narrator tells us, "she guessed she liked the candles and the singing" (*Lila* 28).

On one of her later visits, Lila hears Ames preach and, afterward, walks out with a pew Bible. This marks an important turning point for Lila: as she begins to read and absorb the images of scripture, her perspective on her own life slowly expands. She chooses the opening chapters of Genesis and Ezekiel, and there finds a strangely familiar world.[2] In Genesis, she encounters the creation story and reads "over and over": "He saw that it was good, And the evening and the morning." In Ezekiel, she discovers a book full of fantastic images and apocalyptic warnings. From the first chapter, she reads, "*And out of the midst thereof came the likeness of four living creatures. And this was their appearance: they had the likeness of a man. And every one had four faces, and every one of them had four wings*" (*Lila* 68). And also:

> *And as for thy nativity, in the day thou wast born thy navel was not cut, neither wast thou washed in water to cleanse thee; thou wast not salted at all, nor swaddled at all. No eye pitied thee, to do any of these things*

> unto thee, to have compassion upon thee; but thou wast cast out in the open field, for that thy person was abhorred, in the day that thou wast born. And when I passed by thee, and saw thee weltering in thy blood, I said unto thee, Though thou art in thy blood, live; yea, I said unto thee, Though thou art in thy blood, live.

Lila almost immediately recognizes that this passage is about her—she is the infant weltering in its blood. She thinks, "Ugly old Doll. Who had said to her, Live. Not once, but every time she washed and mended for her, mothered her as if she were a child someone could want. Lila remembered more than she ever let on" (*Lila* 47). The reference to memory here is significant, and we know that among the many events recalled, Lila places special emphasis on the moment when Doll rescues her from the stoop. It is easy to think that this memory is what prepares Lila to later recognize Ezekiel's description of the "weltering" infant, but the opposite seems to be the case. In reality, the temporal order is reversed, and it is the passage from Ezekiel that gives birth to the memory. In the opening pages of the novel, referring to the events of that night, the narrator tells us that "Lila knew it couldn't have been the way she remembered it, as if she were carried along in the wind, and there were arms around her to let her know she was safe, and there was a whisper at her ear to let her know that she shouldn't be lonely" (*Lila* 5). This suggests that Lila's memory of that night may itself be a function of her later exposure to the images of Ezekiel. Not that she invents the memory but rather it receives a particular emphasis and interpretation once it interacts with the image of maternal/divine love depicted in the Old Testament.

We see the same thing occur in Lila's recollection of the day she is left on the steps of the church. Feeling abandoned by everyone, "Lila couldn't move. She wanted to rest her head on a bosom more Doll's than Doll herself, to feel trust rise up in her like that sweet old surprise of being carried off in strong arms, wrapped in a gentleness worn all soft and perfect" (*Lila* 54). Here we again see the possible influence of her reading. As Lila reflects on Ezekiel's use of the word "likeness" ("*And out of the midst thereof came the likeness of four living creatures.*"), she begins to think of her life in similar terms:

> Her name had the likeness of a name. She had the likeness of a woman, with hands but no face at all, since she never let herself see it. She had the likeness of a life, because she was all alone in it. She lived in the likeness of a house, with walls and a roof and a door that kept nothing in and nothing out. And when Doll took her up and swept her away, she had felt a likeness of wings. (*Lila* 68)

Ezekiel's poetry awakens a feeling of longing in Lila. This new appreciation of the possible distance between life and longing is then transferred back into her childhood memories, marking her recollection of the day she is left on the church steps. What, for a child, is experienced in basic terms—maybe sadness or anger—Lila later appreciates in Ezekiel's language. Instead of just a lonely event, she recalls the sorrow of that day as a desire for something more Doll than Doll herself. This, as we have already noticed, is especially significant since Doll (again, with Ezekiel's help) has come to symbolize love and safety more generally. Ezekiel's descriptions have, in this case, been laced together with the content of Lila's past to elicit an appetite for completeness: to find a love more perfect than love.[3]

Because of Lila's ability to recast her past through the images and concepts of the present, we are forced to think more subtly about the experiences we earlier regarded as "anticipations" of her restoration. Initially, we presented things like Lila's encounter with baptism at the camp meeting as fully formed experiences waiting to be developed in Gilead. While this still seems technically correct, the process now looks considerably more complex. Lila's later experiences in Gilead interact with her early memories not just by building off them but by retroactively shaping their significance. This means that the past and present are continuously interacting to mutually inform each other. Lila's new theological vocabulary prepares her to think of her early life in its terms which, then, allow her to see herself more fully represented in a book like Ezekiel. No theological concept becomes more important to this process than the one Lila hears the very first day she visits Ames's church: "resurrection."

As soon as Lila understands what resurrection means, the idea becomes "precious" and, as in her movie theater fantasies, she begins to imagine restoration for others. "The old man might have his wife and his child. She would have Doll, so that would be all right. There would be such crowds of people, but she would look for her until she found her if it took a hundred years" (*Lila* 100). Lila understands "the word 'resurrection' to mean just what she want[s] it to mean," and, in Doll's case, this amounts to being "just the way she used to be, but with death behind her, and all the peace that would come with that." This thought of Doll's peace is so overwhelming that Lila "could almost begin to enjoy her life. She was stealing it, almost, to give it to Doll." She imagines how her current life might seem to Doll—"a very good [one], a comfortable life that she had because Doll had stolen her, and had taken care of her all those years" (*Lila* 96-7). In these restoration-fantasies, Lila casts herself as a kind of thief, "stealing" happiness for the downtrodden. In this Robinhood role, Lila brings joy to others while embracing the continued alienation that all thieves suffer when they flout justice.

As Lila dreams of a new beginning for Doll, John Ames does the same for Lila. On the day of Lila's eventual baptism (and the day after her marriage proposal), Ames confesses, "I was getting along with the damn loneliness well enough. . . . Then I saw you that morning. I saw your face" (*Lila* 85). Though Ames does not go on to explain what exactly he sees, we know that, whatever it is, it becomes the foundation of his love for Lila. In *Gilead,* this moment of intimacy—usually experienced in baptism—is described by Ames as an encounter with a person's existence, their irreducible uniqueness. Once a person is given such a vision, he is connected to that person irrevocably. It is, of course, fitting that such a connection is forged in the act of seeing Lila's face. We see a second reference to it just before Lila receives baptism. Having been asked whether she is prepared to affirm certain articles of faith, Lila replies:

> "Affirm? I don't even know that word. . . . I'm an ignorant woman. Seems like you can't understand that." He stopped, so she did. He looked into her face. "I think I would understand it if it were true. But I don't believe it is. So I don't see the point in acting as if I do." (*Lila* 80)

These scenes show Ames ministering to the heart of Lila's shame and, thus, catalyzing her own resurrection. It is also significant that in the place of affirming the creeds, which Lila is unable to do, Ames finds sufficient answer in her face. His readiness to see Lila in this light seems to have been prepared, as the earlier passage suggests, by Ames's own years of loneliness. His hurt prepares him to attend to her hurt; Lila is baptized and soon married. Of marriage, she admits, "I want this so damn bad. And I hate to want anything" (*Lila* 89).

5 Salvation through (a Second) Baptism

Conversion narratives often highlight a single moment in which a person dramatically turns from their former life. Though there are perhaps anticipations of the change to come (as in Augustine's reading of Cicero or his disappointment with Manichean philosophy), everything comes to a head in an experience that marks a definitive break with what came before (the moment in the garden when the child's voice beckons Augustine to "pick up and read, pick up and read"). If tempted to see such a story in *Lila*, it would perhaps make sense to locate the conversion moment in Lila's christening. As we've already seen, Lila's baptism day was long anticipated by events in her early life and accompanied by other important breakthroughs; she admits the pain of her shame and begins the work of trusting Ames.

Although all this lends merit to the thought that Lila's baptism marks *the* important turning point in her life, it is actually the later decision to "wash off" her baptism that signals Lila's movement into Christianity. Baptism is a symbol both of death and of new life, and Lila most fully embraces this living-death in the moment she washes off her baptism. Her imitation of Christ comes in her decision to bear the mantle of judgment—divine curse—for the sake of those she loves, and it lays the foundation for Robinson's response to Feuerbach, though, as we will see, without accepting his final terms.

Shortly after marrying Ames, Lila is introduced to the doctrine of hell. Ames and Robert Boughton, a longtime friend and fellow-pastor, are discussing the recent return of several Chinese missionaries. During the conversation, Boughton, with an after-dinner matter-of-fact-ness, reflects on the high stakes of such work:

> it seemed to him like a terrible loss of souls, if that's what it was. He was not one to question divine justice, though sometimes he did have to wonder. Anyone would. Which was really not the same as questioning. And the Reverend said, When you think of all the people who lived from Adam to Abraham. Boughton shook his head at the mystery of it. "*We're* a drop in the bucket!" he said. "It's an easy thing to forget!" (*Lila* 20)

The idea that Lila is just a drop in the salvation "bucket" comes as terrifying news, almost as unbelievable as the suggestion that the eternal damnation of the better part of humankind is "an easy thing to forget." For Lila, it's impossible to forget, and her anxiety boils over into a later conversation with Ames. He attempts to allay her fears, saying, "I believe in the grace of God. For me, that is where all these questions end. Why it's pointless to ask them." For Lila, this is unsatisfying. She thinks back on all the acquaintances from her past who, "like most people who lived on earth, did not believe and [were] not baptized" (*Lila* 97); "Doll probably didn't know she had an immortal soul. . . . They knew it was morning when the sun came up. What more was there to know?" (*Lila* 21). More than just their ignorance though, Lila recalls their goodness. In a later conversation, Ames invites a return to the topic with the innocent remark that "God is good."

> "Well," she said, "some of the time."
> "All of the time."
> She said, "I've been tramping around with the heathens. They're just as good as anybody, so far as I can see. They sure don't deserve no hellfire."
> He laughed. "Well, that baby you talk about, cast out and weltering in her blood, the Lord takes her up. He looks after the strays. Especially the strays. That story is a parable, about how He bound himself to

Jerusalem when He told her, 'Live.' It's like a marriage. More than a marriage." (*Lila* 225)

In referencing Ezekiel's weltering infant, Lila is forced to rearrange the analogy, placing God in the role she has hitherto reserved for Doll. It lends a certain tragic irony to Lila's thoughts that Doll, the person she associates with God's compassion, may herself lie outside of God's compassion. This desperate thought requires Lila to, again, recast Ezekiel's analogy. *She* must now be the one who extends compassion—"If Doll was going to be lost forever, Lila wanted to be right there with her" (*Lila* 21).

Lila finally understands how Boughton and Ames can "forget" the damned. One night, lying next to Ames in bed, she remarks, "Maybe you don't have to think about hell because probly nobody you know going to end up there" (*Lila* 102). The implications are clear: Ames and Boughton can live with the idea of hellfire because they do not *love* anyone who will be subject to it. In contrast, the joy of heaven is impossible for those who love the lost. That Ames does not realize this is an indictment both of the narrow extension of his love and also the theology books that have taught him to think about hell without also cultivating a love for the "heathens."

It is for these reasons that Lila is drawn back to the river:

> She had put on her own dress, not one of the nice ones from the Boughtons' attic or the new ones from the Sears, Roebuck catalogue, and her own shoes. No need to worry she might dirty them. When she stepped out the door she felt that good chill, the dark of the morning she used to wake up to every day. The trees stirred in the darkness, and birds made those startled sounds they do when the stars are gone and there is still no sunrise. The river smelled like any river, fishy and mossy and shadowy, and the smell seemed stronger in the dark, with the chink and plosh of all the small life. She eased herself down to the edge of the water and put her hands in it. She took it up in her cupped hands, poured it over her brow, rubbed it into her face and into her hair. Then she did the same thing again, wetting the front of her dress.

And, finally, determined to undo the Trinitarian spell, a third time. "Her hands were so cold she felt them against her face as if they weren't hers at all. The river was like the old life, just itself. Nothing more to it. She thought, It has washed the baptism off me" (*Lila* 21–2).

This scene is reminiscent of the passage from *Housekeeping* in which Ruth experiences her own epiphany on the shore of Lake Fingerbone—the darkness, the chill of the early morning, the smell of fish and moss, and, finally, the water. As it is depicted, with the cupping of the hands and the pouring of the water on the brow, Lila isn't just washing the baptism off. She is rebaptizing herself, reversing the earlier act by restaging its gestures. Because the water has numbed her hands, it even feels as though someone else is touching her face. As soon as the ritual is over, Lila's thoughts turn immediately to Doll:

> Now, if I ever found [her] out there lost and wandering, at least she would recognize me. If there could be no joy for her in whatever was not life, at least she might remember for one second what joy had felt like. Lila thought about that for a while, seeing Doll walking ahead on some old dusty road, nothing on every side of her, and calling out her name so she would turn, and then running into her arms. No, Lila would be sitting on those steps, after it was dark, long after, and then Doll would be there, all out of breath, saying, "Child, child, I thought I was never going to find you!" When the sun had been up a little while she decided she could go back to the Reverend's house. Maybe no one would see her. They would all be in church. (*Lila* 22)

It is fitting that this act of compassion immediately leads Lila to "those steps." The steps which represented Lila's shame and abandonment now receive a theological accent: her damnation. Even still, this is the place where she first experiences love, and the place she must return to repay it.

It can hardly be missed that Lila's decision to court judgment for the sake of love is meant to be seen as an imitation of Christ's sacrifice on the cross. As Paul writes in Galatians, "Christ hath redeemed us from the curse of the law, being made a curse for us."[4] In Romans, Paul makes the remarkable claim that in this too he is prepared to follow Christ. He writes, "For I could wish that myself were accursed from Christ for my brethren, my kinsmen according to the flesh."[5] This last thought, being cursed precisely *by* Christ for the sake of one's "kinsmen," adds something left ambiguous in Christ's case (i.e., that *God* is the source of the curse), and brings Paul into closer contact with Lila. Lila would of course echo Paul's words and, as we have seen, do anything she thought possible to make good on them.

Within Robinson's text itself there is one place where we see an explicit nod to this connection between the cursed Christ and Lila. Late in the novel, after enduring a difficult labor, Lila gives birth to Ames's son. Because the infant is small and the delivery difficult, John hurries to baptize the child:

> The old man took his Bible from the top of the dresser and opened it and read, "But thou art he that took me out of the womb; thou didst make me trust when I was upon my mother's breasts. I was cast upon thee from the womb; thou art my God since my mother bare me. Be not far from me; for trouble is near; for there is none to help." (*Lila* 248)

After the benediction there is silence, and eventually Boughton speaks up: "Yes. I'm a little surprised you chose that text, John. It's a fine text. I just wouldn't have expected it." Boughton's surprise can be accounted for, at least partially, by the quoted verses. As Ames casts his newborn son in the role of the psalm writer, he anticipates a life of woe. However, and perhaps more significantly, the verses that precede those quoted are theologically pregnant. Psalm 22 opens with a cry that will eventually make its way to the lips of Christ: "My God, my God, why hast thou forsaken me?" With these words of apparent despair, Christ suggests he too has courted God's judgment. The love that leads him to the cross also requires divine abandonment.

The New Testament suggests that Christ's true "baptism"—the one his followers are called to join him in—occurs on the cross:

> Know ye not, that so many of us as were baptized into Jesus Christ were baptized into his death? Therefore we are buried with him by baptism into death: that like as Christ was raised up from the dead by the glory of the Father, even so we also should walk in newness of life.

For if we have been planted together in the likeness of his death, we shall be also in the likeness of his resurrection.[6]

Lila's baptism, performed alone and in shame at the water's edge, follows Christ's example in more ways than she can guess. Baptism is a blessed malediction. The disciple follows Christ in becoming a curse for the sake of those he loves. But, as Paul emphasizes, on the other side of this death is resurrection, and, as we will see, in this too Lila follows.

6 Sanctification

If we are right in supposing that Lila's second baptism is, in some important sense, a *Christian* baptism, then we would hope to find a path within the novel by which Lila is able to arrive at the same conclusion. This path would give Lila the ability to see her love for Doll as participating in the love Christ has for the world and, thus, the very thing the hope of resurrection is built upon. Perhaps it shouldn't surprise us that John Ames is the one who leads Lila to this path. His love for Lila—like Lila's for Doll—demands it. "In that eternity of his, where everybody will be happy, how could he feel the lack of her, the loss of her?" (*Lila* 258). Ames slowly finds a way forward through the tangle of Lila's theological worries, culminating in his own imagination for Doll's salvation.

One initial response to the problem of hell is the mystery of grace.[7] As Ames puts it, "I could probably not say more than that life is a very deep mystery, and that finally the grace of God is all that can resolve it. And the grace of God is also a very deep mystery" (*Lila* 31). In some sense, the "mystery" response seems to be a good one. As Robinson will say in other places, it ought to invite a deep humility that makes a person slow to judgment. However, the problem—as Feuerbach clearly foresaw—is that while preserving mystery in individual cases (maybe *she* is elected), it rejects mystery in the more general case—there will be someone or other who exists outside God's grace. And that is hardly consoling.

Sensing the insufficiency of this first answer, Ames reminds Lila that Christ enters into the suffering of the lowly and world-forgotten, and that this imbues them with special dignity (*Lila* 77). However, this too is insufficient. While it might impart a special status to someone's current life, it does nothing to address the looming worry of eternal damnation. How much dignity can Christ's life impart if it does not also prevent eternal punishment?

A third and perhaps more honest response is the nonresponse. Lila asks, "What happens to you if you're lost?" Ames replies, "Lila, you always do ask the hardest questions." And continues,

> There are other things I believe in. God loves the world. God is gracious. I can't reconcile, you know, hell and the rest of it to things I do believe. And feel I understand, in a way. So I don't talk about it very much.... I'm sorry about that. Sorry if you're disappointed. Again. But if I tried to explain I wouldn't believe what I was saying to you. That's lying, isn't it? I'm probably more afraid of that than of anything else. I really don't think preachers ought to lie. Especially about religion. (*Lila* 99)

Here, Ames seems to simply concede to Feuerbach that love and hell cannot be intellectually reconciled. Given this, Ames chooses to pass over the doctrine of hell in silence. This attitude, while in some sense honest, might also lead to the kind of forgetfulness we earlier saw from Boughton, and against which Lila rightly rebels. If one is going to assent to something as horrific as hellfire, there seems to be a duty to carry its burden.

Finally, Ames appears to settle on what we might call a practical rejection view. He says to Lila, "Thinking about hell doesn't help me *live the way I should*. I believe this is true for most people. And thinking that other people might go to hell just feels evil to me, like a very grave sin. So I don't want to encourage anyone else to think that way" (*Lila* 101, emphasis added). At first, this looks like another version of the nonresponse; Ames simply refuses to think about how exactly the world will be divided between the damned and the saved. However, as he clarifies, we see the view is stronger than that. He continues, "Even if you don't assume that you can know in individual cases, it's still a problem to think about people in general as if they might go to hell. *You can't see the world the way you ought to if you let yourself do that*" (*Lila* 101, emphasis added). Not only does Ames resist the thought that any specific person might be an object of divine wrath, it is problematic to think "about people in general" in these terms.

From this last reflection, we can articulate a more general interpretive principle. If a religious doctrine prevents Ames from "living the way he should," then he chooses, for all practical purposes, not "to think that way." This refusal seems importantly different than the kind of culpable forgetfulness we discussed in Boughton's case. Part of what disturbed us about the latter was its apparent negative effect—refusing to think about a person's eternal fate seems to make it all the less likely you'll think about their *current* fate. Ames, on the other hand, believes a practical denial of hell makes it *more likely* he will see people sympathetically. Thus, Ames understands "living the way he should" in ethical-aesthetic terms, meaning he refuses to organize his life around any idea that doesn't encourage proper vision. From other experiences, we know that this vision always includes the dignity of others, but also (and inseparably) their beauty. Since Christ's chief vocation was to see humanity and, accordingly, restore its sight, Ames feels more than licensed to overlook any dogmatic commitment that causes blindness. At the same time, Ames insists on speaking in provisional terms. He says of everything just discussed: "I believe this is true for most people" (*Lila* 101). He holds out the possibility—as slight as it may be—that there might be someone whose ability to "see the world" is enhanced by the doctrine.

We see the fruit of Ames's way of thinking in a vision he shares with Lila. He says to her, "I just want to say one thing, though. If the Lord is more gracious than any of us can imagine, and I'm sure He is, then your Doll and a whole lot of people are safe, and warm, and very happy. And probably a little surprised" (*Lila* 142–3). This vision, along with Ames's thoughts about the practical uselessness of the doctrine of hell, finally allows Lila to understand her love for Doll as Christian love. This means, significantly, that she can connect her love with the thought of resurrection, that "precious" idea she surrenders on the day of her baptism.

7 Resurrection

We notice the idea of resurrection slowly take hold of Lila in her evolving attitude toward Doll's knife. After Lila marries Ames, the knife is brought to their new home and eventually placed on the kitchen table next to the sugar bowl. Lila takes perverse pleasure in the unlikely juxtaposition of the knife and all the other tokens of domesticity. Like Lila herself, the knife doesn't belong and its placement on the table is intended as a constant reminder that this new life has no essential hold on her, its meanness refusing any pretense of assimilation. The knife's significance as a symbol of both Lila's continued isolation and fierce loyalty to Doll is confirmed in her reluctance to let Ames use it. When she discovers that Ames has been using it to pare apples, she snaps: "I never said you could use it." Ames apologizes: "I don't think I did it any harm. I believe you said you used to use it to clean fish." She replies, "That's different." The narrator continues:

> Why was it different? Because it was the only knife she had. And she never slit a fish without thinking she hated the need to use it that way. Hating the need almost made it seem all right. Besides, it was a kind of a little murder, gutting a fish, so when she did it she thought back over her life, and there was something to that. The knife was a potent thing. Other people had houses and towns and names and graveyards. They had church pews. All she had was that knife. And dread and loneliness and regret. That was her dowry. (*Lila* 241)

Despite her almost physical attachment to the knife, there are moments when Lila second-guesses the wisdom of keeping it. Again, awakened out of sleep, "Her first thought was, I have to get that knife off the table. She'd been having her worst dream, with the Reverend's arm carefully across her where her waist would be, with the Reverend breathing at her ear." As Lila's belly swells with Ames's child, she feels herself growing into her new life. Perhaps she should dispose of the knife in the river or at least hide it away.

We see a definitive change in Lila's relationship to the knife after another conversation with Ames. They are both reflecting on the small graces that lightened their years of loneliness. Ames begins:

"I had the church, of course, and Boughton. I had my prayers and my books. 'And my ending is despair, Unless I be relieved by prayer, Which pierces so that it assaults Mercy itself and frees all faults.' Quite a life, really. A very good life. But there was such a silence behind it all. Over it. Beneath it. Sometimes I used to read to myself out loud, just to hear a voice."

"You do that now."

"Do I? Well, by now it's just habit."

"And I think about Doll." Then she said, "I'm keeping that knife. I'll put it out of sight somewhere, but I'm keeping it."

"Fine."

"It ain't very Christian of me. Such a mean old knife. I hate to think he could want it sometime, but he could."

The old man nodded.

Here she was practically calling herself a Christian. (*Lila* 257)

In these few simple lines, Lila finally connects her loyalty to Doll with her new life as "practically" a Christian. With Ames's "practical" theology, not to mention his patient commitment to heal her shame, Lila is prepared to see Gilead not as a challenge and insult to early life but as a blessed culmination. Now, instead of having to hide Doll away, or wield her memory as a barrier between the past and present, Lila sees that the knife belongs at the kitchen table. And that it is precisely for paring apples. Lila has integrated Doll's memory into this new place—imagining restoration for the past and accountability for the present. And her "Christianity" has played an important role in this process. As with Christ's post-resurrection body, Lila's new faith gives her an imagination for how wounds can be healed while still preserving—as a kind of record of love—their scars.

All of these thoughts reach a triumphant culmination in the final passage of the novel, where Lila uses the idea of "eternity" to exercise her love for the world. "Eternity had more of every kind of room in it than this world did. She could even think of wicked old Mack in the light of that other life, looking it over, wondering what the catch was, what the joke was, somehow knowing that she had brought him there. And [Ames's] child. She couldn't bear to be without them." She emphasizes, "It was eternity that let her think like that without a bit of shame." Her mind immediately turns to Doll and the knife:

> So when she told [Ames] she meant to keep that knife and he nodded, she could explain to herself why she meant to keep it. There was no way to abandon guilt, no decent way to disown it. All the tangles and knots of bitterness and desperation and fear had to be pitied. No, better, grace had to fall over them. (*Lila* 260)

In these final thoughts, Lila speaks directly to *Housekeeping*'s Ruth. Though Ruth too turns to the idea of resurrection to assuage her pain, she misuses it. Eternity is not a place made for escape; it is nothing but a temptation when modeled as a place beyond place where one finally leaves behind the pain of life. Lila embraces eternity because her love for life demands a larger arena in which to play itself out. This fantastic condition longs for an infinity in which to unfold and expand and live up to its promise. Like a child on a carousel, or a beating heart, it shouts: again, again, again![8]

Here we also see a response to Feuerbach. While Robinson clearly thinks love will and must triumph over hell, Feuerbach is utterly mistaken to think that the fulfillment of love awaits the final eclipse of faith, a future day when humans learn to live without the mediation of religion. With Lila, we see a life that expands once it embraces a religious vocabulary. The sacredness of an individual soul, baptism, resurrection, eternity: these are ideas that, in proportion to Lila's earnest hope, open up the world as a place of solemn wonder. Even the pain of loneliness screams of transcendence as it draws attention to a kind of ridiculous emotional gratuity: we are capable even of sorrow!

8 Conclusion

Lila concludes with an onrush of joyful realization:

> That's how it is. Lila had borne a child into a world where a wind could rise that would take him from her arms as if there were no strength in them at all. Pity us, yes, but we are brave, she thought, and wild, more

life in us than we can bear, the fire infolding itself in us. That peace could only be amazement, too. (*Lila* 261)

Here we see an explicit nod to *Gilead*. As we discussed previously, early in the novel Lila laments: "There was more shame in life than she could bear." This stood out in sharp contrast with *Gilead*'s: "There is more beauty than our eyes can bear." Now, on the final page of the novel, Lila amends her earlier claim: not unbearable shame, but unbearable *life*!

Each of Lila's references to bravery, wildness, and fire are both important and familiar. *Gilead*, set just a few years in the future, ends with Ames's benediction for his son. He writes: "I love this town. I think sometimes of going into the ground here as a last wild gesture of love—I too will smolder away the time until the great and general incandescence. I'll pray that you grow up a brave man in a brave country" (*Gilead* 247). Perhaps, these thoughts have been simmering in Ames's mind for years and years, awaiting a proper time to bathe a soul in blessing. Or, perhaps, they represent a more recent lesson, knowledge gained from a source both unlikely and unexpected. Whatever their source, *Lila* ends with this promise: "Someday she would tell him what she knew" (*Lila* 261). We should expect, and now have the perspective to appreciate, that *Gilead* is marked by Lila's wisdom. The sun shines brightest on those who stand vigil through the night.

Notes

1. Kathryn Ludwig (2019) discusses Lila's "transient subjectivity," a term itself taken from Paula Geyh's (1993) discussion of "feminine subjectivity" in *Housekeeping*.
2. "She never expected to find so many things she already knew about written down in a book" (*Lila* 176).
3. Kent Eilers makes this same basic point in terms of Ames's influence on Lila. He writes, "Before [meeting] John, Lila could only perceive the world according to the imaginations available to her. Through John—his touch,

their marriage, his words—Lila perceives her memories and with them her self-perception in a new light, according to *his* imagination" (2016, 64).

4 Gal. 3:13.
5 Rom. 9:3.
6 Rom. 6:3-5.
7 See Mark S. M. Scott for a helpful review of Ames's various approaches to answering Lila's questions about fate and hell. Though Scott does not take Ames to offer any "new solution[s]," he praises *Lila* for its creative presentation of preexisting positions on hell. He writes, "[It] enriches the landscape of theodicy by turning over the ground in new ways," "creat[ing] space for more productive dialogue" (2017, 278). In contrast to Scott, we contend that *Lila* does much more than merely make space for "productive dialogue." Robinson does not propose a new answer to an existing theological question as much as she recommends and models an entirely new mode in which such conversations ought to occur. *Lila* is an example of a better way to do theology.
8 Penner makes this point in a slightly different context. She writes, "Lila lingers at gravesites and wonders about unborn children in order to better invest, imaginatively and sympathetically, in life" (2018, 278).

Conclusion

Our Fantastic Condition

The lives of Marilynne Robinson's characters are determined in large part by their ability, or inability, to see each other and themselves as beautiful, as something to be enjoyed. While pondering the problem of Jack, John Ames is reminded of an idea from his favorite theologian, John Calvin:

> Calvin says somewhere that each of us is an actor on a stage and God is the audience. That metaphor has always interested me, because it makes us artists of our behavior, and the reaction of God to us might be thought of as aesthetic rather than morally judgmental in the ordinary sense. . . . [Calvin's image] suggests how God might actually enjoy us. I believe we think about that far too little. It would be a way into understanding essential things, since presumably the world exists for God's enjoyment, not in any simple sense, of course, but as you enjoy the *being* of a child even when he is in every way a thorn in your heart. (*Gilead* 124–5)

God *enjoys* the world. When he creates it and finds it "good," that is not primarily a moral judgment but something more akin to the instinctive delight with which a parent beholds her child, a delight that is inseparable from the simple aesthetic judgment that the child is beautiful. Ames notes that this way of seeing ourselves and others is a "way into understanding essential things," that ultimately the world is as it is, that *we* are as we are, because it was better in precisely this aesthetic sense that things turn out this way. We see the world as God sees it only when we can't help but delight in it.

But it is far from easy to approach the world and our fellow human beings in this way. People are hard to love and (what may be the same thing) hard to find beautiful. They are strange, they resist our efforts to understand them, and they do things that we do not expect of children who delight the divine audience.

In a late passage in *The Gay Science*, Nietzsche muses on the difficulties and rewards of love:

> *One must learn to love.* This happens to us in music: first one must *learn to hear* a figure and melody at all, to detect and distinguish it, to isolate and delimit it as a life in itself; then one needs effort and good will to *stand* it despite its strangeness; patience with its appearance and expression, and kindheartedness about its oddity. Finally comes a moment when we are *used* to it; when we expect it; when we sense that we'd miss it if it were missing; and now it continues relentlessly to compel and enchant us until we have become its humble and enraptured lovers, who no longer want anything better from the world than it and it again. But this happens to us not only in music: it is in just this way that we have *learned to love* everything we now love. We are always rewarded in the end for our good will, our patience, our fair-mindedness and gentleness with what is strange, as it gradually casts off its veil and presents itself as a new and indescribable beauty. That is its *thanks* for our hospitality. Even he who loves himself will have learned it this way—there is no other way. Love, too, must be learned. (GS 334)

Nietzsche clearly expects the title of the aphorism—"one must learn to love"—to be surprising. Love, we might have imagined, is not something you work at but something that befalls you. The beloved crosses your path, and the work is done. The idea is appealing to us because we sense that love is not something we can control, not something that can simply be willed into existence by making a decision or by exerting the requisite effort. But Nietzsche's aphorism suggests that this gives us a misleading and cheapened picture of love. Real love, love that is attentive to what is really there to be loved in the object, is the result of a continuous effort, guided by good will, patience, fair-mindedness, "gentleness with what is strange." When we make these efforts, the object of our love rewards us for our "hospitality" by revealing what it really is, by allowing itself to be at home with us. We do not just will its loveliness into existence, it is true, but our willingness as well as effort to allow the object a space to be what it is plays an important and active role in its revealing itself and its beauty. And it is no irrelevance that Nietzsche puts the point in aesthetic terms, comparing the process to that of appreciating a piece of music. An aesthetic sense, an ability to see and appreciate what is beautiful, and knowledge of what light to present it in so as to make that beauty apparent, is inseparable from the love he describes. Needless to say, Nietzsche applies this not just to our relations to each other but to life in general. Life, in order to be affirmed, must be loved, and that love too must be learned, must take all of the good will, fair-mindedness, and aesthetic sensitivity that we can muster.

The denizens of Robinson's Gilead are all undergoing this learning process, trying to develop the virtues needed really to see each other, and to see their lives, in a way that opens up the "new and indescribable beauty" those things have in them. Certainly, there is much in their life that is strange, much that resists spontaneous affection and easy attachment, much that requires effort and a virtuous disposition in order to come to love. Much, though not all, of the problem is presented through the prism of Jack, whose strangeness is noted by all and whose various failings make him seem almost impossible to love. Ames struggles to forgive and love Jack in *Gilead*, in large part because, as he comes to see, he has not been fair-minded and gentle in the way required to see what is good in him. Glory's struggle in *Home* to accept the role of keeper of the Boughton home is resolved only by an imagined culmination of that role in her ability to welcome Jack's young son back to the home that Jack had so lovingly described to him, a culmination that she can see as beautiful and "wonderful" even if the event itself never happens. Della too is able to love Jack, to see the beauty in his soul in the way that she imagines Jesus must see it, despite what would seem to be failings in him that render him unlovable. Lila's persistent commitment to the goodness and beauty of Doll and the other unseemly figures from her past, despite what would appear from a traditional Christian perspective to be their damned state, makes her more naturally accepting of Jack than the other major characters and lends her outlook the wildness and fire with which her novel comes to a close. For his own part, Jack's desolation is rooted precisely in the fact that he finds it impossible to love himself and instinctively rejects descriptions of himself that would, in his view, dress up his failures as romantic or beautiful. When he quotes to himself the passage from Robert Frost's poem "Acquainted with the Night" ("I have walked out in rain—and back in rain"), he calls the poetry of the description, when applied to himself, a "perjured witness." All that can result from cutting oneself off from the loving gaze that might render one beautiful is despair. To be sure, Jack's skepticism is not unmotivated—we know of his reasons for wanting to avoid hypocrisy and making excuses for his behavior. But Robinson's fiction suggests that his situation is impossible; these scruples, hardwon though they are, undermine any avenue Jack might have had to learn to see the beauty in himself and his life, and thus to escape the perdition his life has always been.

For Nietzsche, Christianity was the mortal enemy of this idea of loving vision. "[T]he Christian decision to find the world ugly and bad," Nietzsche tells us, "has made the world ugly and bad" (GS 130). As we saw in Chapter 1, Nietzsche saw this at work in Christianity in three main, interlocking areas of concern: moralization, sin, and afterlife. Christianity, according to Nietzsche, promotes an overly moralized and judgmental conception of the world. Human beings are naturally sinful, natural rebels against God's monomaniacal power—what they instinctively enjoy in this life must be repressed, or else they will pay for their petty and ineffectual rebellion in the next life. But Nietzsche says not just that Christianity saw the world this way but that the perception had real effects—it "has made the world ugly and bad." On Nietzsche's view, we moderns have inherited this evaluation of our existence, even if (maybe even especially if!) we consider ourselves secular and post-Christian, and wouldn't be caught dead talking earnestly about "sin" or "hell." Like Jack, we find in ourselves an instinctive distrust of the "perjured witness" of any poetry that would attempt to make our lives appear more beautiful and meaningful to us than they now do. We are more realistic than that.[1] We know how painful it is to have high hopes dashed. We are far more comfortable with (or at any rate habituated to) seeing ourselves as insignificant, or perhaps dangerous, incapable of any course of action that could improve our lot, except perhaps (also like Jack) to try our best to be harmless. Anything more, we fear, would be too "presumptuous" (*Jack* 167). Whether we are Christian or not, we are all nihilists now: nothing, with bodies (cf. *Home* 288–9).

In their own ways, Ames, Della, Glory, and Lila all point in a different direction, a direction highly sensitive to Nietzsche's concerns and to our own modern malaise. As far as all of them (and clearly, their creator) are concerned, it is a *Christian* direction. Nietzsche already saw that it was not sufficient to escape the moralized, judgmental, despondent view of the world simply to cease being a Christian. What he failed to see were the resources that Christianity itself could muster to fight that view. There can be a Christianity that insists on God's enjoyment of his creation, rather than on his judgment of rebels against his rule. There can be a Christianity that does not merely pretend to believe in the absolute value of each individual human being, while secretly, "sacredly," insisting on absolute conformity, but really believes, with Ames, that there are "a thousand thousand reasons to live this life, every one of them sufficient" (*Gilead* 243). And there can be a Christianity that can say *this* about the afterlife:

> I feel sometimes as if I were a child who opens its eyes on the world once and sees amazing things it will never know any names for and then has to close its eyes again. I know this is all mere apparition compared to what awaits us, but it is only lovelier for that. There is a human beauty in it. And I can't believe that, when we have all been changed and put on incorruptibility, we will forget our fantastic condition of mortality and impermanence, the great bright dream of procreating and perishing that meant the whole world to us. In eternity this world will be Troy, I believe, and all that has passed here will be the epic of the universe, the ballad they sing in the streets. Because I don't imagine any reality putting this one in the shade entirely, and I think piety forbids me to try. (*Gilead* 57)

The idea of the "human condition" is usually invoked to adopt a tone of world-weariness, of resignation in the face of dashed hopes. But Ames doesn't use it that way—our condition, which he admits does have its limitations, is not lamentable, not even merely acceptable, but *fantastic*. That means it's wonderful, of course, but also that it's something dream-like, almost hard to believe.[2] Our human condition, with all its limitations, is something so glorious as to be the stuff of dreams, of fantastic tales or songs. And the effect, Ames suggests, is so strong that it dominates the life to come. "This world will be Troy," Ames says—the afterlife in Ames's view will not swallow up this one in its significance but will actually be *about* this life, the real thing a reflection of the apparition.

Nietzsche's atheism has long held a strange appeal for Christian believers and theologians, insofar as he takes the problems Christianity seeks to pose so utterly seriously while remaining a staunch atheist. Something similar, but reversed, seems to have taken place with the reception of Robinson's fiction—though it is unapologetically, even aggressively, Christian, it holds a strange appeal for modern secular readers. If we are on the right track, these two phenomena have the same underlying cause: Nietzsche and Robinson both feel acutely the psychological and ultimately existential threat posed by hatred, resentment, and life-denial, and both worry that the modern world stands a good chance of being swallowed up by it. Against it, they both seek to articulate a similar experience, an experience which, when understood, would show us a way out to a new, freer way of life, a way that does justice to the fantastic beings we are. It may be that they can do that better together than they could alone.

Notes

1   "... we have put together among ourselves a rigidly simple account of life in the world, which we honor with the name Reality and which, we now assure one another, must be faced and accepted, even or especially

at the cost of those very things which societies we admire are believed by us to value, for example education, the arts, a humane standard of life for the whole of the community. Science fetches back from its explorations mystery upon mystery, yet somehow we feel increasingly sunk in a world of mere things, in a hard-edged Reality that disallows imagination except to exact tribute from it, in portraits which assert its own power and ferocity, or in interludes and recreations which concede by their triviality that only Reality matters" (Robinson 2005, 76–7).

2 That is, it is like a *fantasy*. The word has roots in the Latin *phantasticus*, which means "imaginary"; the Greek verb *phantazein* means something closer to "picture" or "render visible."

Works Cited

Ameriks, Karl. "The Legacy of Idealism in the Philosophy of Feuerbach, Marx and Kierkegaard." In Karl Ameriks (ed.), *The Cambridge Companion to German Idealism*, 258–80. New York, NY: Cambridge University Press.

Aquinas, Thomas. (2017). *The Summa Theologiae of St. Thomas Aquinas*. Trans. Fathers of the English Dominican Province. Online ed. https://www.newadvent.org/summa/.

Augustine. (1963). *The Confessions of St. Augustine*. Trans. Rex Warner. New York, NY: New American Library.

Barth, Karl. (1933). *The Epistle to the Romans*. Trans. Edwyn C. Hoskyns. New York, NY: Oxford University Press.

Barth, Karl. (1957). "An Introductory Essay." In George Eliot (trans.), Ludwig Feuerbach (ed.), *The Essence of Christianity*. New York, NY: Harper Torchbooks, x–xxxii.

Blue, Daniel. (2016). *The Making of Friedrich Nietzsche: The Quest for Identity, 1844–1869*. New York, NY: Cambridge University Press.

Bradley, Arthur and Andrew Tate. (2010). *The New Atheist Novel: Philosophy, Fiction, and Polemic After 9/11*. New York, NY: Continuum.

Breyfogle, Todd. (April 1994). "Memory and Imagination in Augustine's *Confessions*." *New Blackfriars*, 75 (881): 210–23.

Caver, Christine. (March 1996). "Nothing Left to Lose: *Housekeeping*'s Strange Freedoms." *American Literature*, 68 (1): 111–37.

Crisu, Corina. (2016). "At Home with Transience: Reconfiguring Female Characters of the American West in Marilynne Robinson's *Housekeeping*." In Jason W. Stevens (ed.), *This Life, This World: New Essays on Marilynne Robinson's Housekeeping, Gilead, and Home*, 38–58. Leiden: Brill.

Dawkins, Richard. (2006). *The God Delusion*. New York, NY: Houghton Mifflin Harcourt,.

Dennett, Daniel. (2007). *Breaking the Spell: Religion as a Natural Phenomenon*. New York, NY: Penguin Books.

Domestico, Anthony. (March 2014). "'Imagine a Carthage Sown with Salt': Creeds, Memory and Vision in Marilynne Robinson's *Housekeeping*." *Literature & Theology*, 28 (1): 92–109.

Donnelly, Kelsie. (2017). "(Sub)merged Worlds in Marilynne Robinson's *Housekeeping*." *Irish Journal of American Studies*, 6: 77–87.

Douglas, Christopher. (Fall 2011). "Christian Multiculturalism and Unlearned History in Marilynne Robinson's *Gilead*." *Novel*, 44 (3): 333–52.

Dreyfus, Hubert and Sean Kelly. (2011). *All Things Shining: Reading the Western Classics to Find Meaning in a Secular Age*. New York, NY: Free Press.

Dunbar, Paul Laurence. (2004). *Selected Poems*. New York, NY: Penguin Books.

Ebels-Duggan, Kyla. (2011). "Review of *All Things Shining: Reading the Western Classics to Find Meaning in a Secular Age*." *Notre Dame Philosophical Reviews*, September 9, 2011. https://ndpr.nd.edu/reviews/all-things-shining-reading-the-western-classics-to-find-meaning-in-a-secular-age/.

Eilers, Kent. (2016). "The Beauty and Strangeness of Being: Imagining God in Marilynne Robinson's *Lila*." *Crux: A Journal of Christian Thought and Opinion*, 66 (3): 60–8.

Emerson, Ralph Waldo. (1983). *Essays and Lectures*. Ed. Joel Porte. New York, NY: The Library of America.

Engebretson, Alex. (2017). *Understanding Marilynne Robinson*. Columbia, SC: The University of South Carolina Press.

Evans, Justin. (2014). "Subjectivity and the Possibility of Change in the Novels of Marilynne Robinson." *Renascence*, 66 (2): 131–50.

Feuerbach, Ludwig. (1957). *The Essence of Christianity*. Trans. George Eliot. New York, NY: Harper Torchbooks. (Cited as "EC.")

Frank, Joseph. (1976). *Dostoevsky: The Seeds of Revolt, 1821–1849*. Princeton, NJ: Princeton University Press.

Galehouse, Maggie. (Spring 2000). "Their Own Private Idaho: Transience in Marilynne Robinson's *Housekeeping*." *Contemporary Literature*, 41 (1): 117–37.

Gardner, Thomas. (2001). "Enlarging Loneliness: Marilynne Robinson's *Housekeeping* as a Reading of Emily Dickinson." *The Emily Dickinson Journal*, 10 (1): 9–33.

Garner, Dwight. (2020). "A Minister's Troubled Son Takes Center Stage in Marilynne Robinson's 'Jack.'" *The New York Times*, September 21, 2020, www.nytimes.com/2020/09/21/books/review-jack-marilynne-robinson.html.

Geyh, Paula E. (Spring 1993). "Burning Down the House? Domestic Space and Feminine Subjectivity in Marilynne Robinson's 'Housekeeping.'" *Contemporary Literature*, 34 (1): 103–22.

Gonzalez, Elisa. (March 2021). "No Good Has Come: Marilynne Robinson's Testimony for the White Church." *The Point Magazine*, 24 (March 2021).

Gordon, Peter. (2019). "Either This World or the Next: Do We Need to Give Up God to Embrace Socialism?" *The Nation*, September 2019. https://www.thenation.com/article/archive/martin-hagglund-this-life-socialism-secularism-book-review/.

Gregory, Frederick. (1977). *Scientific Materialism in Nineteenth Century Germany*. Dordrecht/Boston: Reidel.

Hägglund, Martin. (2019). *This Life: Secular Faith and Spiritual Freedom*. New York, NY: Pantheon Books.

Harris, Sam. (2005). *The End of Faith: Religion, Terror, and the Future of Reason*. New York/London: W.W. Norton & Co.

Hart, David Bentley. (2019). *That All Shall Be Saved*. New Haven, CT: Yale University Press.

Hartshorne, Sarah D. (1990). "Lake Fingerbone and Walden Pond: A Commentary on Marilynne Robinson's *Housekeeping*." *Modern Language Studies*, 20 (3): 50–7.

Hegel, G.W.F. (1977). *Phenomenology of Spirit*. Trans. A. V. Miller. New York, NY: Oxford University Press.

Hitchens, Christopher. (2009). *God Is Not Great: How Religion Poisons Everything*. New York/Boston: Hachette.

Hobbs, June Hadden. (Winter 2010). "Burial, Baptism, and Baseball: Typology and Memorialization in Marilynne Robinson's *Gilead*." *Christianity and Literature*, 59 (2): 241–62.

Holberg, Jennifer L. (Winter 2010). "'The Courage to See It': Toward an Understanding of Glory." *Christianity & Literature*, 59 (2): 283–300.

Hopper, Briallen. (2014). "Marilynne Robinson in Montgomery." *Religion & Politics*, December 2014. https://religionandpolitics.org/2014/12/22/marilynne-robinson-in-montgomery/.

Hunt, Lester. (1985). "Politics and Anti-Politics: Nietzsche's View of the State." *History of Philosophy Quarterly*, 2: 453–68.

Keizer, Garrett. (2009). "So Deep a Wound: *Home* and the Novels of Marilynne Robinson." *Religion Dispatches*, June 2009. https://religiondispatches.org/so-deep-a-wound-ihomei-and-the-novels-of-marilynne-robinson/.

Kierkegaard, Søren. (1995). *Works of Love*. Trans. Howard Hong and Edna Hong. Princeton, NJ: Princeton University Press.

Kirkby, Joan. (1986). "Is There Life After Art? The Metaphysics of Marilynne Robinson's *Housekeeping*." *Tulsa Studies in Women's Literature*, 5 (1): 91–109.

Kisner, Jordan. (2020). "Marilynne Robinson's Prodigal Son." *The Atlantic*, October 2020. https://www.theatlantic.com/magazine/archive/2020/10/marilynne-robinsons-lonely-souls/615493/.

Knausgaard, Karl Ove. (2017). *So Much Longing in So Little Space: The Art of Edvard Munch*. New York, NY: Penguin Books.

Larsen, Timothy and Keith Johnson (eds.). (2019). *Balm in Gilead: A Theological Dialogue with Marilynne Robinson*. Downer's Grove, IL: InterVarsity Press.

Lear, Jonathan. (Summer 2012). "Not at Home in Gilead." *Raritan*, 32 (1): 34–52.

Leise, Christopher. (Fall 2009). "'That Little Incandescence': Reading the Fragmentary and John Calvin in Marilynne Robinson's *Gilead*." *Studies in the Novel*, 41 (3): 348–67.

Leiter, Brian. (2002). *Nietzsche on Morality*. New York, NY: Routledge.

Libman, Ben. (2020). "Shells and Spheres of the Self: On Marilynne Robinson's 'Jack,'" *Los Angeles Review of Books*, December 9, 2020. https://www.lareviewofbooks.org/article/shells-and-spheres-of-the-self-on-marilynne-robinsons-jack/.

Löwith, Karl. (1991). *From Hegel to Nietzsche: The Revolution in Nineteenth Century Thought*. Trans. David E. Green. New York, NY: Columbia University Press.

Ludwig, Kathryn. (October 2019). "To Dwell in Grace: Physical and Spiritual Situatedness in Marilynne Robinson's *Lila*." *Humanities*, 8 (4): 163.

Mallon, Anne-Marie. (1989). "Sojourning Women: Homelessness and Transcendence in *Housekeeping*." *Critique: Studies in Contemporary Fiction*, 30 (2): 95–105.

Martin, Herbert Woodward. (2004). "Introduction." *Selected Poems*, by Paul Laurence Dunbar. New York, NY: Penguin Books.

Melville, Herman. (2002). *Moby Dick*. New York: W.W. Norton & Company.

Nietzsche, Friedrich. (1967). *The Will to Power*. Trans. Walter Kaufmann and R. J. Hollingdale. New York, NY: Vintage Press. (Cited as "WP.")

Nietzsche, Friedrich. (1974). *The Gay Science*. Trans. Walter Kaufmann. New York, NY: Random House.

Nietzsche, Friedrich. (1998). *On the Genealogy of Morality*. Trans. Maudemarie Clark and Alan Swensen. Indianapolis, IN: Hackett. (Cited as "GM," by essay and section number.)

Nietzsche, Friedrich. (1999). *The Birth of Tragedy out of the Spirit of Music*. Trans. Ronald Speirs. New York, NY: Cambridge University Press. (Cited as "BT.")

Nietzsche, Friedrich. (2001). *The Gay Science*. Trans. Josefine Nauckhoff and Adrian del Caro. New York, NY: Cambridge University Press. (Cited as "GS.")

Nietzsche, Friedrich. (2002). *Beyond Good and Evil*. Trans. Judith Norman. New York, NY: Cambridge University Press. (Cited as "BGE.")

Nietzsche, Friedrich. (2005a). *The Anti-Christ: The Anti-Christ, Ecce Homo, Twilight of the Idols, and Other Writings*. Trans. Judith Norman. New York, NY: Cambridge University Press. (Cited as "A.")

Nietzsche, Friedrich. (2005b). *Twilight of the Idols: The Anti-Christ, Ecce Homo, Twilight of the Idols, and Other Writings*. Trans. Judith Norman. New York, NY: Cambridge University Press. (Cited as "TI," by section name and number.)

Nietzsche, Friedrich. (2006). *Thus Spoke Zarathustra*. Trans. Adrian del Caro. New York, NY: Cambridge University Press. (Cited as "Z," by section name and number.)

O'Connell, Mark. (2012). "The First Church of Marilynne Robinson." *The New Yorker*, May 2012. https://www.newyorker.com/books/page-turner/the-first-church-of-marilynne-robinson.

Painter, Rebecca. (Winter 2010). "Loyalty Meets Prodigality: The Reality of Grace in Marilynne Robinson's Fiction." *Christianity and Literature*, 59 (2): 321–40.

Painter, Rebecca, and Marilynne Robinson. (Spring 2009). "Further Thoughts on a Prodigal Son Who Cannot Come Home, on Loneliness and Grace: An Interview with Marilynne Robinson." *Christianity and Literature*, 58 (3): 484–92.

Park, Haein. (Spring 2014). "The Face of the Other: Suffering, *Kenosis*, and a Hermeneutics of Love in Dietrich Bonhoeffer's *Letters and Papers from Prison* and Marilynne Robinson's *Gilead*." *Renascence*, 66 (2): 103–18.

Penner, Erin. (Summer 2018). "A Response to Addie Bundren: Restoring Generosity to the Language of Civil Discourse in Marilynne Robinson's *Lila*." *Studies in the Novel*, 50 (2): 277–98.

Plato. (2002). *Five Dialogues: Euthyphro, Apology, Crito, Meno, Phaedo*. Trans. G. M. A. Grube. Indianapolis, IN: Hackett.

Ploeg, Andrew. (2016). "'Trying to Say What Was True': Language, Divinity, Difference in Marilynne Robinson's *Gilead*." *Journal of Language, Literature and Culture*, 63 (1): 1–14.

Ravits, Martha. (1989). "Extending the American Range: Marilynne Robinson's *Housekeeping*." *American Literature*, 61 (4): 644–66.

Robinson, Marilynne. (1980). *Housekeeping*. New York, NY: Picador.

Robinson, Marilynne. (2004). *Gilead*. New York, NY: Farrar, Straus and Giroux.

Robinson, Marilynne. (2005). *The Death of Adam: Essays on Modern Thought*. New York, NY: Picador.

Robinson, Marilynne. (2008). "Credo: Reverence, a Kind of Humility, Corrects Belief's Tendency to Warp or Harden." *Harvard Divinity Bulletin*, 36 (2): 20–32.

Robinson, Marilynne. (2009). *Home*. New York, NY: Picador.

Robinson, Marilynne. (2011). *The Absence of Mind: The Dispelling of Inwardness from the Modern Myth of the Self (The Terry Lectures Series)*. New Haven, CT: Yale University Press.

Robinson, Marilynne. (2012). *When I Was a Child I Read Books*. New York, NY: Farrar, Straus and Giroux.

Robinson, Marilynne. (2014). *Lila*. New York, NY: Farrar, Straus and Giroux.

Robinson, Marilynne. (2020). *Jack*. New York, NY: Farrar, Straus and Giroux.

Robinson, Marilynne, et. al. (Fall 2018–Winter 2019). "Arguing Belief and Unbelief: A Symposium, Session One." *Salmagundi*, 200–1. https://salmagundi.skidmore.edu/articles/123-arguing-belief-and-unbelief-a-symposium-session-one.

Row, Jess. (2020). "Review: Marilynne Robinson's New Novel Tackles Racism, but Glosses over Its History." *Los Angeles Times*, October 6, 2020. https://www.latimes.com/entertainment-arts/books/story/2020-10-06/marilynne-robinson-novel-jack-review.

Ryan, Maureen. (1991). "Marilynne Robinson's *Housekeeping*: The Subversive Narrative and the New American Eve." *South Atlantic Review*, 56 (1): 79–86.

Schaub, Thomas, and Marilynne Robinson. (1994). "An Interview with Marilynne Robinson." *Contemporary Literature*, 35 (2): 231–51.

Schopenhauer, Arthur. (1969). *The World as Will and Representation*, 2 vols. Trans. E. F. J. Payne. Mineola, NY: Dover Press.

Scott, Mark S.M. (Fall 2017). "Wrestling with Existence: Pondering Suffering and Grace in *Lila*." *Toronto Journal of Theology*, 33 (2): 207–17.

Spinks, Lee. (2017). "'The House of Your Church Is Burning': Race and Responsibility in Marilynne Robinson's *Gilead*." *Journal of American Studies*, 52 (1): 141–62.

Stout, Andrew C. (January 2014). "'A Little Willingness to See': Sacramental Vision in Marilynne Robinson's *Housekeeping* and *Gilead*." *Religion and the Arts*, 18 (4): 571–90.

Weber, Max. (2011). *The Protestant Ethic and the Spirit of Capitalism*. Trans. Stephen Kalberg. New York, NY: Oxford University Press.

Young, Julian. (2010). *Friedrich Nietzsche: A Philosophical Biography*. New York, NY: Cambridge University Press.

Index

Adam 28, 36, 51, 60, 99, 193
afterlife 1, 3, 18, 34, 38–40, 58, 208–10
amor fati 8, 43–4, 144 n.13
Aquinas, Thomas 17, 39, 47–8 n.30
asceticism 29–30, 36–7, 40–4
attention 10, 83, 92, 95–8, 106, 108, 159–60, 173
Augustine 29, 82, 96–7, 99, 111 n.8, 192

baptism 128, 185–6, 202
  Ames on 83, 85, 95–6
  of Edward 90
  Feuerbach on 20–1
  of Jack 104–5, 107
  of Lila 10–11, 175, 180–1, 191–9
Barth, Karl 45 n.8, 88–9, 111 nn.5–7
beauty 2, 92, 95, 100–1, 109–10, 157–8, 170, 174, 185, 187, 199, 203, 206–9
  of Jack 151–3, 156, 208
  Kierkegaard on 159–60
Buddhism 4

Calvin, John 28, 82, 110 n.1, 171 n.12, 205
Christian doctrine 127, 191, 199
  of hell 125, 193–4, 197–9
  of original sin 28, 30, 34–8, 131
  of predestination 115, 130–6
  of salvation by grace 28, 132
courage 110, 120, 169
covetise 84, 105–6, 112 n.13

Dante Alighieri 39–40
Dostoevsky, Fyodor 45 n.11
Dreyfus, Hubert 4–5, 11 n.3

Dunbar, Paul Laurence 10, 162–4, 171 nn.16, 18

Eliot, George 46 n.18, 84
Emerson, Ralph Waldo 44, 49 n.36
Eucharist 21, 70, 83, 97–9, 185
Eve 51
existence 91, 148, 184, 187
  Ames on 1, 86–7, 99–101, 154–6, 191

faith 19, 28, 85
  absence of in Jack 127
  of Ames 82, 92–102, 174, 185
  in Hägglund 4
  in modern science 40
Feuerbach, Ludwig Andreas 7–9, 13–22, 27, 45 nn.2–5, 8–11, 46 nn.12–13, 18, 20, 111 n.3, 192
  contradiction between love and faith 174–5, 197–8, 202
  influence on Nietzsche 24, 26, 30, 42, 46 n.20
  John Ames' views of 82–94, 98, 109
finitude 4–5, 15, 53
forgiveness 9–10, 104–9, 128, 130, 207
  shallow 118–19, 126–7, 134
Frost, Robert 161, 208

grace 28, 73, 89, 104, 115, 132, 176, 193, 202
  Ames on 107–10, 197–9
  Augustine on 96–7
  Barth on 89
gratitude 36, 47 n.26
Greek polytheism 4, 31–3

Hägglund, Martin 4–5, 12 n.4
Homer 32–3, 42, 102

homesickness 53–60, 114, 116
hope 44, 76–7, 141, 142 n.4, 144 n.14

ignorance
  as response to loss 58–60, 66–70
imagination 140, 144 n.14, 171 n.14, 203–4 n.3, 210–11 n.1
  Augustine on 97
  Feuerbach on 15–17
  poetic 161–4
  as response to loss 58–60, 70–7, 186–7, 197, 201
  as revelation 97–8
Islam 3–4

joy 82–6, 90–5, 187, 195
  Feuerbach on 14, 16
Judaism 4

Kelly, Sean 4–5, 11 n.3
Kierkegaard, Søren 159–61
Knausgaard, Karl Ove 79 n.19

life-affirmation 2, 6, 53, 77, 81–4, 92–3, 148, 154, 160, 207
  of Ames 2, 81, 108–9, 145 n.17, 174
  Feuerbach on 30
  of Glory 141–2
  of Lila 174, 202–3
  Nietzsche on 42–4
life-denial 1, 3, 6, 7, 171–2 n.21, 210
  in Feuerbach 18–19
  in Hägglund 4–5
  in *Housekeeping* 53–60, 66–75
  in Nietzsche 36–7
  in Plato 42
  in Schopenhauer 28
loneliness 67, 173–4, 176, 202
  of Ames 81, 107, 192
  of Jack 127, 143 n.7
  of Lila 175, 183–4, 191, 200
  of Ruth 71–3, 79 n.22

love 18–19, 36, 38–40, 45 n.11, 82, 84, 94, 96, 106, 108–10, 139–41, 148–9, 153–5, 158–61, 166, 170, 174–5, 184, 187, 189, 190, 194–9, 202, 206–8

Marx, Karl 5, 45 n.4, 84
Melville, Herman 51
memory 60–1, 65–7, 74, 96–9, 105, 111 n.10, 116, 138–9, 172 n.25, 189–90, 201
moralism 3, 31–4

new atheists 3–4, 46 n.13
Nietzsche, Friedrich Wilhelm 22–44, 53, 170, 208–10
  on *amor fati* 43–4, 144 n.13
  on asceticism 36–7, 40–44, 48 n.32, 143 n.8
  on beauty 206–7
  on belief in the afterlife 38–40
  on Christian morality 31–4
  on love 206–7
  on *ressentiment* 35, 47 n.28
  on scientific worldview 40–2
  on sin 34–8
nihilism 2, 7, 37, 40, 174

perception 17, 44, 71–2, 83–4, 93–4
Plato 42, 47 n.23
Prodigal Son 9, 84, 96, 104

race 131–2, 143 n.5, 144 n.16, 165, 167, 172 n.25
relics 61, 64, 70, 79 n.18, 111 n.2, 139–40, 144 n.12, 182
  Lila's knife as 181–2, 200–1
religious arguments 87–8, 93
religious experience 83, 90–2, 98
religious practice 83, 92–9
resurrection 11, 70, 73–7, 98, 175, 187, 190–2, 197, 199–203
ritual 56–7, 59, 63, 83, 195

sacrament   15, 20, 83, 85, 95, 97–8, 105, 111 n.2, 201
sacred   83, 86, 88, 90, 93–6, 98, 105–6, 110, 111 n.11, 118, 168, 209
salvation   59, 135
Schopenhauer, Arthur   27–30
  on the Greeks   32
secret   118, 142 n.2
sex   28–9
Shakespeare   150, 161
shame   32, 203
  of Lila   177–9, 183, 195
sin   31, 34–8, 44, 133–4, 142, 155, 208
  of Jack   115, 124–30
  Schopenhauer's interpretation of original sin   28
slave morality   35–6
socialism   5, 45 n.11, 46 n.12

Strauss, David Friedrich   26–7, 46 n.18

Tertullian   39
theodicy   32, 204 n.7
theology   48–9 n.35, 88, 134, 194, 201, 204 n.7
  Feuerbach's critique of   17–20, 45 n.6

universalism   48 n.31

vision   84, 90, 93, 96, 99–102, 105, 164–5, 169–70, 185, 199
  as aesthetic insight   157–8, 171 n.12, 205–7
  foundational   97–8, 144 n.11

Weber, Max   42, 59
Williams, William Carlos   161

www.ingramcontent.com/pod-product-compliance
Lightning Source LLC
Chambersburg PA
CBHW062217300426
44115CB00012BA/2105